DATE DUE

Demco

For more Kaplan books relating to Medical School
Admissions and the MCAT please visit
http://kaplanpublishing.com

MCAT®
Practice Tests
Eighth Edition

by the staff of Kaplan, Inc.

PUBLISHING

New York

This publication is designed to provide accurate and authoritative information in regard to the subject matter covered. It is sold with the understanding that the publisher is not engaged in rendering legal, accounting, or other professional service. If legal advice or other expert assistance is required, the services of a competent professional should be sought.

©2013 Kaplan, Inc.

Published by Kaplan Publishing, a division of Kaplan, Inc.
395 Hudson Street
New York, NY 10014

Excerpt from "The Old-Fashioned Modernism of John Marin," by Helen Dudar, *Smithsonian* vol. 20, no. 11 (Feb 1990), pp. 20, 52–63, used by permission.

Excerpt from *The First New Nation* by Seymour Martin Lipset, reprinted with permission from Transaction Publishers.

Excerpt from "Selective Incapacitation: A Wolf in Sheep's Clothing?" by Brian Forst, reprinted with the permission of Brian Forst.

Printed in the United States of America

10 9 8 7 6 5 4 3 2 1

ISBN: 978-1-60978-948-0

Contents

Accessing Your Online Practice Tests

With the purchase of this book, you have also gained access to two more full-length, computer-based MCAT exams complete with explanations. To gain access to your additional tests in the Online Companion, simply:

1) Go to http://kaptest.com/mcatpracticetests

2) Enter the password as directed.

3) Click on "Register Now" and follow the on-screen instructions.

4) Once registered, click on the "Go to your Student Homepage" link to access your Online Companion materials.

*Please have a copy of your book with you, since you will need information from it to access your account.

kaptest.com/publishing

The material in this book is up-to-date at the time of publication. However, the Association of American Medical Colleges may have instituted changes in the test after this book was published. Be sure to read carefully the materials you receive when you register for the test.

If there are any important late-breaking developments—or any changes or corrections to the Kaplan test preparation materials in this book—we will post that information online at **kaptest.com/publishing.**

About the Authors

Tessa Cigler, MD
BA (Biochemistry), Harvard University
MD, Duke University

Richard Cohen, PhD
BS (Physics), Brown University
PhD (Physics), University of Maryland

William Dracos, MBA
BA (Biology), Duke University
MBA, Duke University

Sascha Dublin, MD, PhD
BA (Renaissance Studies), Brown University
MD/PhD, University of Washington
School of Medicine

Richard Friedland, DPM
BA (Biology), Ithaca College
DPM, Pennsylvania College of Podiatric Medicine

Sharon Klotz
BS (Physics), Massachusetts Institute of Technology

Andy Koh, MD
BA (Biology), Harvard University
BA (English Literature), Oxford University
MD, Harvard Medical School

Karl Lee, MA
BA (Chemistry), Amherst College
MA (Physical Chemistry), Harvard University

Alan Levine, MS
BA (Mathematics), Rice University
MS (Chemistry), University of Houston

Michael Manley, MD
BS (Psychobiology), University of California,
Los Angeles
MD, University of California, San Diego

Leslie Manley, PhD
BA (Biochemistry & Cell Biology),
University of California, San Diego
PhD (Physiology & Pharmacology),
University of California, San Diego

Eileen A. McDonnell, JD
BA (English Literature), CUNY
JD, Fordham University

Ingrid Multhopp
BA (English Literature), University of Chicago

Stacie Orell
BA (Biology), University of Pennsylvania

Rochelle Rothstein, MD
BA (Biology), Princeton University
MD, University of California, San Diego

Evan Skowronski, PhD
BS (Chemistry), Duke University
PhD (Microbiology), Loma Linda University

Andrew Taylor
BA (Biology), Boston University

Special Thanks:
Kim Bowers, Owen Farcy, Joanna Graham, Adam Grey, Keith Lubeley, Walter Niedner, Deeangelee Pooran-Kublall, and Amjed Saffarini for all the tireless work in making this publication possible.

How to Use
This Book

Congratulations on buying the best MCAT workbook available: *MCAT Practice Tests*. Kaplan's *MCAT Practice Tests* provides you with key subject-specific MCAT strategies and four full-length practice tests—two in this book, and two in the online companion—along with thorough, detailed explanations.

Before you start practicing with the MCAT-style tests in this book and the online companion, it's important that you have a fundamental understanding of the science content tested on the MCAT, including college-level biology, general chemistry, organic chemistry, and physics. Additionally, you should be familiar with the format and style of the MCAT.

If you already have a strong understanding of the sciences tested and the format of the MCAT, then you're ready to begin practicing with *MCAT Practice Tests*. However, if you feel that you need more extensive content review, you should consider using Kaplan's *MCAT Premier* or *Kaplan MCAT Review: Complete 5-Book Series*. Either of these can be used as a companion to this book and will cover all the science necessary for the MCAT in detail, provide additional practice sets, and discuss strategies for every area of the test.

Here's how to use the various components of the *MCAT Practice Tests*:

STEP ONE: READ THE MCAT STRATEGIES SECTION

Kaplan's live MCAT course has helped more people get into medical school than all other MCAT courses combined. In this section, we've distilled the main techniques and approaches from our course into a clear, easy-to-grasp format. We'll introduce you to the idiosyncrasies of the MCAT and show you how to take control of the test-taking experience on all levels.

Test Material
Specific methods and strategies for tackling MCAT passages and questions in all subjects.

Test Expertise
Item-specific techniques, as well as advice on how to pace yourself on each section and how to decide when to answer questions and when to guess. We'll teach you how the peculiarities of a standardized test can be used to your advantage.

Test Mentality
The proper attitude for executing all you've learned and for facing the MCAT with confidence.

STEP TWO: TAKE KAPLAN'S FULL-LENGTH PRACTICE MCATS

After you've learned valuable test strategies, take the full-length practice tests—timed exams—as a test run for the real thing. The first two practice tests are found right in your book, but the third and fourth tests can be accessed online for a true test-like experience. Visit **kaptest.com/ mcatpracticetests** to set up your online companion account and access these resources. (Have your book close at hand when you do so, as it will be needed for activation.)

STEP THREE: REVIEW TO SHORE UP WEAK POINTS

The explanations for every question on all four of your practice tests are included in this book and online so you can understand your mistakes. Try not to confine your review to the explanations of the questions you've gotten wrong. Instead, read all the explanations to reinforce key concepts and sharpen your skills. After you review each test, if you find your performance was weak in any particular area, make sure to remember that topic as a weakness, and review that material (starting with chapters two and three of section one of this book) before Test Day.

FOR MORE PRACTICE

Kaplan's *MCAT Premier* and *MCAT Subject Review* are personalized study programs that integrate online components. They are feature in-depth reviews of all the science topics covered on the MCAT, as well as additional practice sets and more full-length practice tests. You can use them independently or in conjunction with this book. You can also contact the Association of American Medical Colleges to receive the MCAT practice tests it publishes:

MCAT Care Team
Association of American Medical Colleges
Section for Applicant Assessment Services
2450 N Street NW
Washington, DC 20037-1127
Phone: 202-828-0690
aamc.org/mcat
mcat@aamc.org

Different people have different learning styles. If after spending some time with this book, you feel that a live course with more individualized instruction and extensive opportunity for practice is what you need, consider taking a Kaplan MCAT course.

If you would like more information on Kaplan's MCAT prep courses, please call us at **1-800-KAP-TEST.** You can also contact us on the Web at **www.kaptest.com.**

MCAT Strategies

Introduction to the MCAT

- Understand how the MCAT is structured and scored.
- Learn to take control of the test using the MCAT Mindset.

The Medical College Admission Test, affectionately known as the MCAT, is different from any other test you've encountered in your academic career. It's not like the knowledge-based exams from high school and college, whose emphasis was on memorizing and regurgitating information. Medical schools can assess your academic prowess by looking at your transcript. The MCAT isn't even like other standardized tests you may have taken, where the focus was on proving your general skills.

Medical schools use MCAT scores to assess whether you possess the foundation upon which to build a successful medical career. Though you certainly need to know the content to do well, the stress is on thought process, because the MCAT is above all else a thinking test. That's why it emphasizes reasoning, critical and analytical thinking, reading comprehension, data analysis, and problem-solving skills.

The MCAT's power comes from its use as an indicator of your abilities. Good scores can open doors. Your power comes from preparation and mindset, because the key to MCAT success is knowing what you're up against. And that's where this section of this book comes in. We'll explain the philosophy behind the test, review the sections one by one, show you sample questions, share some of Kaplan's proven methods, and clue you in to what the test makers are really after. You'll get a handle on the process, find a confident new perspective, and achieve your highest possible scores.

THE MCAT

Several years ago, the Association of American Medical Colleges (AAMC) changed the MCAT from a paper and-pencil-exam to a computer-based test (CBT). Information about the CBT is included below.

MCAT CBT

Format	U.S. — All administrations on computer International — Most on computer with limited paper and pencil in a few isolated areas
Breaks	Optional break after each section
Length of MCAT Day	Approximately 5.5 hours
Test Dates	Multiple dates in January, April, May, June, July, August, and September
Delivery of Results	Within 30 days; or if scores are delayed, notification will be posted online at aamc.org/mcat Electronic
Security	Government-issued ID Electronic thumbprint Electronic signature verification
Testing Centers	Small computer testing sites

As of January 2013, the MCAT will no longer include the Writing Sample section. Although Writing Sample scores will remain valid for three years after the last administration of that section, students who take the test in 2013 and afterwards will not have to write essays. Instead of the Writing Sample, students will encounter an optional Experimental Section at the end of their official MCAT. The Experimental Section does not affect test takers' scores in any way and will be offered as a voluntary exercise at the end of the examination.

The AAMC has included the Experimental Section in the 2013 test to prepare for the changes that the MCAT will undergo in 2015. The 2015 MCAT will be an eight-hour-long test on four sections: Biological and Biochemical Foundations of Living Systems; Chemical and Physical Foundations of Biological Systems; Psychological, Social and Biological Foundations of Behavior; and Critical Analysis and Reasoning Skills. Scoring will be similar to the current 1–15 scale, and each section will receive its own score. The inclusion of these four sections in the 2015 MCAT means that students taking that test will not only need to have a background in the basic natural sciences (biology, chemistry, organic chemistry, and physics), but will also need to be familiar with new topics, including biochemistry, psychology, and sociology.

While the upcoming changes to the MCAT in 2015 are complex and potentially intimidating, rest assured that if you plan to take the MCAT *before* then, this book will prepare you for exactly what you will see on your test.

PLANNING FOR THE TEST

As you look toward your preparation for the MCAT, consider the following advice.

Complete your core course requirements as soon as possible. Take a strategic eye to your schedule and get core requirements out of the way now.

Take the MCAT once. The MCAT is a notoriously grueling standardized exam that requires extensive preparation. It is longer than the graduate admissions exams for business school (GMAT, $3\frac{1}{2}$ hours), law school (LSAT, $3\frac{1}{2}$ hours), and graduate school (GRE, $3\frac{1}{2}$ hours). You do not want to take it twice. Plan and prepare accordingly.

Go online and sign up for a local Kaplan pre-med edge event to get the latest information on the new test.

THE ROLE OF THE MCAT IN ADMISSIONS

More and more people are applying to medical school, and more and more people are taking the MCAT. It's important for you to recognize that while a high MCAT score is a critical component in getting admitted to top med schools, it's not the only factor. Medical school admissions officers weigh grades, interviews, MCAT scores, level of involvement in extracurricular activities, as well as personal essays.

In a Kaplan survey of 130 pre-med advisors, 84 percent called the interview a "very important" part of the admissions process, followed closely by college grades (83 percent) and MCAT scores (76 percent). Kaplan's college admissions consulting practice works with students on all these issues so they can position themselves as strongly as possible. In addition, the AAMC has made it clear that scores will continue to be valid for three years and that the scoring of the computer-based MCAT will not differ from that of the paper-and-pencil version.

REGISTRATION

The only way to register for the MCAT is online. The registration site is aamc.org/mcat.

You will be able to access the site approximately six months before your test date. Payment must be made by MasterCard or Visa.

Go to aamc.org/mcat/registration.htm and download *MCAT Essentials* for information about registration, fees, test administration, and preparation. For other questions, contact

MCAT Care Team
Association of American Medical Colleges
Section for Applicant Assessment Services
2450 N Street NW
Washington, DC 20037
aamc.org/mcat
Email: mcat@aam.org

Don't drag your feet gathering information. You'll need time not only to prepare and practice for the test but also to get all your registration work done.

ANATOMY OF THE MCAT

Before mastering strategies, you need to know exactly what you're dealing with on the MCAT. Let's start with the basics: The MCAT is, among other things, an endurance test.

If you can't approach it with confidence and stamina, you'll quickly lose your composure. That's why it's so important that you take control of the test.

The MCAT consists of three timed sections: Physical Sciences, Verbal Reasoning, and Biological Sciences. Later in this section of the book, we'll take an in-depth look at each MCAT section, including sample question types and specific test-smart hints, but here's a general overview, reflecting the order of the test sections and number of questions in each.

PHYSICAL SCIENCES

Time	70 minutes
Format	52 multiple-choice questions:
	7 passages with 4–7 questions each;
	13 discrete questions (not passage-based)
What it tests	basic general chemistry concepts, basics physics concepts, analytical reasoning, data interpretation

VERBAL REASONING

Time	60 minutes
Format	40 multiple-choice questions:
	7 passages with 4–7 questions each
What it tests	critical reading

BIOLOGICAL SCIENCES

Time	70 minutes
Format	52 multiple-choice questions
	7 passages with 4–7 questions each
	13 discrete questions (not passage-based)
What it tests	basic biology concepts, basic organic chemistry concepts, analytical reasoning, data interpretation

EXPERIMENTAL SECTION

Time	45 minutes
Format	32 multiple-choice questions
What it tests	any skills from previous sections, plus psychology, sociology, biochemistry

The sections of the test always appear in the same order:

Physical Sciences
[optional 10-minute break]
Verbal Reasoning
[optional 10-minute break]
Biological Sciences
[optional 10-minute break]
Experimental Section

SCORING

Each MCAT section receives its own score. Physical Sciences, Verbal Reasoning, and Biological Sciences are each scored on a scale of 1–15, with 15 as the highest. (As of January 2013, there will also be an optional Experimental Section after the three scored sections, but this final section will have no effect on your score; in fact, the medical schools that see your MCAT score won't even know whether or not you chose to complete it.)

The number of multiple-choice questions that you answer correctly per section is your "raw score." Your raw score will then be converted to yield the "scaled score"—the one that will fall somewhere in that 1–15 range. These scaled scores are reported to medical schools as your MCAT scores.

All multiple-choice questions are worth the same amount—one raw point—and *there's no penalty for guessing.* That means that *you should always select an answer for every question, whether you get to that question or not!* This is an important piece of advice, so pay it heed. Never let time run out on any section without selecting an answer for every question.

Your score report will tell you—and your potential medical schools—not only your scaled scores but also the national mean score for each section, standard deviation, national scoring profile for each section, and your percentile ranking.

WHAT'S A GOOD SCORE?

There's no such thing as a cut-and-dried "good score." Much depends on the strength of the rest of your application (if your transcript is first-rate, the pressure to strut your stuff on the MCAT isn't as intense) and on where you want to go to school (different schools have different score expectations). Here are a few interesting statistics.

For each MCAT administration, the average scaled scores are approximately 8s for Physical Sciences, Verbal Reasoning, and Biological Sciences. You need scores of at least 10–11s to be considered competitive by most medical schools, and if you're aiming for the top you've got to do even better and score 12s and above.

You don't have to be perfect to do well. For instance, on the AAMC's Practice Test 5, you could get as many as 10 questions wrong in Verbal Reasoning, 17 in Physical Sciences, and 16 in Biological Sciences and still score in the 80th percentile. To score in the 90th percentile, you could get as many as 7 wrong in Verbal Reasoning, 12 in Physical Sciences, and 12 in Biological Sciences. Even students who receive the highest scaled scores usually get a handful of questions wrong.

It's important to maximize your performance on every question. Just a few questions one way or the other can make a big difference in your scaled score. Here's a look at recent score profiles so you can get an idea of the shape of a typical score distribution.

Physical Sciences			Verbal Reasoning		
Scaled Score	Percent Achieving Score	Percentile Rank Range	Scaled Score	Percent Achieving Score	Percentile Rank Range
15	0.1	99.9–99.9	15	0.1	99.9–99.9
14	1.2	98.7–99.8	14	0.2	99.7–99.8
13	2.5	96.2–98.6	13	1.8	97.9–99.6
12	5.1	91.1–96.1	12	3.6	94.3–97.8
11	7.2	83.9–91.0	11	10.5	83.8–94.2
10	12.1	71.8–83.8	10	15.6	68.2–83.7
9	12.9	58.9–71.1	9	17.2	51.0–68.1
8	16.5	42.4–58.5	8	15.4	35.6–50.9
7	16.7	25.7–42.3	7	10.3	25.3–35.5
6	13.0	12.7–25.6	6	10.9	14.4–25.2
5	7.9	04.8–12.6	5	6.9	07.5–14.3
4	3.3	01.5–04.7	4	3.9	03.6–07.4
3	1.3	00.2–01.4	3	2.0	01.6–03.5
2	0.1	00.1–00.1	2	0.5	00.1–01.5
1	0.0	00.0–00.0	1	0.0	00.0–00.0
Scaled Score Mean = 8.1 Standard Deviation = 2.32			Scaled Score Mean = 8.0 Standard Deviation = 2.43		

Biological Sciences		
Scaled Score	Percent Achieving Score	Percentile Rank Range
15	0.1	99.9–99.9
14	1.2	98.7–99.8
13	2.5	96.2–98.6
12	5.1	91.1–96.1
11	7.2	83.9–91.0
10	12.1	71.8–83.8
9	12.9	58.9–71.1
8	16.5	42.4–58.5
7	16.7	25.7–42.3
6	13.0	12.7–25.6
5	7.9	04.8–12.6
4	3.3	01.5–04.7
3	1.3	00.2–01.4
2	0.1	00.1–00.1
1	0.0	00.0–00.0

Scaled Score
Mean = 8.2
Standard Deviation = 2.39

WHAT THE MCAT REALLY TESTS

It's important to grasp not only the nuts and bolts of the MCAT, so you'll know *what* to do on Test Day, but also the underlying principles of the test so you'll know *why* you're doing what you're doing. We'll cover the straightforward MCAT facts later. Now it's time to examine the heart and soul of the MCAT to see what it's really about.

THE MYTH

Most people preparing for the MCAT fall prey to the myth that the MCAT is a straightforward science test. They think something like this:

"It covers the four years of science I had to take in school: biology, chemistry, physics, and organic chemistry. It even has equations. OK, so it has Verbal Reasoning, but that section is just to see if we're literate, right? The important stuff is the science. After all, we're going to be doctors."

Well, here's the little secret no one seems to want you to know: The MCAT is not just a science test; it's also a thinking test. This means that the test is designed to let you demonstrate your thought process, not only your thought content.

The implications are vast. Once you shift your test-taking paradigm to match the MCAT modus operandi, you'll find a new level of confidence and control over the test. You'll begin to work with the nature of the MCAT rather than against it. You'll be more efficient and insightful as you prepare for the test, and you'll be more relaxed on Test Day. In fact, you'll be able to see the MCAT for what it is rather than for what it's dressed up to be. We want your Test Day to feel like a visit with a familiar friend instead of an awkward blind date.

THE ZEN OF MCAT

Medical schools do not need to rely on the MCAT to see what you already know. Admission committees can measure your subject-area proficiency using your undergraduate coursework and grades. Schools are most interested in the potential of your mind.

In recent years, many medical schools have shifted pedagogic focus away from an information-heavy curriculum to a concept-based curriculum. Currently, more emphasis is placed on problem solving, holistic thinking, and cross-disciplinary study. Be careful not to dismiss this important point, figuring you'll wait to worry about academic trends until you're actually in medical school. This trend affects you right now, because it's reflected in the MCAT. Every good tool matches its task. In this case, the tool is the test used to measure you and other candidates, and the task is to quantify how likely it is that you'll succeed in medical school.

Your intellectual potential—how skillfully you annex new territory into your mental boundaries, how quickly you build "thought highways" between ideas, how confidently and creatively you solve problems—is far more important to admission committees than your ability to recite Young's modulus for every material known to humanity. The schools assume they can expand your knowledge base. They choose applicants carefully because expansive knowledge is not enough to succeed in medical school or in the profession. There's something more. And it's this "something more" that the MCAT is trying to measure.

Every section on the MCAT tests essentially the same higher-order thinking skills: analytical reasoning, abstract thinking, and problem solving. Most test takers get trapped into thinking they are being tested strictly about biology, chemistry, etc. Thus, they approach each section with a new outlook on what's expected. This constant mental gear shifting can be exhausting, not to mention counterproductive. Instead of perceiving the test as parsed into radically different sections, you need to maintain your focus on the underlying nature of the test: It's designed to test your thinking skills, not your information-recall skills. Each test section thus presents a variation on the same theme.

WHAT ABOUT THE SCIENCE?

With this perspective, you may be left asking these questions: "What about the science? What about the content? Don't I need to know the basics?" The answer is a resounding "Yes!" You must be fluent in the different languages of the test. You cannot do well on the MCAT if you don't know the basics of physics, general chemistry, biology, and organic chemistry. We recommend that you take one year each of biology, general chemistry, organic chemistry, and physics before taking the MCAT and that you review the content in this book thoroughly. Knowing these basics is just the beginning of doing well on the MCAT. That's a shock to most test takers. They presume that once they recall or relearn their undergraduate science, they are ready to do battle against the MCAT. Wrong! They merely have directions to the battlefield. They lack what they need to beat the test: a copy of the test maker's battle plan!

You won't be drilled on facts and formulas on the MCAT. You'll need to demonstrate the ability to reason based on ideas and concepts. The science questions are painted with a broad brush, testing your general understanding.

TAKE CONTROL: THE MCAT MINDSET

In addition to being a thinking test, as we've stressed, the MCAT is a standardized test. As such, it has its own consistent patterns and idiosyncrasies that can actually work in your favor. This is the key to why test preparation works. You have the opportunity to familiarize yourself with those consistent peculiarities—to adopt the proper test-taking mindset.

The following are some overriding principles of the MCAT Mindset that will be covered in depth in the chapters to come:

- Read actively and critically.
- Translate prose into your own words.
- Save the toughest questions for last.
- Know the test and its components inside and out.
- Do MCAT-style problems in each topic area after you've reviewed it.
- Allow your confidence to build on itself.
- Take full-length practice tests a week or two before the test to break down the mystique of the real experience.
- Learn from your mistakes—get the most out of your practice tests.
- Look at the MCAT as a challenge, the first step in your medical career, rather than as an arbitrary obstacle.

And that's what the MCAT Mindset boils down to: Taking control. Being proactive. Being on top of the testing experience so that you can get as many points as you can as quickly and as easily as possible. Keep this in mind as you read and work through the material in this book and, of course, as you face the challenge on Test Day.

Now that you have a better idea of what the MCAT is all about, let's take a tour of the individual test sections. Although the underlying skills being tested are similar, each MCAT section requires that you call into play a different domain of knowledge. So, though we encourage you to think of the MCAT as a holistic and unified test, we also recognize that the test is segmented by discipline and that there are characteristics unique to each section. In the overviews, we'll review sample questions and answers and discuss section-specific strategies. For each of the scored sections—Physical Sciences, Verbal Reasoning, and Biological Sciences—we'll present you with the following:

- **The Big Picture**
  You'll get a clear view of the section and familiarize yourself with what it's really evaluating.

- **A Closer Look**
  You'll explore the types of questions that will appear and master the strategies you'll need to deal with them successfully.

- **Kaplan Tips**
  The key approaches to each section are outlined for reinforcement and quick review.

Physical and Biological Sciences

2

- Find out why abstract thinking is much more important than memorization on the MCAT.

- Review the content areas you can expect to find on the actual MCAT.

- Learn key strategies to help you answer both passage–based questions and discrete questions.

THE BIG PICTURE

The two science sections on the MCAT, Physical and Biological, are similar in their format, though their content obviously differs. In each 70-minute section, you'll find 7 passages, each followed by 4–7 multiple-choice questions, along with 13 stand-alone multiple-choice questions (also referred to as *discretes*) not based on any passage. The Physical Sciences section is comprised of physics and general chemistry; the questions are approximately evenly divided in content though mixed throughout the section. The Biological Sciences section consists of biology and organic chemistry questions mixed throughout, with greater emphasis on biology (specifically, on DNA and genetics).

The passages, each 250–300 words in length, will describe experiments, situations, or ideas from which questions are drawn. The information may be presented in the guise of journal or textbook articles, experimental research, data analysis, or scientific-style editorials. When reading the science passages, you should think about extracting information—not meaning and structure as in Verbal Reasoning. Consider the passages to be data that you must interpret and understand to be able to apply them to the specific needs of the questions. The passage-and-question structure allows you to demonstrate many skills, among them the following:

- Understanding the science presented in the passage, no matter how obscure or foreign it is to you
- Confidently connecting elements of your scientific "repertoire" to new situations
- Quickly assessing the kinds of situations feasible given the information in the passage

The stand-alone questions will draw on your knowledge of particular concepts or themes in the respective sciences. They're "wild cards" in the sense that you cannot group them in any formal way; in fact, they appear scattered throughout the sections. Ranging in scope from a quantitative problem to a conceptual thought experiment, they are the test maker's way of randomly tapping into your knowledge base.

THE MCAT ATTITUDE

It's important to approach both science sections with the same mindset: MCAT science is just a window into your mind. The test makers are trying to see how you reason, how you solve problems, and how well you command your knowledge. They are not after a data dump from your core memory. It's crucial that you demonstrate conceptual understanding of scientific material and show proficiency in applying scientific themes in new situations. This is the kind of mental flexibility that will get you a great MCAT score.

Abstract Thinking

Another way to describe flexibility is as a form of abstraction. To think abstractly is to lift ideas out of a specific context and place them in a new context. It's a skill that allows you passage into seemingly unfamiliar territory, and on the MCAT, that could mean the question around the corner. In the science sections, this skill is tested repeatedly.

For example, passages may provide hypothetical scenarios or describe experiments you've never seen before. You'll need to take the unfamiliar and make it familiar, and that's where abstract thinking comes in. If you understand the basic framework of experimental design and scientific method, you won't be overwhelmed by an unfamiliar context. You'll be able to "rise above" the details rather than get tripped up by them.

What About Formulas and Math?

Contrary to what you may presume, the MCAT is not a math-intensive test. Despite the scientific language on the MCAT, there is nothing more mathematically complex than algebra, exponents, logs, and a little bit of trig. There is no calculus, differential equations, or matrix mechanics. You may need to recall sine and cosine for standard angles, though such values are often provided if necessary. That's it! No higher math.

Similarly, many of the scientific formulas necessary to work through problems and answer questions will be provided on the test. This is just an indicator of how negligible is the value of "straight memorization." You gain little by having every nitty-gritty formula easily accessible unless you also have a broad understanding of what the formulas mean, what they imply, what their units indicate, how they relate to one another, and how to navigate among them.

In light of our discussion of concept-based testing, it makes sense that the MCAT will not reward you merely for the "brute force" of memorization. There will rarely be an opportunity on the MCAT to crunch away algebraically on a formula. The information you're given won't fit neatly into formulas. If it did, the MCAT would be nothing but a memory-and-algebra test. And, as we've discussed, it is much more. Again, you should not be concerned with memorizing formulas. You should be concerned with *understanding* formulas. The key point is that once you understand the scientific concepts behind a formula, you hardly need the formula itself anymore. Though this applies mostly to physics and chemistry, the underlying theme is relevant for both science sections: Think, don't compute!

A CLOSER LOOK

What follows is a review of the content areas you can expect to find in the science sections of the MCAT. This is not to suggest that your MCAT will cover all of these topics; instead, use this list as a guideline of the content that could possibly show up. All these areas are covered in detail in Kaplan's *MCAT Premier* book.

PHYSICAL SCIENCES
PHYSICS
- Basic Units/Kinematics
- Newtonian Mechanics
- Force and Inertia
- Thermodynamics
- Fluids/Solids
- Electrostatics
- Magnetism
- Circuits
- Periodic Motion, Waves, Sound
- Light and Optics
- Atomic Phenomena
- Nuclear Physics

GENERAL CHEMISTRY
- Quantum Numbers
- Hund's Rule/Electron Configuration
- Periodic Table
- Reaction Types
- Balancing Equations
- Bonding
- Formal Charge/VSEPR Theory
- Intermolecular Forces
- Chemical Kinetics/Equilibrium
- Thermodynamics/Entropy
- Ideal Gas Law
- Phases of Matter
- Solutions
- Acids and Bases
- Electrochemistry

BIOLOGICAL SCIENCES
BIOLOGY
- Eukaryotic and Prokaryotic Cells
- Membrane Traffic
- Cell Division—Mitosis and Meiosis
- Embryogenesis
- Enzymatic Activity
- Cellular Metabolism
- Muscular and Skeletal Systems
- Digestive System
- Respiratory and Circulatory Systems
- Lymphatic System
- Immune System
- Homeostasis
- Endocrine System
- Nervous System
- Molecular Genetics/Inheritance
- Viruses
- Evolution

ORGANIC CHEMISTRY
- Nomenclature
- Stereochemistry
- Mechanisms
- Carboxylic Acids
- Amines
- Spectroscopy
- Carbohydrates and Lipids
- Hydrolysis and Dehydration
- Amino Acids and Proteins
- Oxygen-Containing Compounds
- Hydrocarbons
- Laboratory Techniques
- IR and NMR Spectroscopy

SAMPLE PASSAGE AND QUESTIONS

This is probably your first chance to see what the passages, passage-based questions, and stand-alone questions will look like in the science sections. An answer key is provided, but try to work through these samples without consulting it. We'll use the following passage and questions to highlight general strategies. You'll find more MCAT-style practice questions at the end of each content review subject area.

Passage

A physics class is attempting to measure the acceleration due to gravity, g, by throwing balls out of classroom windows. They performed the following two experiments:

Experiment 1

Two class members lean out of different windows at the same height, h = 5.2 m, above the ground and drop two different balls. One ball is made out of lead and has a mass of 5 kg. The other ball is made out of plastic and has a mass of 1 kg. The students measure the velocity of the lead ball just before impact with the ground and find it to be 10 m/s. They also find that when the plastic ball hits the ground it bounces, and its momentum changes by 18 kg · m/s.

Experiment 2

Instead of dropping the plastic ball, a student throws the ball out of a higher window and observes its projectile motion. The ball is thrown from a height of 10 m above the ground with a velocity of 4 m/s directed at an angle of 30° above the horizontal. (Note: Assume that the air resistance is negligible unless otherwise stated.)

Passage-Based Questions

1. The students did not account for air resistance in their measurement of g in Experiment 1. How does the value of g they obtained compare with the actual value of g?

    A. The value of g obtained in Experiment 1 is greater than the actual value of g because air resistance increases the time it takes the balls to fall from the windows to the ground.

    B. The value of g obtained in Experiment 1 is greater than the actual value of g because air resistance decreases the kinetic energy of the balls just before impact.

    C. The value of g obtained in Experiment 1 is less than the actual value of g because air resistance decreases the velocity of the balls just before impact.

    D. The value of g obtained in Experiment 1 is less than the actual value of g because air resistance decreases the time it takes the balls to fall from the windows to the ground.

2. Which of the following would change the measured value of g in Experiment 1?

    I. Increasing the mass of the earth
    II. Using balls having a different mass but the same volume
    III. Throwing the balls horizontally instead of dropping them vertically

    A. I only
    B. III only
    C. I and II only
    D. II and III only

3. In Experiment 1, the change in momentum that the plastic ball experiences when it bounces off the ground does NOT depend on (Note: Assume that the collision is perfectly elastic.)

    A. the velocity of the ball just before impact.
    B. the mass of the ball.
    C. the mass of the earth.
    D. the volume of the ball.

4. In Experiment 2, what was the maximum height above the window reached by the plastic ball? (Note: The acceleration due to gravity is $g = 9.8$ m/s^2, sin 30° = 0.50, and cos 30° = 0.866.)

    A. 10.2 cm
    B. 20.4 cm
    C. 30.6 cm
    D. 61.2 cm

5. In a third experiment, a student throws the lead ball out of the same window used in Experiment 1 with a velocity of 3 m/s in the horizontal direction. What is the ratio of the work done by gravity on the lead ball in the first experiment to the work done by gravity on the ball in the third experiment?

    A. 1:1
    B. 1:3
    C. 1:9
    D. 3:1

Discrete Questions

6. In the figure below, the velocity vector of a particle is represented at successive times t. Which of the following best represents the acceleration vector?

$$\longrightarrow \;\; \longrightarrow \; \rightarrow \; \leftarrow \; \longleftarrow \; \longleftarrow$$

$$t = 0 \quad t = 1 \quad t = 2 \quad t = 3 \quad t = 4 \quad t = 5$$

　　A. $\longrightarrow$
　　B. $\longleftarrow$
　　C. The acceleration changes direction.
　　D. The acceleration is zero.

7. All of the following statements are true of most transition elements EXCEPT

　　A. they have partially filled d subshells.
　　B. they have extremely high ionization energies.
　　C. they exhibit metallic character.
　　D. they have multiple oxidation states.

8. A patient is taking a drug that has the side effect of being a sympathetic nervous system inhibitor. Which of the following would most likely be seen as a result of this drug?

　　A. Decreased bowel motility
　　B. Decreased heart rate
　　C. Increased pupil diameter
　　D. Decreased blood supply to skin

Were You Able to Think Abstractly?

Did you get bogged down in details, or were you able to rise above them? Were you able to come up with your own answers before looking at the choices? As you review the following answer explanations, you'll be able to assess your performance and pick up important strategies.

ANSWER REVIEW

Passage

The passage describes a series of experiments performed by some students. As you read, you should be making notes in the margins or underlining important information (i.e., height = 5.2 meters, mass = 5 kg, etc.). You might make a chart to list out the respective "given" data for each experiment:

Experiment 1
2 balls
masses for each
height
final velocity for lead ball
plastic ball: change in momentum

Experiment 2
height
initial velocity
angle above horizon

Passage-Based Questions

1. **C**

   This is a question you could answer without reference to the passage. It's really asking about how a measurement of *g* would change depending on whether or not air resistance is considered (with all other variables presumed constant). Because air resistance is a force working in the opposite direction from gravity, it's a force of resistance, like friction. Therefore, it slows down the motion of the ball, making it take longer to fall the same distance. Thus, the velocity just before impact decreases when air resistance is considered. We know that *g* is proportional to the square of the velocity (from solving for *g* in $v^2 = v_0^2 + 2ad$, where *a* would be *g* and *d* would be the height). If the velocity is less (because the ball takes more time to travel the same distance if we consider air resistance), then *g* will also be less than the measured value. This line of reasoning rules out **choices (A)** and **(B)**. **Choice (D)** says that air resistance *decreases* the time it takes for the ball to fall. But we just discussed that resistance *adds* to the time for travel. So **choice (C)** is correct.

Key Strategy: A chart helps you organize what you know from the passage so you can access the information quickly while answering the questions. Remember, you're reading for data—not for meaning or structure. Be sure, however, that you understand the context of every piece of data you collect.

Key Strategy: Don't read more complexity into a question than is there. In some cases, passage-based questions will actually be testing in a "pseudo-discrete" style with little or no reference back to the passage.

2. A

This Roman numeral–style question asks what factors would change the measured value of g in the first experiment. Be careful to consider only the information from Experiment 1 when answering this question.

Let's consider the first statement. If it's wrong, then you can eliminate any answer choice that has it listed. If you decide it is true, then you must choose an answer that includes it in its list of numerals. In the first experiment, the students neglected air resistance, so we have only gravity to consider. The first statement requires that we think about how g is related to the mass of the earth. You should recall that the gravitational force between an object and the earth is $G = mM/R^2$, where G is the universal gravitational constant, m is the mass of the object, M is the mass of the earth, and R is the distance between. But remember also that the weight of an object $= mg$. We can equate these two forces ($mM/R^2 = mg$) to solve for $g = GM/R^2$. Therefore, changing the mass of the earth would indeed change the value of g. So Statement I is true, and you can eliminate **choices (B)** and **(D)**. Now we need consider only Statement II to decide between **(A)** and **(C)**. Let's look at Statement II. It says that using balls with different mass but the same volume would change g. We know that in Experiment 1, the students ignored air resistance, so the volume of the balls is not relevant. What about the mass? Well, we saw above that g is independent of the object's mass. So Statement II is not true, and **choice (A)** is correct.

If you were unsure about Statement I, though, you'd have to work through Statement III to decide which answer choice is correct. The key to the third statement is realizing that vertical trajectory will be unchanged by any initial horizontal velocity. The same vertical force—gravity— will be at work. So Statement III is untrue, confirming **(A)** as the correct answer choice.

Key Strategy: Use the structure of a Roman numeral question to your advantage! Eliminate choices as soon as you find them to be inconsistent with the truth or falsehood of a statement in the stimulus. Similarly, consider only those choices that include a statement that you've already determined to be true.

Key Strategy: You don't have to consider the statements in order. Knowing about any one of them will get you off to a great start answering the question, so if you're unsure about the first statement, go on to the second or third.

3. D

This question asks about which variable is *not* a factor in determining the change in momentum for the plastic ball in Experiment 1. You'll be looking for the answer that does not play a role in the momentum shift. One of the first things to note is that you're given a hint about the collision between the ball and the ground—it is elastic, implying that both kinetic energy and momentum are conserved during the collision. The question stimulus tells you, then, that at the time of impact, the two surfaces act like solid, hard surfaces (like billiard balls) with no energy lost to the collision.

Because the mass of the ball doesn't change, its change in momentum is dependent on its change in velocity. So change in momentum = $mv_{final} - mv_{initial}$. In considering the answers, however, there is no need to painstakingly step through calculations. One choice jumps out as inconsistent. **Choice (D)** mentions a variable—the volume of the ball—that has no bearing on the ball's change in momentum. All the other choices mention variables that are relevant in considering the change in momentum of the ball as it hits the earth.

Key Strategy: Don't do more work than you have to on the test. Work smart. The MCAT rewards test takers who can save time by seeing a creative strategy (e.g., looking for a variable that's not relevant rather than plodding through every choice, solving equations, and wasting time).

4. **B**

Be careful to read the question. It asks for the maximum height above the window reached by the plastic ball in Experiment 2. Since we're looking for maximum height, we know the vertical velocity will be 0 (when the ball stops and turns around to fall back to the ground). From the passage, we know that the ball's initial velocity is 4 meters per second at an angle of 30°. The initial vertical velocity component is $4 \times$ sine 30, or $4 \times 1/2$, which is 2 meters per second. Using kinematics, we know that $v^2 - v_0^2 = 2ay$, where a is acceleration and y is distance. We know $v_0 = 2$ meters per second; we can estimate g to be 10 meters per second squared. Solving the equation, we see that y maximum = 0.2 meters or 20 centimeters. This is closest to **choice (B)**, the correct answer. The height of the window doesn't even come into play. Notice that **choice (D)** derives from using the cosine rather than sine of 30° to find the vertical component of velocity. **Choice (A)** results from a simple calculation error. **Choice (C)** is incorrect as well.

Key Strategy: Estimate whenever you can to save time.

Key Strategy: Don't get flustered by unnecessary information. In this case, you had more information than you needed to solve the problem. Don't just plug in numbers and hope for a match. Think before you calculate!

5. **A**

You're asked for a ratio. The implication is that some component of the problem is not solvable, so don't expect to work with actual numbers. In this case, you need to compare the work done in two different scenarios. We need to know that work is force through a distance, or $F \times d$. Since gravity works only along the vertical axis, we need to know the vertical distance traveled by both balls to compare the work done. In both cases, the ball drops 5.2 meters. The ball mentioned in the question has some horizontal velocity, but this has no bearing on the vertical dynamics. So the distance traveled by the balls in the two different experiments is the same. Furthermore, because the mass is identical, the work done is the same. The ratio is 1:1—or **choice (A)**.

Key Strategy: In many cases with ratio questions, you will not be able to solve for actual numbers. You may have to work with relationships, fractions, and formulas to arrive at the solution.

Key Strategy: We reviewed these questions in order, but you don't have to do the questions in order. Start with the ones that seem most feasible, and mark and return to the ones that seem difficult or time-intensive.

Discrete Questions

6. **B**

This question is a great example of how the MCAT rewards the careful thinker. You're told that the vectors represent successive measurements of velocity for a particle. You're then asked which answer choice best represents the acceleration vector. Without having actual numbers to work with, you have to be able to construct a relationship between velocity and acceleration and "visualize" that relationship using vectors. The way to approach this question is to ask yourself, "What is the connection between velocity and acceleration?" Once you answer that, you can begin to home in on an appropriate answer choice. So what *is* the relationship? Recall that, dimensionally, acceleration is velocity per unit time or displacement per time squared. Theoretically speaking, acceleration is the *rate of change of velocity through a period of time.*

The answer choice will be a vector that matches the general rate of change among the given velocity vectors. At $t = 0$, the velocity is positive and at a maximum. At $t = 1$, it is still positive but the magnitude has decreased, indicating a *deceleration*. At $t = 2$, the velocity is still positive but is diminished in magnitude even more. What the vectors are describing is a particle, mass, car, thing, object, or whatever that is slowing down. At $t = 3$, something that looks a little tricky happens: the velocity becomes negative but with the same magnitude as $t = 2$. The object we're tracking has changed direction from "forward" to "reverse." The trend continues through $t = 4$ and $t = 5$; we see that the particle is going faster (greater magnitude) but in the opposite direction from its original orientation. Let's get a picture of what we've just figured out. A particle—suppose it's a car—is moving forward at some velocity. It slows down, stops at some point, and then reverses direction and speeds up.

OK, now that we understand the stimulus, we're ready to tackle the answer choices. Remember, we're looking for acceleration. We said earlier that acceleration is the rate of change in velocity. Even though the velocity vectors change direction, the acceleration vector maintains its negative direction throughout the time sampled. So even though the car speeds up in the "negative" direction, its acceleration remains negative. It continually *decelerates* throughout its movement. The implication is that the force acting on the car is in a direction *opposing* the original direction of movement. Once this clicks, the correct answer—**choice (B)**—leaps out as correct.

Let's step through the others. **Choice (A)** suggests that the particle keeps accelerating, but the velocity vectors get *smaller* in magnitude at first, not larger. So even if you forgot that the "negative acceleration" for time markers 3, 4, and 5 has a negative direction, there's no way **choice (A)** makes sense. **Choice (C)** replicates the behavior of the velocity vectors, and if you're not thinking carefully, you may fall for this choice because it *seems* to be consistent with the information you're given. **Choice (D)** presumes that you may visually "add up" all the vectors in the stimulus rather than apply them. If you do try to add them, you'll get a sum of 0. However, that sum is *not* the acceleration. In fact, it's the total *displacement*. The car essentially moves forward, slows to a stop, and then reverses, speeding up back to its original position.

Key Strategy: Understand the question clearly before you move to the answer choices. Otherwise, you'll be vulnerable to persuasive but incorrect choices.

Key Strategy: Use reason. Don't compute.

7. **B**

This question has the "all EXCEPT" format, which means you're looking for the answer that is the *exception* (i.e., it's *not* true). The stimulus asks about transition elements. Before you rush to the answer choices, think about what you know of transition elements. They're in the middle of the periodic table and have partially filled *d* subshells. You might also recall that their electrons are loosely held by the nucleus and they are sometimes called *transition metals*.

Choice (B)—they have high ionization energies—is the correct choice because its statement about transition elements is false. Transition elements are easy to ionize because their electrons are not strongly bound. **Choice (A)** can't be the correct choice because it says something *true* about transition elements. **Choice (C)** is also true—they do exhibit metallic properties because their electrons are mobile. **Choice (D)** is also true about transition elements; they can lose electrons from both *s* and *d* orbitals, resulting in multiple oxidation states.

Key Strategy: When answering a question in the "all EXCEPT" format, remember that you're looking for the choice that is *not* true.

Key Strategy: When answer questions in the "all EXCEPT" format, be sure to consider all the answer choices to be confident you've picked the most appropriate one.

8. **B**

This question is based on various functions of the different branches of the nervous system. Specifically, it requires knowledge of the pathways innervated by the sympathetic division of the autonomic nervous system. The autonomic nervous system is divided into two branches: the sympathetic and the parasympathetic. The sympathetic system mediates the "fight or flight" responses that ready the body for action. The parasympathetic system innervates those pathways that return the body to its normal state following fight or flight. The sympathetic system prepares the body by increasing heart rate, inhibiting digestion, causing vasoconstriction of blood vessels in the skin, and promoting pupil dilation.

From this list of functions, you can eliminate **choices (A)**, **(C)**, and **(D)** since they're all functions of the sympathetic nervous system and would, therefore, not be likely responses to a drug that inhibits the activity of the sympathetic system. By the process of elimination, you see that **choice (B)** is the correct answer. Since sympathetic innervation normally increases heart rate, of the four choices, an inhibitor of the system would most likely result in a *decrease* in heart rate.

<u>Key Strategy</u>: If you approach a discrete question that tests specific knowledge you do not possess, skim the choices carefully to see if you can glean any clues or information from them. If not, guess quickly, don't look back, and move on. You don't have time to waste.

KAPLAN TIPS

READING THE PASSAGES

- Passages may sound difficult or unfamiliar. Don't be daunted!
- Make notes on scratch paper or draw diagrams to help you summarize the information presented.

FACING THE QUESTIONS

- You can skip around. Tackle the easiest questions first, leaving the harder ones for later. The difficult questions are worth the same as the easy ones.
- Use numerical approximations when you can. Don't do any long calculations.
- Base your answers on the passage, not on your own knowledge.
- Use a process of elimination to get to the right answer or to increase your chances of guessing the right answer
- If you don't know an answer, guess! Try to do so while you're still working on the passage so you won't have to reread it later. There's no penalty for wrong answers. Leave no question unanswered!

Verbal Reasoning

3

- Practice "taking possession" of Verbal Reasoning passages by reading actively.
- Learn strategies for answering each of the six Verbal Reasoning question types.

THE BIG PICTURE

The Verbal Reasoning section is perhaps the most recognizable section of the MCAT, because it's similar to the reading comprehension sections of other standardized tests. It's 60 minutes long and consists of 7 passages, with anywhere from 4 to 7 questions per passage. The passages, often complex, are drawn from the social sciences, philosophy, and other humanistic disciplines, as well as from the natural sciences.

The Verbal Reasoning section tests your ability to do the following:

- Read critically and actively.
- "Possess," or truly comprehend, written material.
- Capture the essence of a passage by recognizing its main idea.
- Intuit a writer's tone
- Draw inferences/conclusions.

The passages you'll confront on Test Day probably won't be fun to read. Odds are, they'll be boring. If they're too engaging, check the cover. You may be taking the wrong test! As part of the challenge, you must be able to concentrate and glean meaning regardless of the nature of the text. This will involve working through your resistance to dry passages and overcoming any anxiety or frustration you feel. The more control you can muster, the quicker you can move through each passage, through the questions, and to a higher score. Remember, Verbal Reasoning isn't there to entertain you or to provide relief from the science but to put you through a mental obstacle course.

DO YOU NEED TO STUDY FOR VERBAL REASONING?

Don't make the mistake that so many MCAT participants make in underestimating the challenge of the Verbal Reasoning section. Sometimes it falls under the shadow cast by the looming science sections. Also, students figure that there isn't anything to "study" for this section. Be aware that the scoring gradient for Verbal Reasoning is very steep. It's hard to get a good score, so you can't afford to be cavalier. Some medical schools add all your MCAT scores together for a composite score—if you blow off Verbal Reasoning, you could kill your composite. Practice Verbal Reasoning as you would the other test sections and challenge yourself to acquire the specialized reading skills required on the MCAT.

HOW TO READ ACTIVELY

Usually we read for entertainment or information. Rarely do we read critically, to understand how the writer organizes ideas and uses detail to support themes. MCAT Verbal Reasoning requires that you abandon standard reading habits and take on the role of a critical, or active, reader. This means that you create a mental model of the passage while you're reading, capturing each idea the author constructs and making it part of your vision of the passage.

This can happen only if you resist feeling overwhelmed by the themes in the passage. If you're too awed by the author or bored by the subject matter, you won't be able to take possession of the passage. This notion of "taking possession" is the key to active reading. It means that you keep a distance from the words and that you remain analytical rather than get emotional.

Your goals from the outset of the passage are to figure out what the author is saying and how the ideas are linked. Every passage contains one main idea. You can usually figure it out in the first few lines of the passage and redefine your sense of it as you move through the passage. When you're done reading, you should be able to state the main idea in your own words. Being an active reader means that you constantly ask yourself what the author intends and how that intention is conveyed and supported. Successfully answering the questions depends on your ability to glean the author's point quickly, to map out the passage in your mind, and to assess the inferences.

Pay Attention to Structure
The structure of each passage can help you organize a mental map. You know, for example, that each paragraph will explore a new angle of the main idea or provide detail associated with a key idea. The MCAT Verbal Reasoning passages are, for the most part, very logical in their construction. They may contain complicated words or ideas, but their structure is very manageable, even predictable. Look for certain keywords (e.g., *consequently*) or phrases (e.g., *on the other hand*) that hold ideas together and can alert you as to what's ahead in the passage.

Some test takers feel more anchored as they read the passage if they've scoped out the questions first. As a rule, however, doing so won't save you time or effort. Most of the questions will require that you demonstrate a general understanding of the passage's main idea and overall construction—neither of which can be derived from any particular section of the passage. You need to read for meaning and for organization whether or not you've reviewed the questions.

A CLOSER LOOK

Here's a chance to begin familiarizing yourself with Verbal Reasoning passages and questions and to learn how to approach them. You'll have more opportunities to practice this section in the content review section of this book; for now, we want to open your eyes to structure and strategy.

SAMPLE PASSAGE AND QUESTIONS

As you read through the MCAT-style passage below, try to articulate the main idea to yourself. Read actively and critically. Consider what the author is trying to say and how the ideas are communicated. You might want to pause between paragraphs to digest what you've read and put the ideas into your own words.

In a real MCAT situation, you'll need to be time-conscious while you read. For now, just go at whatever pace feels comfortable to you. Keep in mind that the passages you'll see on the MCAT can come from history, philosophy, the arts, and other disciplines and can vary in length and complexity.

In 1948, *Look* magazine polled America's art critics and major artists, among them Edward Hopper, Stuart Davis, and Charles Burchfield, for a consensus on the creative spirit who could be pronounced the best of the age. It is a fair measure of the art establishment's limited attention span that a generation after John Marin was crowned prince of painters by his peers, his name had begun to fade. New styles raced in to seize the interest of the gallery and museum worlds; fashion embraced Abstract Expressionism, then thrilled to the distancing imagery of Pop Art and later, for about five minutes, went gaga over a frail phenomenon labeled Op Art. To be sure, Marin's death in 1953 was the occasion for lavish obituary tributes. But mention him today to a reasonably literate American or a cultured, well–traveled European, and likely as not, the response will be a puzzled stare.

That is not only odd but hard to understand. Marin's legacy embraces more than 3,000 works, many of them memorable. There are prime etchings; splendid, if demanding, oils; and, in the main, watercolors—2,500 of them, amazing in color, design, and complexity. He seemed to have set down everything in a transport of excitement, as if he were recording themes for a fevered gavotte. Indeed, he once wrote of the acts of drawing and painting as "a sort of mad wonder dancing."

Everything that came from Marin's loving hand radiated spontaneity. Here, it appeared, was a natural, creative spirit: a lucky man who was freed, rather than constrained, by his magnanimous imagination. In truth, hardly anything Marin turned out was unrehearsed. The paintings that hinted at the impetuosity of an artist struggling to convey the "warring, pushing, pulling forces" of his surroundings were, as often as not, studio works. Even his letters, with their blithe disregard for punctuation, were discovered to be the result of many drafts.

As a husband and father, Marin lived a life of singular regularity. He had one wife and, as far as anyone knows, no extramarital entanglements. When he put away his paints at the end of his working day, Marin became a man of simple, harmless pleasures. Late pictures show a wiry-looking figure with a long, thin Yankee nose, the parched skin of a farmer, and a humorous mouth that often held a cigarette. No one ever saw him down more drink than was good for his speech or balance. His idea of fun was a good game of billiards.

The contrast between the art and the man who made it was extreme, fascinating, and a trifle baffling. Marin's pictures were daring, the work of a sophisticated eye, an unfailing imagination, a virtuoso hand; some of them verge on elegant abstraction, although he looked down on abstract art. He hated efforts to interpret his art—or for that matter anyone else's. The attitude is not uncommon to artists, particularly American artists, but Marin's distrust of the critical and academic establishments verged on the fanatic. "Intellectuals," he once pronounced, "have in their makeup a form of Nazism."

1. The main point of the passage is to

   A. explain why John Marin's work was virtually forgotten after his death.
   B. consider the contrast between Marin's artistic style and his personal life and habits.
   C. argue that the art establishment was unable to reach a consensus on the "best of the age" because of its limited attention span.
   D. suggest that Marin's vivacious watercolors were a reaction against Nazism in the art world.

2. Of the following, the author of the passage is most likely

   A. a contemporary painter.
   B. a magazine art critic.
   C. an investigative reporter.
   D. a museum curator.

3. The author refers to Op Art in order to

   A. place Marin's art within a specific category or genre.
   B. identify the origins of Marin's artistic style.
   C. emphasize the fleeting popularity of artistic styles.
   D. compare Marin's stylistic simplicity with later psychedelic trends.

4. The author's attitude toward Marin may be described as one of

   A. grudging approval.
   B. playful irreverence.
   C. flippant disrespect.
   D. reverent appreciation.

5. The passage discusses all of the following aspects of Marin's life EXCEPT his

   A. political beliefs.
   B. physical appearance.
   C. artistic style.
   D. family life.

6. In saying that intellectuals "have in their makeup a form of Nazism", Marin most probably means that

   A. the academic establishment is clearly fascist in its structure.
   B. intellectuals often have leftist political and social leanings.
   C. critics often misread extremist political messages in the works of artists.
   D. the criticism and interpretation of art represents a sort of tyranny.

7. The author characterizes Marin's work as

   A. fevered and energetic.
   B. simple and colorful.
   C. constrained and precise.
   D. tortured and impenetrable.

8. The author characterizes Marin's paintings as "studio works" to make the point that

   A. Marin's painting exhibited the influences of many studio artists.
   B. despite attempts at objectivity, Marin's works expressed the academic biases of his time.
   C. although Marin's work seemed spontaneous, it was the result of precise crafting.
   D. Marin's paintings never reflected his complexity and vivid imagination.

Did You Catch the Main Idea?

The author's intent was to contrast John Marin's flamboyant artistic style with his subdued personal life. We get the first hint of this theme in the second paragraph, where the author describes the ostensible mechanism by which Marin created his art ("mad wonder dancing"). The idea is further developed in the next paragraph, where we get the sense that the process through which Marin produced art was not as it seemed ("In truth, hardly anything Marin turned out was unrehearsed.") The fourth paragraph describes the subject's personal life, showing it to be as dull as his art was wild. The last paragraph begins with a clear statement of the passage's main idea; the rest of the paragraph solidifies the intent of the passage.

There's more to understanding the passage than just being able to figure out the main idea. You have to construct a mental outline of the structure of the passage so you'll be able to refer back to it while you answer the questions. The questions following a passage test your understanding of the passage, its structure, its implications, and its tone. It's important that you gather information about the passage as you read so you'll be able to answer the questions quickly and confidently.

ANSWER REVIEW

1. **B**

   Choice (B) has the proper scope to reflect the main idea. **choice (A)** makes reference to a minor point in the first paragraph, **choice (C)** distorts an idea from the passage and magnifies a detail, and **choice (D)** connects two ideas presented separately.

2. **B**

   The citation after the passage and the general tone of the writing suggest that "magazine art critic" is most fitting. Were the writer a painter, we would expect more information about the artwork. An investigative reporter would have a confrontational tone. Finally, we might expect that a museum curator would focus more on Marin's artwork and its effect on the public rather than on the relationship between his art and his life.

3. **C**

   Go back to the passage to find the reference. We find it in conjunction with the writer's implication that the art world has a short attention span. This is most consistent with **choice (C)**. **Choices (A)** and **(B)** mistakenly connect Op Art to the work of Marin, a connection the author does not make in the passage. **Choice (D)** assumes a comparison also not drawn from the passage.

4. **D**

   Only **choice (D)** matches the overall tone of the passage. Most Tone questions have adjectives and nouns in the answer choices. Remember that both must match the passage for the choice to be correct.

5. **A**

   This type of question requires that you find an exception. **Choice (A)**—political beliefs—is the only aspect among the answer choices not discussed in the passage. If you misinterpreted Marin's "Nazi" quote as being political instead of philosophical, you might have had a hard time answering this question.

6. **D**

   Here, you must show that you interpreted the quote correctly. Marin used the *Nazism* to describe a repressive, tyrannical system of criticism—not a political attitude. Only **choice (D)** resonates with the metaphorical interpretation of the phrase.

7. **A**

   The answer can't be found in a particular line from the passage. You must conclude the best answer based on the attitude and tone of the passage. **Choice (A)** accurately reflects the writer's characterizations of Marin's work. **Choice (B)** might be tempting because the writer *does* describe Marin as simple, but in reference to his personal life, not his art. **Choice (C)** describes Marin's life as depicted by the author but has no connection to his art. Finally, **choice (D)** conveys too much negativity to match the tone of the passage.

8. **C**

   Refer back to see how the sentence functions in the passage. We see that the author was trying to suggest that despite their seeming spontaneity, Marin's paintings were actually quite "crafted." **Choice (C)** is thus consistent with the intent of the passage. **Choice (A)** is a tricky interpretation of the sentence. **Choice (B)** sounds erudite, but it has no relation to the passage whatsoever. Lastly, **choice (D)** makes an illogical leap to conclude that Marin's paintings showed no imagination, but the passage never suggests this is the case.

SIX QUESTION TYPES

There are six Verbal Reasoning question styles you'll find on the MCAT: Main Idea, Detail, Inference, Application, Tone, and Logic. Familiarity with the question types helps you anticipate the kinds of answers you should be choosing. The ability to anticipate correct answers will speed up your testing time, give you extra confidence, and—ultimately—boost your score!

1. Main Idea

Description: Main Idea questions ask for a restatement of the author's main point, the primary idea, or the overall gist of the passage. Question 1 in the preceding sample is a Main Idea question, because it's asking you for the point of the Marin excerpt.

Strategy: Look for the answer that best matches the scope of the main theme. Wrong answers will be either too narrow or too broad in their restatement of the author's main point or will distort it in some way.

Strategy Applied: If you looked for the "big idea" of the preceding sample passage as you read it, you see that your interpretation of the author's purpose matches only one answer, that there was a sharp contrast between Marin's artistic style and personal life.

2. Detail

Description: Detail questions require you to recall a specific point from the passage or to relocate it using information from the question stem. Correct answers will be those that approximate information directly from the passage. One type of Detail question—"Scattered Detail"—will ask you to consider many details from various places in the passage and may ask you to identify a detail as an exception among the answer choices. For example: "The author uses as evidence all the following except . . . ." Question 5 in the preceding sample is a Scattered Detail question because it requires that you recall or look back to the passage to determine a characteristic of Marin's life that is not mentioned.

Strategy: Refer to any notes you made on your scratch paper or to notes in your mental outline to identify the detail under consideration. If the question is in the "all EXCEPT" format, you should be looking for the exception choice that fits the stimulus. By all means, look back to the passage. You're not supposed to memorize details!

Strategy Applied: In the case of the sample, you're looking for the exception, so you should ask yourself, "Does this fit the stimulus?" for each answer choice. The answer is no for only one—the passage does not discuss Marin's political beliefs.

3. Inference

<u>Description</u>: Inference questions ask you to make a small logical leap from the passage to another idea that would be consistent with the main idea. Correct answers to Inference questions will have the proper degree of "distance" from the passage itself—not so close as to be a detail but not so far as to be illogical.

<u>Strategy</u>: Choose an answer that is consistent with the passage but is not a simple restatement of information already presented.

<u>Strategy Applied</u>: There wasn't an Inference question in the sample, but let's say that you were asked how Marin's work was affected by critical interpretation. Since you're told that Marin did not like interpretation of his or anyone else's art, you can infer that he would not adjust his art to suit the critics and that his work would be unaffected.

4. Application

<u>Description</u>: Application questions ask you to take an essential idea from the passage and relate it to a different context. These questions may set up analogies or metaphors; you'll need to figure out how they relate to one another and determine which one presents an idea that parallels the passage. Question 2 in the sample is an Application question because it asks you to use what you know about the passage to guess at the source of the passage.

<u>Strategy</u>: Pick an answer choice that effectively "translates" an idea from the passage into a new context or scenario.

<u>Strategy Applied</u>: Taking what you know about the sample passage (the author's point of view and tone) and applying this to a scenario outside the passage (the source of the piece), you can judge that the author was most likely a magazine art critic.

5. Tone

<u>Description</u>: Questions of Tone require you to identify the author's attitude or opinion about a passage's subject matter. Such questions may be focused on a detail or may refer to the tone of the whole passage. Question 4 from the sample passage is an example of a Tone question because it asks you to determine the author's attitude.

<u>Strategy</u>: Go with the answer choice that is consistent with your "gut feel" from the passage—positive, neutral, or negative.

<u>Strategy Applied</u>: Based on the first paragraph in the sample passage, you know that the author holds Marin in high esteem, so the correct answer about the author's tone will have to reflect a completely positive attitude. Only one choice does so.

6. Logic

<u>Description</u>: Logic questions require that you analyze the function of certain portions of the passage. You may be asked how a particular detail serves the purpose of the passage, or you may be asked about overall passage structure. A Logic question is derived from the overall plan and layout of the passage—not from the specifics contained within the passage. Question 8 in the sample is a Logic question because it asks you about the role of a test element in logical structure of the passage.

<u>Strategy</u>: Refer to your mental map and passage outline, the key to all Logic questions. Choose an answer that maintains the integrity of your passage blueprint.

<u>Strategy Applied</u>: In the sample, you're asked to determine the meaning of the term *studio works*. To do so, you need to read a few sentences back from the term and figure out its context. You clearly see, then, that *studio works* refers to artistic pieces crafted through a deliberate process.

KAPLAN TIPS

GETTING OFF ON THE RIGHT FOOT

- You usually won't save time by scanning the questions before reading the passage, as most of the questions are based on a holistic understanding of the passage. Besides, having the questions in mind can distract you from focusing on the passage.
- Read the opening lines of each paragraph slowly and carefully to "orient" yourself to the subject matter and its main point.
- Read for the Main Idea, which is often, but not always, expressed in the opening lines.

READING THE PASSAGES

- Read actively!
- Don't get emotional. Read with distance.
- Don't judge the passages. You'll need to overcome the hurdle of reading material that doesn't interest you.
- Create a mental map.
- Feel free to make notes on scratch paper.
- Don't try to memorize details. Know the purpose of the detail, not the detail itself.
- Look for structural keywords to help you anticipate new ideas in the passage.
- Check the citation at the end of the passage. It may give clues about tone or context.

FACING THE QUESTIONS

- When you're finished reading, don't rush to the questions. Take a moment to rephrase the main idea to yourself.
- Remember that wrong answer choices will distort or reverse the author's main point, blow a detail out of proportion, confuse or misplace details, or be totally irrational. Use a process of elimination to increase your chances of getting to the right answer.
- You should look back at the passage to find or clarify details while you're answering the questions.
- Answer questions based on the passage—not based on outside knowledge.
- If you don't know an answer, guess! Try to do so while you're still working on the passage so you won't have to reread it later. There's no penalty for wrong answers. Leave no question unanswered!

Test Expertise

4

HIGHLIGHTS

- Learn Kaplan's Five Basic Principles of Test Expertise.
- Find out how to pace yourself during each section of the MCAT.
- Make sure you know the smartest way to handle the answer grid.

The first year of medical school is a frenzied experience for most students. Faced with the requirements of a rigorous work schedule, students either learn to prioritize and budget their time or else fall hopelessly behind. It's no surprise, then, that the MCAT, the test specifically designed to predict success in the first year of medical school, is a high-speed, time-intensive test. It demands excellent time-management skills as well as that sine qua non of the successful physician—grace under pressure.

It's one thing to answer a Verbal Reasoning question correctly; it's quite another to answer several correctly in a limited time frame. And the same goes for Physical and Biological Sciences—it's a whole new ball game once you move from doing an individual passage at your leisure to handling a full section under actual timed conditions. Time pressure is a factor that affects virtually every test taker.

So when you're comfortable with the content of the test, your next challenge will be to take it to the next level—test expertise—which will enable you to manage the all-important time element of the test.

THE FIVE BASIC PRINCIPLES OF TEST EXPERTISE

On some tests, if a question seems particularly difficult, you'll spend significantly more time on it, as you'll probably be given more points for correctly answering a hard question. Not so on the MCAT. Remember: Every MCAT question, no matter how hard, is worth a single point. There's no partial credit or A for effort. And since there are so many questions to do in so little time, you'd be a fool to spend ten minutes getting a point for a hard question and then not have time to get a few quick points from three easy questions later in the section.

Given this combination—limited time, all questions equal in weight—you've got to develop a way of handling the test sections to make sure you get as many points as you can as quickly and easily as you can. Here are the principles that will help you do that.

1. FEEL FREE TO SKIP AROUND

One of the most valuable strategies to help you finish the sections in time is to learn to recognize and deal first with the questions that are easier and more familiar to you. That means you must temporarily skip those that promise to be difficult and time consuming, if you feel comfortable doing so. You can always come back to these at the end, and if you run out of time, you're much better off not getting to questions you may have had difficulty with, rather than not getting to potentially feasible material. Of course, because there's no guessing penalty, always put an answer to every question on the test, whether you get to it or not. (It's not practical to skip passages, so do those in order.)

This strategy is difficult for most test takers; we're conditioned to do things in order. But give it a try when you practice. Remember, if you do the questions in the exact order given, you're letting the test makers control you. But you control how you take this test. On the other hand, if skipping around goes against your moral fiber and makes you a nervous wreck—don't do it. Just be mindful of the clock and don't get bogged down with the tough questions.

2. LEARN TO RECOGNIZE AND SEEK OUT QUESTIONS YOU CAN DO

Another thing to remember about managing the test sections is that MCAT questions and passages, unlike items on the SAT and other standardized tests, are not presented in order of difficulty. In fact, the test makers scatter the easy and difficult questions throughout the section, in effect rewarding those who actually get to the end. Don't lose sight of what you're being tested for along with your reading and thinking skills: efficiency and cleverness.

Don't waste time on questions you can't do. We know that skipping a possibly tough question is easier said than done; we all have the natural instinct to plow through test sections in their given order. But it just doesn't pay off on the MCAT. The computer won't be impressed if you get the toughest question right. If you dig in your heels on a tough question, refusing to move on until you've cracked it, well, you're letting your ego get in the way of your test score. A test section (not to mention life itself) is too short to waste on lost causes.

3. USE A PROCESS OF ANSWER ELIMINATION

Using a process of elimination is another way to answer questions both quickly and effectively. There are two ways to get all the answers right on the MCAT. You either know all the right answers, or you know all the wrong answers. Since there are three times as many wrong answers, you should be able to eliminate some if not all of them. By doing so, you either get to the correct response or increase your chances of guessing the correct response. You start out with a 25 percent chance of picking the right answer, and with each eliminated answer, your odds go up. Eliminate one, and you'll have a $33\frac{1}{3}$ percent chance of picking the right one; eliminate two, and you'll have a 50 percent chance; and, of course, eliminate three, and you'll have a 100 percent chance. Increase your efficiency by actually crossing out the wrong choices. Remember to look for wrong-answer traps when you're eliminating. Some answers are designed to seduce you by distorting the correct answer.

4. REMAIN CALM

It's imperative that you remain calm and composed while working through a section. You can't allow yourself to become so rattled by one hard reading passage that it throws off your performance on the rest of the section. Expect to find at least one killer passage in every section, but remember, you won't be the only one to have trouble with it. The test is curved to take the tough material into account. Having trouble with a difficult question isn't going to ruin your score—but getting upset about it and letting it throw you off track will. When you understand that part of the test maker's goal is to reward those who keep their composure, you'll recognize the importance of not panicking when you run into challenging material.

5. KEEP TRACK OF TIME

Of course, the last thing you want to happen is to have time called on a particular section before you've gotten to half the questions. Therefore, it's essential that you pace yourself, keeping in mind the general guidelines for how long to spend on any individual question or passage. Have a sense of how long you have to do each question so you know when you're exceeding the limit and should start to move faster.

When working on a section, always remember to keep track of time. Don't spend a wildly disproportionate amount of time on any one question or group of questions. Also, give yourself 30 seconds or so at the end of each section to fill in answers for any questions you haven't gotten to.

SECTION-SPECIFIC PACING

Let's now look at the section-specific timing requirements and some tips for meeting them. Keep in mind that the times per question or passage are only averages; there are bound to be some that take less time and some that take more. Try to stay balanced. Remember, too, that every question is of equal worth, so don't get hung up on any one. Think about it: If a question is so hard that it takes you a long time to answer it, chances are you may get it wrong anyway. In that case, you'd have nothing to show for your extra time but a lower score.

VERBAL REASONING

Allow yourself approximately eight to ten minutes per passage and respective questions. It may sound like a lot of time, but it goes quickly. Keep in mind that some passages are longer than others. On average, give yourself about three or four minutes to read and then four to six minutes for the questions.

PHYSICAL AND BIOLOGICAL SCIENCES

Averaging over each section, you'll have about 1 minute and 20 seconds per question. Some questions, of course, will take more time, some less. A science passage plus accompanying questions should take about eight to nine minutes, depending on how many questions there are. Discrete questions can take anywhere from a few seconds to a minute or more. Again, the rule is to do your best work first. Also, don't feel that you have to understand everything in a passage before you go on to the questions. You may not need that deep an understanding to answer questions, since a lot of information may be extraneous. You should overcome your perfectionism and use your time wisely.

COMPUTER-BASED TESTING STRATEGIES

ARRIVE AT THE TESTING CENTER EARLY

Get to the testing center early to jump-start your brain. However, if they allow you to begin your test early, decline.

USE THE MOUSE TO YOUR ADVANTAGE

If you are right-handed, practice using the mouse with your left hand for Test Day. This way, you'll increase speed by keeping the pencil in your right hand to write on your scratch paper. If you are left-handed, use your right hand for the mouse.

KNOW THE TUTORIAL BEFORE TEST DAY

You will save time on Test Day by knowing exactly how the test will work. Click through any tutorial pages and save time.

PRACTICE WITH SCRATCH PAPER

Going forward, always practice using scratch paper when solving questions because this is how you will do it on Test Day. Never write directly on a written test.

GET NEW SCRATCH PAPER

Between sections, get a new piece of scratch paper even if you only used part of the old one. This will maximize the available space for each section and minimize the likelihood of running out of paper to write on.

MARK INCOMPLETE WORK

If you need to go back to a question, clearly mark the work you've done on the scratch paper with the question number. This way, you will be able to find your work easily when you come back to tackle the question.

LOOK AWAY AT TIMES

Taking the test on computer leads to faster eye-muscle fatigue. Use the Kaplan strategy of looking at a distant object at regular intervals. This will keep you fresher at the end of the test.

PRACTICE ON THE COMPUTER

This is the most critical aspect of adapting to computer-based testing. As with anything else, to perform well on computer-based tests, you must practice. Spend time reading passages and answering questions on the computer. You often will have to scroll when reading passages.

Test Mentality

5

- Learn Kaplan's Four Basic Principles of Good Test Mentality.
- Find out how to handle stress leading up to and during the exam.
- Review Kaplan's Top Ten MCAT Tips.

In this section, we first glanced at the content that makes up each specific section of the MCAT, focusing on the strategies and techniques you'll need to tackle individual questions and passages. Then we discussed the test expertise involved in moving from individual items to working through full-length sections. Now we're ready to turn our attention to the often overlooked attitudinal aspects of the test, to put the finishing touches on your comprehensive MCAT approach.

THE FOUR BASIC PRINCIPLES OF GOOD TEST MENTALITY

Knowing the test content arms you with the weapons you need to do well on the MCAT. But you must wield those weapons with the right frame of mind and in the right spirit. Otherwise, you could end up shooting yourself in the foot. This involves taking a certain stance toward the entire test. Here's what's involved.

1. TEST AWARENESS

To do your best on the MCAT, you must always keep in mind that the test is like no other you've taken before, both in terms of content and in terms of the scoring system. If you took a test in high school or college and got a number of the questions wrong, you wouldn't receive a perfect grade. But on the MCAT, you can get a handful of questions wrong and still get a "perfect" score. The test is geared so that only the very best test takers are able to finish every section. But even these people rarely get every question right.

What does this mean for you? Well, just as you shouldn't let one bad passage ruin an entire section, you shouldn't let what you consider to be a subpar performance on one section ruin your performance on the entire test. If you allow that subpar performance to rattle you, it can have a cumulative negative effect, setting in motion a downward spiral. It's that kind of thing that could potentially do serious damage to your score. Losing a few extra points won't do you in, but losing your cool will.

Remember, if you feel you've done poorly on a section, don't sweat it. Chances are it's just a difficult section and that factor will already be figured into the scoring curve. The point is, remain calm and collected. Simply do your best on each section, and once a section is over, forget about it and move on.

2. STAMINA

You must work on your test-taking stamina. Overall, the MCAT is a fairly grueling experience, and some test takers simply run out of gas on the last section. To avoid this, you must prepare by taking a few full-length practice tests in the weeks before the test so that on Test Day, those three sections will seem like a breeze. (Well, maybe not a breeze, but at least not a hurricane.)

Take the full-length practice tests included in this book. You'll be able to review answer explanations and assess your performance. For additional practice material, visit the Association of American Medical Colleges website (aamc.org) to order the MCAT Practice Tests it publishes. The AAMC also sells online access to six full-length practice tests. Test 3 is available at the AAMC website free of charge. Tests 4, 5, 7, 8, 9, 10, and 11 are available for purchase.

Your best option, if you have time, would be to take the full Kaplan course. We'll give you access to all the released material plus loads of additional material (more than 1,000 MCAT-style passages in total) so you can really build up your MCAT stamina. You'll also have the benefit of our expert live instruction on every aspect of the MCAT. To go this route, call 1-800-KAP-TEST or visit kaptest.com for on site and online Kaplan class schedules.

Reading this chapter is a great start in your preparation for the test, but it won't get you your best score. That can happen only after lots of practice and skill building. You've got to train your brain to be test smart! Kaplan has been helping people do that for over 65 years, so giving us a call would be a great way to move your test prep into high gear!

3. CONFIDENCE

Confidence feeds on itself, and unfortunately, so does the opposite of confidence—self-doubt. Confidence in your ability leads to quick, sure answers and a sense of well-being that translates into more points. If you lack confidence, you end up reading the sentences and answer choices two, three, or four times, until you confuse yourself and get off track. This leads to timing difficulties, which only perpetuate the downward spiral, causing anxiety and a tendency to rush to finish sections.

If you subscribe to the MCAT Mindset we've described, however, you'll gear all of your practice toward the major goal of taking control of the test. When you've achieved that goal—armed with the principles, techniques, strategies, and approaches set forth in this book—you'll be ready to face the MCAT with supreme confidence. And that's the one sure way to score your best on Test Day.

4. THE RIGHT ATTITUDE

Those who approach the MCAT as an obstacle, who rail against the necessity of taking it, who make light of its importance, who spend more time making fun of the AAMC than studying for the test usually don't fare as well as those who see the MCAT as an opportunity to show off the reading and reasoning skills that the medical schools are looking for. Don't waste time making value judgments about the MCAT. It is not going to go away, so deal with it. Those who look forward to doing battle with the MCAT—or, at least, who enjoy theopportunity to distinguish themselves from the rest of the applicant pack—tend to score better than do those who resent or dread it.

It may sound a little dubious, but take our word for it: Attitude adjustment is a proven test-taking technique. Here are a few steps you can take to make sure you develop the right MCAT attitude:

- Look at the MCAT as a challenge but try not to obsess over it; you certainly don't want to psyche yourself out of the game.
- Remember that, yes, the MCAT is obviously important, but, contrary to what some premeds think, this one test will not single-handedly determine the outcome of your life.
- Try to have fun with the test. Learning how to match your wits against the test makers can be a very satisfying experience, and the reading and thinking skills you'll acquire will benefit you in medical school as well as in your future medical career.
- Remember that you're more prepared than most people. You've trained with Kaplan. You have the tools you need plus the know-how to use those tools.

QUICK TIPS FOR THE DAYS JUST BEFORE THE EXAM

- The best test takers do less and less as the test approaches. Taper off your study schedule and take it easy on yourself. Give yourself time off, especially the evening before the exam. By that time, if you've studied well, everything you need to know is firmly stored in your memory bank.
- Positive self-talk can be extremely liberating and invigorating, especially as the test looms closer. Tell yourself things such as "I will do well," rather than "I hope things go well"; "I can," rather than "I cannot." Replace any negative thoughts with affirming statements that boost your self-esteem.
- Get your act together sooner rather than later. Have everything (including choice of clothing) laid out in advance. Most important, make sure you know where the test will be held and the easiest, quickest way to get there. You'll have great peace of mind by knowing that all the little details—gas in the car, directions, etc.—are set before the day of the test.
- Go to the test site a few days in advance, particularly if you are especially anxious. Better yet, bring some practice material and do at least a section or two.

- Forego any practice on the day before the test. It's in your best interest to marshal your physical and psychological resources for 24 hours or so. Even racehorses are kept in the paddock and treated like royalty the day before a race. Keep the upcoming test out of your consciousness; go to a movie, take a pleasant hike, or just relax. Don't eat junk food or tons of sugar. And, of course, get plenty of rest the night before—just don't go to bed too early. It's hard to fall asleep earlier than you're used to, and you don't want to lie there worrying about the test.

HANDLING STRESS DURING THE TEST

The biggest stress monster will be the test itself. Fear not; there are methods of quelling your stress during the test.

- Keep moving forward instead of getting bogged down in a difficult question. You don't have to get everything right to achieve a fine score. So don't linger out of desperation on a question that is going nowhere even after you've spent considerable time on it. The best test takers skip difficult material temporarily in search of the easier stuff. They mark the questions that require extra time and thought.
- Don't be thrown if other test takers seem to be working more busily and furiously than you are. Don't mistake the other people's sheer activity as signs of progress and higher scores.
- Keep breathing! Weak test takers tend to share one major trait: They don't breathe properly as the test proceeds. They might hold their breath without realizing it or breathe erratically or arrhythmically. Improper breathing hurts confidence and accuracy. Just as important, it interferes with clear thinking.
- Some quick isometrics during the test—especially if concentration is wandering or energy is waning—can help. Try this: Put your palms together and press intensely for a few seconds. Concentrate on the tension you feel through your palms, wrists, forearms, and up into your biceps and shoulders. Then quickly release the pressure. Feel the difference as you let go. Focus on the warm relaxation that floods through the muscles. Now you're ready to return to the task.
- Here's another isometric that will relieve tension in both your neck and eye muscles. Slowly rotate your head from side to side, turning your head and eyes to look as far back over each shoulder as you can. Feel the muscles stretch on one side of your neck as they contract on the other. Repeat five times in each direction.

With what you've just learned here, you're armed and ready to do battle with the test. This book and your studies have given you the information you'll need to answer the questions. It's all firmly planted in your mind. You also know how to deal with any excess tension that might come along, both when you're studying for and taking the exam. You've experienced everything you need to tame your test anxiety and stress. You're going to get a great score.

KAPLAN'S TOP TEN MCAT TIPS

1. **Relax!**

2. **Remember: It's primarily a thinking test.** Never forget the purpose of the MCAT: It's designed to test your powers of analytical reasoning. You need to know the content, as each section has its own particular "language," but the underlying MCAT intention is consistent throughout the test.

3. **Feel free to skip around within each section.** Attack each section confidently. You're in charge. Move around between questions if you feel comfortable doing so. Work your best areas first to maximize your opportunity for MCAT points. Don't be a passive victim of the test structure!

4. **For passage-based questions, choose an answer based on the information given.** Be careful not to be "too smart for your own good." Passages—especially those that describe experimental findings (an MCAT favorite, by the way)—often generate their own data. Your answer choices must be consistent with the information in the passage, even if that means an answer choice is inconsistent with the science of ideal theoretical situations.

5. **Avoid wrong-answer traps.** Try to anticipate answers before you read the answer choices. This helps boost your confidence and protects you from persuasive or tricky incorrect choices. Most wrong answer choices are logical twists on the correct choice.

6. **Think, think, think!** We said it before, but it's important enough to say again: Think. Don't compute.

7. **Don't look back.** Don't spend time worrying about questions you had to guess on. Keep moving forward. Don't let your spirit start to flag, or your attitude will slow you down. You can recheck answers within a section if you have time left, but don't worry about a section after time has been called.

8. **Practice for the MCAT on the computer.** The MCAT is a computer-based test, and you will perform better on Test Day if you practice on the computer. This means that the online companion to this book, which includes two additional MCAT-style computer-based exams, will be a huge asset to your Test Day preparation. For additional computer-based practice, you should investigate Kaplan's *MCAT Premier* book, which includes another three computer-based practice exams, or visit the AAMC website (aamc.org). And as mentioned earlier in this chapter, a full Kaplan course includes all of the above material, plus thousands more practice questions and our expert MCAT teachers.

9. **Don't leave any questions unanswered.** There are no points taken off for wrong answers, so if you're not sure of an answer, guess. And guess quickly, so you'll have more time to work through other questions.

10. **Call us! We're here to help! 1-800-KAP-TEST.** Or visit us on the Web at kaptest.com.

Section Two

Full-Length Practice Tests

Full-Length Practice Test 1

MCAT OVERVIEW

PHYSICAL SCIENCES

Time	70 minutes
Format	52 multiple-choice questions:
	7 passages with 4–7 questions each;
	13 discrete questions (not passage-based)

VERBAL REASONING

Time	60 minutes
Format	40 multiple-choice questions:
	7 passages with 4–7 questions each

BIOLOGICAL SCIENCES

Time	70 minutes
Format	52 multiple-choice questions:
	7 passages with 4–7 questions each;
	13 discrete questions (not passage-based)

Instructions for Taking the Full-Length Practice Test

Before taking this Full-Length Practice Test, find a quiet place where you can work uninterrupted.

Use the answer grid on the following page to record your answers. Time yourself according to the time limits shown at the beginning of each section. Keep in mind that you'll be taking the real test on the computer.

You'll find the answer key, the score converter, and detailed answer explanations following the test.

Good luck.

Answer Grid — Questions 1–144 (options A B C D)

1. Ⓐ Ⓑ Ⓒ Ⓓ
2. Ⓐ Ⓑ Ⓒ Ⓓ
3. Ⓐ Ⓑ Ⓒ Ⓓ
4. Ⓐ Ⓑ Ⓒ Ⓓ
5. Ⓐ Ⓑ Ⓒ Ⓓ
6. Ⓐ Ⓑ Ⓒ Ⓓ
7. Ⓐ Ⓑ Ⓒ Ⓓ
8. Ⓐ Ⓑ Ⓒ Ⓓ
9. Ⓐ Ⓑ Ⓒ Ⓓ
10. Ⓐ Ⓑ Ⓒ Ⓓ
11. Ⓐ Ⓑ Ⓒ Ⓓ
12. Ⓐ Ⓑ Ⓒ Ⓓ
13. Ⓐ Ⓑ Ⓒ Ⓓ
14. Ⓐ Ⓑ Ⓒ Ⓓ
15. Ⓐ Ⓑ Ⓒ Ⓓ
16. Ⓐ Ⓑ Ⓒ Ⓓ
17. Ⓐ Ⓑ Ⓒ Ⓓ
18. Ⓐ Ⓑ Ⓒ Ⓓ
19. Ⓐ Ⓑ Ⓒ Ⓓ
20. Ⓐ Ⓑ Ⓒ Ⓓ
21. Ⓐ Ⓑ Ⓒ Ⓓ
22. Ⓐ Ⓑ Ⓒ Ⓓ
23. Ⓐ Ⓑ Ⓒ Ⓓ
24. Ⓐ Ⓑ Ⓒ Ⓓ
25. Ⓐ Ⓑ Ⓒ Ⓓ
26. Ⓐ Ⓑ Ⓒ Ⓓ
27. Ⓐ Ⓑ Ⓒ Ⓓ
28. Ⓐ Ⓑ Ⓒ Ⓓ
29. Ⓐ Ⓑ Ⓒ Ⓓ
30. Ⓐ Ⓑ Ⓒ Ⓓ
31. Ⓐ Ⓑ Ⓒ Ⓓ
32. Ⓐ Ⓑ Ⓒ Ⓓ
33. Ⓐ Ⓑ Ⓒ Ⓓ
34. Ⓐ Ⓑ Ⓒ Ⓓ
35. Ⓐ Ⓑ Ⓒ Ⓓ
36. Ⓐ Ⓑ Ⓒ Ⓓ
37. Ⓐ Ⓑ Ⓒ Ⓓ
38. Ⓐ Ⓑ Ⓒ Ⓓ
39. Ⓐ Ⓑ Ⓒ Ⓓ
40. Ⓐ Ⓑ Ⓒ Ⓓ

41. Ⓐ Ⓑ Ⓒ Ⓓ
42. Ⓐ Ⓑ Ⓒ Ⓓ
43. Ⓐ Ⓑ Ⓒ Ⓓ
44. Ⓐ Ⓑ Ⓒ Ⓓ
45. Ⓐ Ⓑ Ⓒ Ⓓ
46. Ⓐ Ⓑ Ⓒ Ⓓ
47. Ⓐ Ⓑ Ⓒ Ⓓ
48. Ⓐ Ⓑ Ⓒ Ⓓ
49. Ⓐ Ⓑ Ⓒ Ⓓ
50. Ⓐ Ⓑ Ⓒ Ⓓ
51. Ⓐ Ⓑ Ⓒ Ⓓ
52. Ⓐ Ⓑ Ⓒ Ⓓ
53. Ⓐ Ⓑ Ⓒ Ⓓ
54. Ⓐ Ⓑ Ⓒ Ⓓ
55. Ⓐ Ⓑ Ⓒ Ⓓ
56. Ⓐ Ⓑ Ⓒ Ⓓ
57. Ⓐ Ⓑ Ⓒ Ⓓ
58. Ⓐ Ⓑ Ⓒ Ⓓ
59. Ⓐ Ⓑ Ⓒ Ⓓ
60. Ⓐ Ⓑ Ⓒ Ⓓ
61. Ⓐ Ⓑ Ⓒ Ⓓ
62. Ⓐ Ⓑ Ⓒ Ⓓ
63. Ⓐ Ⓑ Ⓒ Ⓓ
64. Ⓐ Ⓑ Ⓒ Ⓓ
65. Ⓐ Ⓑ Ⓒ Ⓓ
66. Ⓐ Ⓑ Ⓒ Ⓓ
67. Ⓐ Ⓑ Ⓒ Ⓓ
68. Ⓐ Ⓑ Ⓒ Ⓓ
69. Ⓐ Ⓑ Ⓒ Ⓓ
70. Ⓐ Ⓑ Ⓒ Ⓓ
71. Ⓐ Ⓑ Ⓒ Ⓓ
72. Ⓐ Ⓑ Ⓒ Ⓓ
73. Ⓐ Ⓑ Ⓒ Ⓓ
74. Ⓐ Ⓑ Ⓒ Ⓓ
75. Ⓐ Ⓑ Ⓒ Ⓓ
76. Ⓐ Ⓑ Ⓒ Ⓓ
77. Ⓐ Ⓑ Ⓒ Ⓓ
78. Ⓐ Ⓑ Ⓒ Ⓓ
79. Ⓐ Ⓑ Ⓒ Ⓓ
80. Ⓐ Ⓑ Ⓒ Ⓓ

81. Ⓐ Ⓑ Ⓒ Ⓓ
82. Ⓐ Ⓑ Ⓒ Ⓓ
83. Ⓐ Ⓑ Ⓒ Ⓓ
84. Ⓐ Ⓑ Ⓒ Ⓓ
85. Ⓐ Ⓑ Ⓒ Ⓓ
86. Ⓐ Ⓑ Ⓒ Ⓓ
87. Ⓐ Ⓑ Ⓒ Ⓓ
88. Ⓐ Ⓑ Ⓒ Ⓓ
89. Ⓐ Ⓑ Ⓒ Ⓓ
90. Ⓐ Ⓑ Ⓒ Ⓓ
91. Ⓐ Ⓑ Ⓒ Ⓓ
92. Ⓐ Ⓑ Ⓒ Ⓓ
93. Ⓐ Ⓑ Ⓒ Ⓓ
94. Ⓐ Ⓑ Ⓒ Ⓓ
95. Ⓐ Ⓑ Ⓒ Ⓓ
96. Ⓐ Ⓑ Ⓒ Ⓓ
97. Ⓐ Ⓑ Ⓒ Ⓓ
98. Ⓐ Ⓑ Ⓒ Ⓓ
99. Ⓐ Ⓑ Ⓒ Ⓓ
100. Ⓐ Ⓑ Ⓒ Ⓓ
101. Ⓐ Ⓑ Ⓒ Ⓓ
102. Ⓐ Ⓑ Ⓒ Ⓓ
103. Ⓐ Ⓑ Ⓒ Ⓓ
104. Ⓐ Ⓑ Ⓒ Ⓓ
105. Ⓐ Ⓑ Ⓒ Ⓓ
106. Ⓐ Ⓑ Ⓒ Ⓓ
107. Ⓐ Ⓑ Ⓒ Ⓓ
108. Ⓐ Ⓑ Ⓒ Ⓓ
109. Ⓐ Ⓑ Ⓒ Ⓓ
110. Ⓐ Ⓑ Ⓒ Ⓓ
111. Ⓐ Ⓑ Ⓒ Ⓓ
112. Ⓐ Ⓑ Ⓒ Ⓓ
113. Ⓐ Ⓑ Ⓒ Ⓓ
114. Ⓐ Ⓑ Ⓒ Ⓓ
115. Ⓐ Ⓑ Ⓒ Ⓓ
116. Ⓐ Ⓑ Ⓒ Ⓓ
117. Ⓐ Ⓑ Ⓒ Ⓓ
118. Ⓐ Ⓑ Ⓒ Ⓓ
119. Ⓐ Ⓑ Ⓒ Ⓓ
120. Ⓐ Ⓑ Ⓒ Ⓓ

121. Ⓐ Ⓑ Ⓒ Ⓓ
122. Ⓐ Ⓑ Ⓒ Ⓓ
123. Ⓐ Ⓑ Ⓒ Ⓓ
124. Ⓐ Ⓑ Ⓒ Ⓓ
125. Ⓐ Ⓑ Ⓒ Ⓓ
126. Ⓐ Ⓑ Ⓒ Ⓓ
127. Ⓐ Ⓑ Ⓒ Ⓓ
128. Ⓐ Ⓑ Ⓒ Ⓓ
129. Ⓐ Ⓑ Ⓒ Ⓓ
130. Ⓐ Ⓑ Ⓒ Ⓓ
131. Ⓐ Ⓑ Ⓒ Ⓓ
132. Ⓐ Ⓑ Ⓒ Ⓓ
133. Ⓐ Ⓑ Ⓒ Ⓓ
134. Ⓐ Ⓑ Ⓒ Ⓓ
135. Ⓐ Ⓑ Ⓒ Ⓓ
136. Ⓐ Ⓑ Ⓒ Ⓓ
137. Ⓐ Ⓑ Ⓒ Ⓓ
138. Ⓐ Ⓑ Ⓒ Ⓓ
139. Ⓐ Ⓑ Ⓒ Ⓓ
140. Ⓐ Ⓑ Ⓒ Ⓓ
141. Ⓐ Ⓑ Ⓒ Ⓓ
142. Ⓐ Ⓑ Ⓒ Ⓓ
143. Ⓐ Ⓑ Ⓒ Ⓓ
144. Ⓐ Ⓑ Ⓒ Ⓓ

Physical Sciences Test

Time: 70 minutes—Questions 1–52

DIRECTIONS: Most of the questions in the following Physical Sciences test are organized into groups, with a descriptive passage preceding each group of questions. Study the passage, then select the single best answer to each question in the group. Some of the questions are not based on a descriptive passage; you must also select the best answer to these questions. If you are unsure of the best answer, eliminate the choices that you know are incorrect, then select an answer from the choices that remain. A periodic table is provided below for your use with the questions.

A Periodic Table of the Elements

1	2	3	4	5	6	7	8	9	10	11	12	13	14	15	16	17	18
1 H 1.0																	2 He 4.0
3 Li 6.9	4 Be 9.0											5 B 10.8	6 C 12.0	7 N 14.0	8 O 16.0	9 F 19.0	10 Ne 20.2
11 Na 23.0	12 Mg 24.3											13 Al 27.0	14 Si 28.1	15 P 31.0	16 S 32.1	17 Cl 35.5	18 Ar 39.9
19 K 39.1	20 Ca 40.1	21 Sc 45.0	22 Ti 47.9	23 V 50.9	24 Cr 52.0	25 Mn 54.9	26 Fe 55.8	27 Co 58.9	28 Ni 58.7	29 Cu 63.5	30 Zn 65.4	31 Ga 69.7	32 Ge 72.6	33 As 74.9	34 Se 79.0	35 Br 79.9	36 Kr 83.8
37 Rb 85.5	38 Sr 87.6	39 Y 88.9	40 Zr 91.2	41 Nb 92.9	42 Mo 95.9	43 Tc (98)	44 Ru 101.1	45 Rh 102.9	46 Pd 106.4	47 Ag 107.9	48 Cd 112.4	49 In 114.8	50 Sn 118.7	51 Sb 121.8	52 Te 127.6	53 I 126.9	54 Xe 131.3
55 Cs 132.9	56 Ba 137.3	57 La * 138.9	72 Hf 178.5	73 Ta 180.9	74 W 183.9	75 Re 186.2	76 Os 190.2	77 Ir 192.2	78 Pt 195.1	79 Au 197.0	80 Hg 200.6	81 Tl 204.4	82 Pb 207.2	83 Bi 209.0	84 Po (209)	85 At (210)	86 Rn (222)
87 Fr (223)	88 Ra 226.0	89 Ac † 227.0	104 Rf (261)	105 Db (262)	106 Sg (263)	107 Bh (264)	108 Hs (269)	109 Mt (268)	110 Ds (269)	111 Rg (272)	112 Uub (277)	113 Uut (284)	114 Uuq (289)	115 Uup (288)	116 Uuh (292)	117 Uus (291)	118 Uuo (293)

*	58 Ce 140.1	59 Pr 140.9	60 Nd 144.2	61 Pm (145)	62 Sm 150.4	63 Eu 152.0	64 Gd 157.3	65 Tb 158.9	66 Dy 162.5	67 Ho 164.9	68 Er 167.3	69 Tm 168.9	70 Yb 173.0	71 Lu 175.0
†	90 Th 232.0	91 Pa (231)	92 U 238.0	93 Np (237)	94 Pu (244)	95 Am (243)	96 Cm (247)	97 Bk (247)	98 Cf (251)	99 Es (252)	100 Fm (257)	101 Md (258)	102 No (259)	103 Lr (260)

GO ON TO THE NEXT PAGE.

Passage 1 (Questions 1–5)

When light enters the eye, it forms an image on the retina. First, light from the object passes through the cornea, a converging lens within the eye, and then through a liquid known as the aqueous humor. After this, it passes through a second crystalline converging lens into the eyeball, which is filled with a fluid known as the vitreous humor. The light is refracted by the cornea and by the crystalline lens and is focused on the retina, which transmits electrical impulses along the optic nerve to the brain.

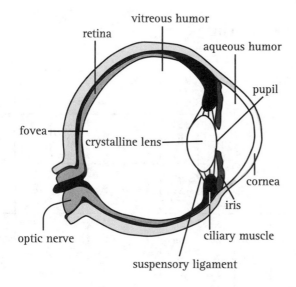

The cornea has a constant focal length and is responsible for most of the refraction of the light from the object. The crystalline lens has a variable focal length, which enables the eye to focus the image on the retina, even though the object distance varies. The focal length of the crystalline lens is varied by tensing and relaxing the ciliary muscle that surrounds the lens. It is relaxed when focusing on a distant object and tensed when focusing on a near object. It is important to note that when the ciliary muscle is tensed, the lens assumes a more spherical shape, thus decreasing the focal length.

The cornea and the crystalline lens may be considered two thin lenses in contact and, therefore, thought of as a single converging lens at a distance of 2.0 centimeters from the retina. When an object is at an infinite distance away, the focal length of the lens is equal to the distance between the lens and the retina. When the distance to the object is appreciably smaller, the focal length of the lens changes so that the image is still focused on the retina.

There are several defects of vision. The two most common are myopia and hyperopia. Myopia, or nearsightedness, is caused when the image of an object at infinity is focused in front of the retina. Hyperopia, or farsightedness, is caused when an object at infinity is focused behind the retina. (Note: In the following questions, assume that the distance from the lens to the retina is 2 cm.)

1. The index of refraction of the vitreous humor is greater than the index of refraction of the aqueous humor, which is greater than the index of refraction of air. What is the relationship of the speed of light in each of these media?

   A. Fastest in air, slower in aqueous humor, slowest in vitreous humor
   B. Fastest in vitreous humor, slower in aqueous humor, slowest in air
   C. Equal in all three
   D. Depend on the index of refraction of the lenses which separate the media

2. For a normal eye to focus on an object 20 cm away, what is the required focal length of the eye's lens?

   A. 0.05 cm
   B. 1.8 cm
   C. 2.0 cm
   D. 2.2 cm

GO ON TO THE NEXT PAGE.

3. Two converging lenses are in contact. If the focal lengths are each 5 cm, what is the equivalent focal length of the combination?

   A. 0.1 cm
   B. 2.5 cm
   C. 5.0 cm
   D. 10.0 cm

4. A myopic person's eye has a relaxed focal length of 1.9 cm. What is the maximum distance from the eye at which she can see an object clearly, and what is the magnification of the lens for an object at this point?

   A. $0 = 1$ cm, $m = -\dfrac{1}{2}$
   B. $0 = 38$ cm, $m = -\dfrac{1}{38}$
   C. $0 = 38$ cm, $m = -\dfrac{1}{19}$
   D. $0 = 50$ cm, $m = -\dfrac{1}{50}$

5. Which of the following is true of the image formed on the retina?

   I. It is real.
   II. It is inverted.
   III. It is reduced.

   A. I only
   B. I and II only
   C. II and III only
   D. I, II, and III

GO ON TO THE NEXT PAGE.

Passage II (Question 6-11)

A mixture of two volatile solvents that exhibits ideal behavior will boil when the total vapor pressure is equal to the atmospheric pressure. The concentration of the more volatile component will always be greater in the vapor than in the solution. If the vapor above the boiling mixture is condensed and boiled again, it will be even richer in the more volatile component. With successive condensations and boilings, it is possible to separate the individual components. This process is known as fractional distillation.

There are, however, a number of solvent systems that do not behave ideally and, consequently, cannot be separated. Figure 1 shows a boiling-point diagram for a system that is called a *minimum-boiling azeotrope*. In a system such as this, the attraction between unlike molecules is weaker than the attraction between like molecules; as a result, the solution boils at a lower temperature than the pure components. Systems that have a maximum on the boiling-point diagram are called *maximum-boiling azeotropes*. Fractional distillation of these nonideal systems will, at best, give one pure component and the azeotrope.

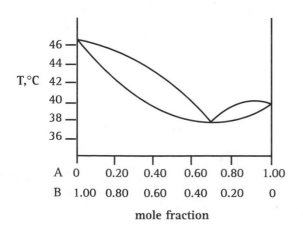

Figure 1

6. Which of the following best describes the mechanism by which two substances form a maximum-boiling azeotrope?

   A. Each substance increases the specific heat of the other.
   B. Each substance decreases the specific heat of the other.
   C. Each substance increases the vapor pressure of the other.
   D. Each substance decreases the vapor pressure of the other.

7. Which of the following combinations would be likely to form a minimum-boiling azeotrope?

   A. Water and chlorobenzene
   B. Water and nitric acid
   C. Water and hydrogen peroxide
   D. Water and acetone

8. Which of the following shows the boiling point of an aqueous sodium chloride solution as a function of the percent sodium chloride in the solution by weight?

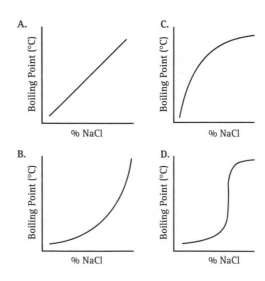

9. Based on Figure 1, if a mixture of Solution A and Solution B boils at 40°C, what is the mole fraction of B in the vapor?

   A. 0.04 or 0.70
   B. 0.20 or 0.40
   C. 0.30 or 0.96
   D. 0.60 or 0.80

10. An ethanol and water solution can be distilled to, at best, a 95 percent ethanol solution, which boils at 78°C. What can be said about this mixture?

    A. It is a minimum-boiling azeotrope with water as the most volatile component.
    B. It is a minimum-boiling azeotrope with ethanol as the most volatile component.
    C. It is a maximum-boiling azeotrope with water as the most volatile component.
    D. It is a maximum-boiling azeotrope with ethanol as the most volatile component.

11. Which of the following describes the effect on boiling point when a nonvolatile solute is added to a liquid?

    A. $\Delta T_b = K_b M$
    B. $\Delta T_b - K_b / M$
    C. $\Delta T_b = K_b m$
    D. $\Delta T_b = K_b / m$

GO ON TO THE NEXT PAGE.

Passage III (Questions 12–17)

Robert Millikan is credited with showing experimentally that the electron has a definite, finite charge. His experiment, in a somewhat simplified form, is described below. The setup is shown in Figure 1.

Two horizontal parallel plates, A and B, are placed 1 cm apart and are insulated from one another. A potential difference V_{AB} is applied across the plates, producing an electric field between them.

Drops of oil between 10^{-6} and 10^{-5} cm in diameter are sprayed through a hole in the top plate into the electric field. The drops accumulate electric charge and are, therefore, affected by the electric field. In the case of a negatively charged drop, the potential difference across the plates is adjusted until the drop is motionless, the gravitational force being exactly balanced by the upward electrostatic force. The mass of the droplet and the potential difference across the plates is measured, and from this, the electric charge on the drop can be determined. This procedure is then repeated with another drop.

Millikan found, when he calculated the electric charge required from the balanced forces, that the measured charges were integer multiples of a specific electric charge. This "unit" charge was assumed to be the charge of a single electron. (Note: Acceleration due to gravity = 9.8 m/s²; density of oil = 800 kg/m³.)

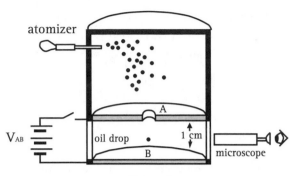

Figure 1

12. What is the electric field between the plates in Figure 1 if the voltage V_{AB} is 20 volts?

   A. 0.02 V/m
   B. 0.2 V/m
   C. 20 V/m
   D. 2×10^3 V/m

13. What is the direction of an electric field between the plates that holds a negatively charged droplet motionless?

   A. Upward
   B. Downward
   C. To the left
   D. To the right

14. If the separation of the plates is reduced, but the potential difference across them remains constant, which of the following statements must be true?

   I. The electric field increases.
   II. The magnetic field increases.
   III. The capacitance increases.

   A. I only
   B. I and II only
   C. I and III only
   D. II and III only

GO ON TO THE NEXT PAGE.

15. An oil drop is stationary within an electric field of 490 V/m that is set up between two parallel plates. If the volume of the oil drop is 4×10^{-19} m³, how many excess electrons does it carry? (Note: The fundamental unit of charge e $= 1.6 \times 10^{-19}$ C.)

A. 1
B. 4
C. 10
D. 40

16. A negatively charged droplet has a mass of 5×10^{-16} kg and carries a charge of 8×10^{-18} C. The droplet falls through the hole in the upper plate when the electric field is 0 V/m. How does the drop move within the plates as the electric field is increased slowly from 0 V/m to 800 V/m? (Note: Assume that the drop remains between the plates at all times.)

A. It moves downward, stops, then moves upward.
B. It moves downward, accelerating all the time.
C. It moves downward, stops, then moves downward again.
D. It moves downward, stops, and remains stationary.

17. A drop of oil of mass 5×10^{-16} kg is at rest on the bottom plate of a parallel plate combination when the electric field is zero. An electric field of 4×10^{3} V/m is then applied between the plates, accelerating the drop toward the top plate. What will be the resultant acceleration of the drop if it carries a negative charge of 3×10^{-18} C? (Note: Neglect the effects of air resistance.)

A. 9.8 m/s²
B. 14.2 m/s²
C. 24.0 m/s²
D. 28.4 m/s²

Questions 18 through 20 are NOT based on a descriptive passage.

18. What is the calcium concentration of a solution formed by adding 1 mol of $CaCl_2$ to 1 L of distilled water at 298K?

A. $1M$
B. $1m$
C. $2M$
D. $2m$

19. Two blocks of the same density are completely submerged in water. One block has a mass equal to m and volume equal to V. The other has a mass equal to $2m$. What is the ratio of the first block's apparent weight to the second block's apparent weight?

A. 1:1
B. 1:2
C. 2:1
D. 4:1

GO ON TO THE NEXT PAGE.

20. In the arrangement shown below, a current flows from P to Q, and the ammeter A_1 reads 3.0 A. If each ammeter has negligible resistance, what is the reading on ammeter A_2?

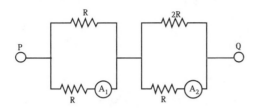

A.   1.0 A
B.   1.5 A
C.   2.0 A
D.   4.0 A

GO ON TO THE NEXT PAGE.

Passage IV (Questions 21–25)

The most commonly used electric lights in homes today are incandescent. Incandescent light is created by applying a potential difference to a filament of thin, high-resistance wire. Electrons moving in the current collide with atoms in the wire, transferring energy to these atoms. This energy is dissipated in the form of radiation, almost all of which is in the infrared range. When the wire becomes hot enough, the spectrum produced begins to enter the red end of the visible range. As the temperature of the resistor increases, the visible spectrum produced becomes closer to the spectrum of white light. However, a high temperature decreases the life of the light bulb by increasing the rate of vaporization of the filament. Early incandescent lamps used vacuum bulbs; later on, filling the bulb with an inert gas became common. The gas distributes the light more evenly over the visible spectrum and increases the life of the filament.

Fluorescent lights work by an entirely different method. An electric arc is created between two electrodes in a tube in which a small amount of mercury has been vaporized. The mercury produces ultraviolet light, and this light is then intercepted by a phosphor that coats the inside of the glass tube. The phosphor absorbs the ultraviolet and emits visible radiation of a longer wavelength. The wavelength produced can be controlled by varying the phosphor composition. A "warm white" lamp produces more light on the red end of the spectrum than does a "cool white" lamp.

With the recent interest in the effect of light on mood, a market has developed for lamps that simulate the spectrum of outdoor light. The natural light spectrum on a sunny day is of more or less equal intensity over the range from 540 to 700 nanometers, although the intensity is lower at shorter wavelengths, particularly from about 400 to 460 nanometers. On a cloudy day, the greatest natural light intensity occurs on the blue end of the spectrum, with the red end somewhat less intense. Of course, the greatest difference between the artificial light generally used in homes and natural light is the intensity.

21. Why does an incandescent light have a longer life when an inert gas is used rather than a vacuum?

    A. The filament vaporizes more slowly.
    B. Heat is removed from the filament.
    C. The bulb is less likely to implode when subjected to vibration.
    D. The gas directly absorbs energy from the electrons in the filament.

22. An advertiser argues that incandescent lights are not adequate for improving mood on a cloudy day because they do not provide enough light of short wavelength. What argument could be made against this position?

    A. Incandescent lights provide mostly light of short wavelength.
    B. Outdoor light is more intense at longer wavelengths on a sunny day than on a cloudy day.
    C. Outdoor light is more intense at shorter wavelengths on a sunny day than on a cloudy day.
    D. The spectrum produced by electric lights is irrelevant since their intensity is so low.

GO ON TO THE NEXT PAGE.

23. Which of the lamps described in the passage can produce excess exposure to ultraviolet radiation when operating normally?

    A. Incandescent lamps only
    B. Fluorescent lamps only
    C. Both incandescent and fluorescent lamps
    D. Neither kind of lamp

24. Which kind of lamps, incandescent or fluorescent, are more efficient?

    A. Incandescent lamps, because they release all of the radiation they originally produce
    B. Fluorescent lamps, because they produce only radiation in the visible range
    C. Incandescent lamps, because no energy is lost in the conversion of energy from one wavelength to another
    D. Fluorescent lamps, because they multiply the intensity of radiation as it is converted from ultraviolet to visible light

25. What would a manufacturer of fluorescent lamps have to do in order to change his "warm white" lamps to "cool white" lamps?

    A. Change the amount of mercury vapor in the lamp to produce less ultraviolet light.
    B. Change the thickness of the glass tube to get a greater index of refraction.
    C. Change the composition of the electrodes to produce a weaker electric arc.
    D. Change the composition of the phosphor to emit more light at the blue-violet end of the spectrum.

GO ON TO THE NEXT PAGE.

Passage V (Questions 26–30)

Band theory explains the conductivity of certain solids by stating that the atomic orbitals of the individual atoms in the solid merge to produce a series of atomic orbitals comprising the entire solid. The closely spaced energy levels of the orbitals form bands. The band corresponding to the outermost occupied subshell of the original atoms is called the valence band. If partially full, as in metals, it serves as a conduction band through which electrons can move freely. If the valence band is full, then electrons must be raised to a higher band for conduction to occur. The greater the band gap between the separate valence and conduction bands, the poorer is the material's conductivity. Figure 1 shows the valence and conduction bands of a semiconductor, which is intermediate in conductivity between conductors and insulators.

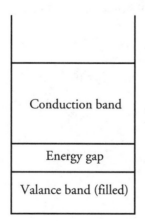

Figure 1

When silicon, a semiconductor with tetrahedral covalent bonds, is heated, a few electrons escape into the conduction band. Doping the silicon with a few phosphorus atoms provides unbonded electrons that escape more easily, increasing conductivity. Doping with boron produces holes in the bonding structure, which may be filled by movement of nearby electrons within the lattice. When a semiconductor in an electric circuit has excess electrons on one side and holes on the other, electron flow occurs more easily from the side with excess electrons to the side with holes than in the reverse direction.

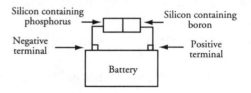

Figure 2

26. Why is iron a good conductor of electricity?

    A. Its *3d* electrons only partially fill the valence band.
    B. The band gap is small.
    C. The *4s* and *3d* orbitals form a filled valence band.
    D. The energy levels of the atomic orbitals are closely spaced.

GO ON TO THE NEXT PAGE.

27. How could heat be expected to increase the conductivity of a semiconductor?

    I. By reducing collisions between moving electrons
    II. By breaking covalent bonds
    III. By raising electrons to a higher energy level

    A. I only
    B. III only
    C. I and III only
    D. II and III only

28. Why do phosphorus and boron atoms enhance the conductivity of silicon?

    A. Their electronegativity differs from that of silicon.
    B. They have different numbers of valence electrons.
    C. Their semimetallic nature makes them good semiconductors.
    D. They are better conductors than silicon even as pure substances.

29. The energy gap for pure silicon is about 1.1 electron volts. If a 1.5 volt electrical potential is connected across a sample of silicon,

    A. the electrons would jump to the conduction band, and the silicon would conduct.
    B. the holes in the silicon lattice would move.
    C. the energy gap would be lowered.
    D. the silicon would not conduct.

30. If the semiconductor orientation in Figure 2 were reversed so that the boron-doped silicon were on the left and the phosphorus-doped silicon on the right, what could be said about the electron flow of the new setup?

    A. The electron flow is easier in the new direction than in that of Figure 2.
    B. The electron flow is the same in either direction.
    C. The electron flow is harder in the new direction than in that of Figure 2.
    D. The electrons cannot flow.

GO ON TO THE NEXT PAGE.

31. When an electron falls from $n = 3$ to $n = 2$ in a hydrogen atom, what is the value of the energy released, given that A is the energy needed to remove an electron from the ground state of a hydrogen atom to an infinite distance from the atom?

    A. 0.14 A
    B. 0.17 A
    C. 1.00 A
    D. 5.00 A

32. A Boeing 737 aircraft has a mass of 150,000 kg and a cruising velocity of 720 km/hr. Its engines can create a total thrust of 200,000 N. If air resistance, change in altitude, and fuel consumption can be ignored, how long does it take for the plane to reach its cruising velocity starting from rest?

    A. 100 s
    B. 150 s
    C. 540 s
    D. 1,944 s

33. If the pK_a of a weak acid is 5, the pH will be 6

    A. when the concentration of dissociated acid is one-tenth the concentration of undissociated acid.
    B. when half the acid is dissociated.
    C. when the concentration of dissociated acid is ten times the concentration of undissociated acid.
    D. only after a base has been added.

34. A certain metal plate is completely illuminated by a monochromatic light source. Which of the following would increase the number of electrons ejected from the surface of the metal?

    I. Increasing the intensity of the light source
    II. Increasing the frequency of the light source
    III. Increasing the surface area of the metal plate

    A. I only
    B. I and II only
    C. I and III only
    D. II and III only

35. An apparatus is set up to measure the standard potential of a chemical reaction. When the apparatus is in operation, which of the following correctly describes of the movement of electrons?

    A. Through the ammeter to the anode
    B. Through the ammeter to the cathode
    C. Through the voltmeter to the anode
    D. Through the voltmeter to the cathode

GO ON TO THE NEXT PAGE.

Passage VI (Questions 36–41)

Aggregated gas molecules, known as clusters, are found in abundance in the upper atmosphere. Atmospheric scientists have devised several ways of artificially synthesizing clusters, which are bound together by weak intermolecular forces. The most common method of producing bimolecular clusters in the laboratory is via a supersonic nozzle. Such a nozzle consists of a tiny pinhole, a few microns in diameter, through which a gas under high pressure (up to 100 atm) expands into a vacuum chamber. During expansion the molecules collide with one another, and many "stick together" as clusters. Conditions such as pressure and nozzle diameter can be adjusted to favor clusters containing different numbers of molecules.

The strength of the forces holding these aggregations together can be determined by irradiating samples with a laser. The threshold frequency of light needed to break the clusters down into their constituent molecules is used to derive t`he energy of the clusters. Table 1 shows several types of intermolecular attractive forces and examples of clusters for which each type of force predominates. In contrast to the strengths of these intermolecular forces, the strength of a chemical bond is typically tens of thousands of wavenumbers.

Table 1

FORCE	STRENGTH (cm^{-1})	EXAMPLES
H-bonding	~1,200 – 2,000	F–H • • • F–H
Dipole–Dipole	~30 – 1,000	HCl • • • SO_2
Dipole–Induced Dipole	~20 – 500	H_2O • • • Ar
Dispersion	~3 – 150	Ar • • • Ar

36. What is meant by the "energy of the clusters" mentioned in the second paragraph of the passage?

A. The energy released when the clusters formed
B. The energy shared among the molecules of clusters
C. The bond energy of the molecules in clusters
D. The energy released when clusters break up

37. If clusters are broken up using lasers in the near-infrared to the radio-frequency range of the spectrum, what frequencies could be used to break a chemical bond?

A. Far infrared
B. Microwave
C. Ultraviolet
D. Red light

38. What is the strongest intermolecular interaction between H_2O and CH_3OH molecules?

A. Dipole–dipole
B. Dipole–induced dipole
C. H-bonding
D. Dispersion

GO ON TO THE NEXT PAGE.

39. What type of intermolecular force(s) can exist between two neon atoms?

    I. Dispersion forces
   II. Dipole–induced dipole
  III. Dipole–dipole

    A. I only
    B. II only
    C. I and II only
    D. I and III only

40. The example given in Table 1 of a system exhibiting dipole–dipole interactions shows the molecule SO_2. What is the shape of this molecule?

    A. Linear
    B. Bent
    C. T-shaped
    D. Trigonal planar

41. If a cluster can be broken up by a photon with a wave number of 1,000 cm^{-1}, what is the cluster's energy?

(Note: Planck's constant $= 6.6 \times 10^{-34}$ J • s.)

    A. 6.6×10^{-31} J
    B. 6.6×10^{-29} J
    C. 2.0×10^{-26} J
    D. 2.0×10^{-20} J

GO ON TO THE NEXT PAGE.

Passage VII (Questions 42–47)

A bomb calorimeter measures the heat of combustion of unknown materials. Inside a pressurized heavy-duty steel canister (the "bomb") filled with pure oxygen gas is placed a compressed disc of the unknown sample, through which a fine wire runs. The wire is connected to electrodes on the canister and is ignited with a jolt of electricity. Both sample and wire burn rapidly in the oxygen, raising the calorimeter's temperature.

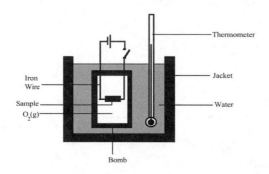

Figure 1 Bomb Calorimeter

The energy of combustion ΔE_{comb} of the sample may be determined from the sample's heat capacity C_v at constant volume, the rise in temperature of the calorimeter ΔT, and the heat capacity of the iron wire C_{Fe}. We assume that sufficient oxygen is available in the bomb to allow the combustion reaction to go to completion.

$$\Delta E_{comb} = (C_v\,\Delta T - C_{Fe}\,m_{Fe})/m_{sample} \quad \text{[Equation I]}$$
$$C_{calorimeter} = -\Delta E/\Delta T \quad \text{[Equation II]}$$

The following experimental data were taken by a student.

Property	Value
m_{sample}	1.3916 g
m_{wire}	0.0068 g
C_{Fe}	1,400 cal/g
$C_{calorimeter}$	2,417 cal/°C
T_i	25.01 °C
T_f	29.93 °C
C_v	8,541.9 cal/g

Table 1 Bomb Calorimetry of Sample

From the data listed in Table 1, the student determined that the sample was benzophenone, $(C_6H_5)_2CO$.

42. Which expression gives the correct energy of combustion for benzophenone?

A. $\Delta E_{comb} = 13\Delta E_{f,CO_2} + 5\Delta E_{f,H_2O} - \Delta E_{f,benzophenone}$

B. $\Delta E_{comb} = \Delta E_{f,benzophenone} + \Delta E_{f,O_2} - \Delta E_{f,CO_2} - \Delta E_{f,H_2O}$

C. $\Delta E_{comb} = \Delta E_{f,benzophenone} + 15\Delta E_{f,O_2} + 13\Delta E_{f,CO_2} + 5\Delta E_{f,H_2O}$

D. $\Delta E_{comb} = 13\Delta E_{f,CO_2} + 5\Delta E_{f,H_2O} - \Delta E_{f,benzophenone} - \Delta E_{f,CO_2}$

GO ON TO THE NEXT PAGE.

43. Below is a plot of the temperature of the calorimeter versus time:

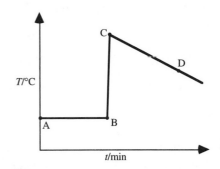

Which point on the graph represents *Tf*?

A. A
B. B
C. C
D. D

44. About how many moles of oxygen were consumed in the calorimeter?

A. 0.001 mol
B. 0.01 mol
C. 0.1 mol
D. 1 mol

45. About how much energy was required to raise the calorimeter's temperature by 4.92 °C?

A. 2.4 kJ
B. 12 kJ
C. 30 kJ
D. 490 J

46. Which of the following two assumptions is (are) invoked when using a bomb calorimeter to measure energy of combustion?

   I. The system is adiabatic with respect to the environment.

  II. The system maintains an approximately constant pressure throughout the process.

A. I only
B. II only
C. I and II
D. Neither I nor II

47. What is the molar heat capacity of the iron wire?

A. 1.4 kcal/mol
B. 9.5 cal/mol
C. 25 cal/mol
D. 78 kcal/mol

GO ON TO THE NEXT PAGE.

Questions 48 through 52 are NOT based on a descriptive passage.

48. Which form of energy transfer occurs most readily in a vacuum?

   A. Convection
   B. Conduction
   C. Radiation
   D. Two of the above

49. $^{204}_{84}$PO undergoes radioactive decay with a half-life of 3.8 hours by emitting alpha particles. Two moles of pure $^{204}_{84}$PO are isolated and put on a scale. After 7.6 hours, a reading of the sample's mass is made. Its mass is found to be

   A. 201 grams.
   B. 203 grams.
   C. 400 grams.
   D. 402 grams.

50. A sound wave that has a velocity of 10,000 ft/s and a frequency of 1,000 Hz is emitted by a source at rest. When the source is moving at a constant velocity of 2,000 ft/s, what is the ratio of the wavelength that would be heard by a stationary observer behind the moving source to an observer in front of the moving source?

   A. 1:1
   B. 2:3
   C. 3:2
   D. 9:11

51. Gas A is at 30°C and gas B is at 20°C. Both gases are at 1 atmosphere. What is the ratio of the volume of 1 mole of gas A to 1 mole of gas B?

   A. 1:1
   B. 2:3
   C. 3:2
   D. 303:293

52. Which of the following elements has an ionic radius that is larger than its atomic radius?

   A. Na
   B. K
   C. Mg
   D. Cl

STOP.

IF YOU FINISH BEFORE TIME HAS EXPIRED, CHECK YOUR WORK.
YOU MAY GO BACK TO ANY QUESTION IN THIS PART ONLY.

Verbal Reasoning Test

Time: 60 minutes—Questions 53–92

DIRECTIONS: There are six passages in this Verbal Reasoning test. Each passage is followed by several questions. After reading a passage, select the one best answer to each question. If you are not certain of an answer, eliminate the alternatives that you know to be incorrect and then select an answer from the remaining alternatives.

Passage 1 (Questions 53–58)

Although many may argue with my stress on the continuity of the essential traits of American character and religion, few would question the thesis that our business institutions have reflected the constant emphasis in the American value system on individual achievement. From the earliest comments of foreign travelers down to the present, individuals have identified a strong materialistic bent as being a characteristic American trait. The worship of the dollar, the desire to make a profit, the effort to get ahead through the accumulation of possession—all have been credited to the egalitarian character of the society; that is, to the absence of aristocracy. As Tocqueville noted in his discussion of the consequences of a democracy's destruction of aristocracy: "They have swept away the privileges of some of their fellow creatures which stood in their way, but they have opened the door to universal competition." And a study of the comments on American workers of various nineteenth-century foreign travelers reveals that most of these European writers, among whom were a number of socialists, concluded that "social and economic democracy in America, far from mitigating compensation for social status, intensified it. . . ."

American secular and religious values both have facilitated the "triumph of American capitalism" and fostered status striving. The focus on equalitarianism and individual opportunity has also prevented the emergence of class consciousness among the lower classes. The absence of a socialist or labor party, and

the historic weakness of American trade-unionism, appear to attest to the strength of values which depreciated a concern with class. The growth of a large trade-union movement during the 1930s, together with the greater political involvement of labor organizations in the Democratic party, suggested to some that the day—long predicted by Marxists—was arriving in which the American working class would finally follow in the footsteps of its European brethren. Such changes in the structure of class relations seemed to these observers to reflect the decline of opportunity and the hardening of class lines. To them, such changes could not occur without modification in the traditional value system. . . .

A close examination of the character of the American labor movement, however, suggests that it, like American religious institutions, may be perceived as reflecting the basic values of the larger society. Although unions, like all other American institutions, have changed in various ways consistent with the growth of an urban industrial civilization, the essential traits of American trade unions, as of business corporations, may still be derived from key elements in the American value system. . . .

Although the American labor movement is similar to others in many respects, it differs from those of other stable democracies in ideology, class solidarity, tactics, organizational structure, and patterns of leadership behavior. American unions are more conservative; they are more narrowly self-interested; their tactics are more militant; they are

GO ON TO THE NEXT PAGE.

more decentralized in their collective bargaining; and they have more full-time salaried officials, who are on the whole much more highly paid. . . . American unions have also organized a smaller proportion of the labor force than have unions in these other nations.

53. If the claims made in the passage about American and foreign labor unions are correct, how would they be expected to react during a strike against a corporation?

   A. American labor unions would be less likely than foreign unions to use violence against a corporation.
   B. American labor unions would be more likely than foreign unions to use violence against a corporation.
   C. American labor unions would be less likely than foreign unions to bargain with a corporation.
   D. American labor unions would be more likely than foreign unions to bargain with a corporation.

54. Based on the passage, which of the following is (are) NOT true?

   I. American society emphasizes class solidarity over individual achievement.
   II. American unions are less interested in non-labor issues than unions in other democracies.
   III. American labor organizations and American religious institutions share some of the same values.

   A. I only
   B. II only
   C. II and III
   D. I, II, and III

GO ON TO THE NEXT PAGE

55. Suppose that an American union decides that its members should take an active part in national politics. What effect would this information have on the author's view of American unions?

A. It would support that view.

B. It would contradict that view.

C. It would neither support nor contradict that view.

D. It would support that view only if it could be shown that getting involved in politics was for society's good.

56. In the context of the passage, the phrase *strong materialistic bent* (paragraph 1) refers to

A. European socialists' view of aristocrats.

B. European travelers' concern with democracy.

C. American society's emphasis on acquiring wealth.

D. American religion's criticism of secular values.

57. According to the passage, all of the following have influenced the outlook of the American labor movement EXCEPT

A. secular values.

B. religious values.

C. urban industrial civilization.

D. foreign labor movements.

58. According to the passage, which of the following is a part of the "traditional value system"?

A. Class solidarity

B. Individual achievement

C. Urban industrialization

D. Marxist ideology

GO ON TO THE NEXT PAGE.

Passage II (Questions 59–64)

There are a great many points about coral reefs that remain subjects of scientific puzzlement. One mystery concerns the relationship between *Scleractinia*, the coral type whose colonization produces reefs, and their symbiotic partners the *zooxanthellae*, the unicellular algae present in the corals' endodermic tissues. It is known that each symbiont plays an integral part in the formation of a reef's protective limestone foundation. The coral polyps secrete calceous exoskeletons which cement themselves into an underlayer of rock, while the algae deposit still more calcium carbonate, which reacts with sea salt to create an even tougher limestone layer. It is also known that, due to the algal photosynthesis, the reef environment is highly oxygen-saturated, while the similarly high amounts of carbon dioxide are carried off rapidly. All this accounts for the amazing renewability of coral reefs despite the endless erosion caused by wave activity. However, the precise manner in which one symbiont stimulates the secretion of calcium carbonate by the other remains unclear.

Scientists have also proposed various theories to explain the transformation of "fringing reefs," those connected above sea level to land masses, into "barrier reefs, " which are separated from shorelines by wide lagoons, and then into free-floating atolls. Though the theory postulated by Charles Darwin is considered at least partially correct, some scientists today argue that the creation of the reef forms has more to do with the rise of sea level that accompanied the end of the Ice Age than with the gradual submergence of the volcanic islands to which the fringing reefs were originally attached. However, recent drillings at Eniwetak atoll have uncovered a large underlay of volcanic rock, which suggests that Darwin's explanation may have been more valid after all.

Even the name given to the reefs is something of a misnomer. The *Scleractinia* themselves generally comprise no more than 10 percent of the biota of the average reef community: *zooxanthellae* can account for up to 90 percent of the reef mass, along with *foraminifera,* annelid worms, and assorted mollusks. Moreover, the conditions under which reef growth occurs are determined by the needs of the algae, not the corals. Reefs can flourish only in shallow, highly saline waters above 70°F, because the algae require such circumstances; yet non-reef-building corals—corals which lack the algal presence—occur worldwide under various environmental conditions, from the Arctic to the Mediterranean, home of the red coral prized for jewelry. The most likely reason that the term *coral reefs* persists is that the brilliant variety of coral shapes and colors makes aesthetic considerations more vivid than biological ones.

59. All of the following are puzzling to reef scientists EXCEPT

   A. how the *zooxanthellae* stimulate *Scleractinia* to secrete calcium carbonate.
   B. how barrier reefs become separated from land masses by vast expanses of water.
   C. how the reef environment reaches such high levels of oxygen saturation.
   D. how fringing reefs develop into barrier reefs and then into atolls.

GO ON TO THE NEXT PAGE

60. Some scientists consider the term *coral reef* a misnomer because

    A. the beautiful shapes and colors of reefs are produced by the *Scleractinia* rather than the *zooxanthellae.*
    B. the coral portion of a reef has little to do with the reef's survival.
    C. non–reef-building corals are found throughout the world.
    D. the majority of a reef's substance comprises *zooxanthellae, foraminifera,* annelid worms, and assorted molluscs while a small portion comprises the *Scleractinia.*

61. Opponents of Darwin's theory regarding coral reef transformation would disagree with which of the following statements?

    A. Coral reefs change from fringing reefs to barrier reefs and then into free-floating atolls.
    B. Atolls are farther from land masses than are barrier reefs.
    C. Fringing reefs inevitably developed into barrier reefs because volcanic islands gradually sank into the ocean.
    D. As a result of the end of the Ice Age, increased expanses of water aided in the transformation of fringing reefs into barrier reefs.

62. Based on the passage, which of the following is probably an assumption of scientists studying coral reefs?

    A. The theories of reef evolution through glacial melting and through volcanic subsidence are mutually exclusive.
    B. The three main types of coral reefs did not develop independently of one another.
    C. *Zooxanthellae* are always found with coral.
    D. Intense calcification single-handedly protects reefs from destruction by waves and other natural causes.

63. According to the author, the theory proposed by Charles Darwin

    A. is less persuasive on the topic of reef formation in light of recent discoveries.
    B. shows that each type of coral reef developed by separate, distinct processes.
    C. accurately described the transformation of fringing reefs into atolls.
    D. focused on the idea of submerging volcanic islands.

64. Suppose that marine biologists discovered that the calceous exoskeletons produced by coral polyps stimulate the zooxanthellae to deposit calcium carbonate via a chemical stimulus. How would this finding be relevant to the study of reefs?

    A. It would explain how reefs maintain a high level of oxygen saturation.
    B. It would clarify the symbiotic relationship between *Scleractinia* and *zooxanthellae* during their formation of the protective limestone foundation.
    C. It would identify the chemical components of the reef's protective layer.
    D. It would explain the intense colors and formations often seen in coral reefs.

GO ON TO THE NEXT PAGE.

Passage III (Questions 65–69)

Archaeopteryx lithographica lived during the latter part of the Jurassic period, approximately 150 million years ago, just south of what today is central Germany. This ancient creature, which combined a reptilian body and tail with birdlike wings and feathers, has provided a wealth of information about the evolution of flight in birds. However, fossil and skeletal studies indicate that it was not capable of flight. . . .

None of the *Archaeopteryx* fossils discovered to date, including the most mature specimens, exhibits an ossified or bony sternum, the wide bone that extends from the chest to the pelvic area in most modern birds. The main purposes of this structure are to protect internal organs during flight and to act as a sturdy anchoring point for the enormous pectoral muscles necessary for flight. There is no indication that *Archaeopteryx* ever developed strong pectoral muscles, and perhaps this is one reason why it never developed a sternum. Instead, it retained reptilian gastral ribs, thin braces in the abdominal region, which were not attached to the skeleton and which served only to support and protect internal organs. These fishbonelike structures appear too fragile to have supported pectoral muscles. Researchers believe that flight would have been highly unlikely in an animal with such skeletal characteristics.

Furthermore, the bones in the manus of *Archaeopteryx* do not seem to have been fused. In modern birds, these bones are fused in order to support the wing. In addition, the ulna of modern birds is marked with small knobs where feathers are anchored firmly to the bone by ligaments. The ulna in *Archaeopteryx*, however, is smooth, indicating that its feathers were not firmly anchored into the skeleton.

Finally, the skeletal characteristics of *Archaeopteryx* seem to indicate that this animal was most adapted to terrestrial movement. Its hind legs and pelvis closely resemble those of bipedal theropods and dinosaurs, suggesting that, like these other bipeds, it was adept at running along the ground. In contrast to the posture of modern birds, whose bodies are suspended at the pelvis like a seesaw with the thighbones horizontal, it stood up on its hind legs with its long reptilian tail serving to balance it as well as enhance its ability to coordinate abrupt changes of direction while running. In modern birds, all that remains of the tail is a shrunken, fused structure called a pygostyle. Although the foot of *Archaeopteryx* was birdlike, with fused metatarsals, it was also adapted to running and serves as further evidence that this ancient animal had probably not developed the faculty of flight. . . .

Despite the fact that *Archaeopteryx lithographica* possessed many birdlike features, including wings and advanced feathers, most of the fossil evidence of its existence overwhelmingly indicates that this animal was not capable of flight. By way of its peculiar mix of features, it seems to represent a kind of transitionary phase, illustrating an evolutionary leap from reptile to bird and providing insight into the development of flight. . . .

GO ON TO THE NEXT PAGE

65. Suppose that scientists have recently found the skeleton of a bird capable of flight embedded in pre-Jurassic period rock. What effect would this discovery most likely have on their thinking about *Archaeopteryx lithographica*?

    A. It would support the view that *Archaeopteryx lithographica* represented a transitionary species between reptiles and birds.
    B. It would undermine the view that *Archaeopteryx lithographica* represented a transitionary species between reptiles and birds.
    C. It would neither support nor undermine the view that *Archaeopteryx lithographica* represented a transitionary species between reptiles and birds.
    D. It would support the view that *Archaeopteryx lithographica* failed to develop the pectoral muscles necessary for flight.

66. Based on information in the passage, which of the following statements is NOT true?

    A. *Archaeopteryx lithographica's* skeleton is similar to the skeleton of a modern bird.
    B. *Archaeopteryx lithographica's* tail played a larger role in its daily life than the tail of a modern bird plays in its daily life.
    C. Scientists have studied *Archaeopteryx lithographica* in order to learn about the development of flight.
    D. *Archaeopteryx lithographica* shared some characteristics in common with dinosaurs.

67. In the context of the passage, the phrase *wealth of information* (paragraph 1) refers to

    A. knowledge of recent research projects on the evolution of flight.
    B. knowledge about *Archaeopteryx lithographica's* skeletal structure.
    C. knowledge acquired by scientists studying the development of birds.
    D. knowledge of fossil discoveries in what is now central Germany.

68. The author suggests which of the following about *Archaeopteryx lithographica*?

    A. It did not have as well-developed a tail as a modern bird.
    B. Its wings had a different function than the wings of a modern bird.
    C. It was less intelligent than a modern bird.
    D. Its skeletal structure made it much larger than a modern bird.

69. Researchers believe that *Archaeopteryx* differs from modern birds for all of the following reasons EXCEPT

    A. a lack of feathers.
    B. pectoral muscle development.
    C. ossification of the sternum.
    D. knobs found on the ulna.

GO ON TO THE NEXT PAGE.

Passage IV (Questions 70–76)

Light has been used as a beacon to mariners for thousands of years, for as long as man has taken to the sea. From the first primitive light beacons evolved the modern lighthouse, found on almost every waterway and coast in the world. To the uneducated eye, all of these lighthouses, despite their distinct locations, seem to be irrelevant variations on a homogeneous design. However, nothing could be further from the truth; from height to lenses, each lighthouse is as unique as the landscape that surrounds it.

There is not one feature of a lighthouse that is arbitrary. By day, the varying color patterns painted on lighthouses help sailors distinguish their location along the coastline. These patterns, known as "daymarks," are usually a combination of white, black, or red and can be painted in broad bands or spirals, and none is alike.

The earliest modern lighthouses employed a catoptric light system that used parabolic silver mirrors to reflect lamplight into a concentrated beam. Often, this bowl- or cone-shaped reflector would be made to spin around the lamp, rotating the beam in the "searchlight" manner typical of many lighthouses. An everyday example of a catoptric light system can be found in a common household flashlight. In 1822, a revolutionary, multi-prismatic lens designed by Jean Augustin Fresnel ushered in the dioptric optical system for lighthouses, able to produce a five-times more powerful beam using the same light source as the catoptric system. Instead of reflecting the light, the Fresnel lens, which is actually a series of concentric rings of segmental lenses, refracted it.

By 1860, every existing lighthouse in the United States had been converted to a Fresnel lens, and to fully take advantage of this more powerful light beam, lighthouses built after the lens's introduction stood much taller than their predecessors. Later, an even more effective optical system known as the catadioptric system was developed, which was a hybrid of the two earlier systems. By 1900, most lighthouses began to convert to electricity and use incandescent bulbs. Prior to that, lanterns fueled by wood, coal, or oil served as a lighthouse's source light for the optical system.

The patterns of light beams emitted from these three different systems are as varied and individual as daymarker patterns. Each lighthouse has its own characteristic intervals of light and eclipse. These intervals, known as nightmarks or signatures, are set in specific patterns defined with such names as flashing, occulting, group flashing, or group occulting. Beacons that are characterized as "flashing" have intervals of darkness that are longer in duration than the intervals of light; "occulting" lights display the opposite of this pattern. "Group flashing" or "group occulting" light patterns are simple groups of small flashes or eclipses. Obviously, there is no flash-eclipse pattern to a steady, uninterrupted "fixed" light, but rare patterns known as fixed flashing do exist; in such patterns, the beacon's light fluctuates between a higher- and lower-beam intensity. What distinguishes each lighthouse is the rate of repetition for the intervals of flash and eclipse or fixed flashing. This unique repetition rate is called a period, and each lighthouse's period is charted in U.S. Coast Guard publications known as light lists. In addition to a lighthouse's nightmarks, its daymarks are included in these charts as well. Smart sailors still value these charts because they know that long after their fragile radios and radar rust into uselessness, the stalwart lighthouses will still be standing tall.

GO ON TO THE NEXT PAGE

70. The author's primary purpose is to

    A. detail the specific functions of a lighthouse.
    B. illustrate a point made by the author.
    C. offer an unbiased opinion.
    D. enumerate lighthouse facts.

71. Based on the passage, which of the following is probably NOT true of lighthouses?

    A. The earliest lighthouses were bonfires built on the shore to guide fishermen back to the beach.
    B. Up until very recently, the capturing and defending of lighthouses was often of strategic naval importance during a war.
    C. A lighthouse's "period" is randomly assigned from a list.
    D. The tallest standing lighthouse has a catadioptric light system.

72. Based on the information in the passage, the author would most likely agree with which statement?

    A. Daymarks on a lighthouse are ancillary to nightmarks.
    B. Daymarks and nightmarks are representative of an esoteric language.
    C. In purpose and design, daymarks and nightmarks are frequently not utilitarian.
    D. A lighthouse with an operative catadioptric system no longer needs daymarks.

73. According to the passage, which of the following statements is (are) true of catoptric light systems?

    I. They were installed in lighthouses built prior to the 1820s.
    II. They use refraction to create a concentrated light beam.
    III. Only a few remain in American lighthouses today.

    A. I only
    B. III only
    C. I and II only
    D. I and III only

74. Based on the passage, it can be inferred that all of the following employ either a catoptric or dioptric light system EXCEPT a

    A. headlight.
    B. flashlight.
    C. film projector.
    D. lantern.

75. According to the passage, an operational lighthouse must

    A. have a generic period.
    B. be of at least a certain height.
    C. possess distinct daymarks and nightmarks.
    D. use a catadioptric optical system.

76. Based on the final sentence of the passage, it can be inferred that the author would describe a sailor who relies solely on technology as a means of navigation as

    A. a typical example of the contemporary mariner.
    B. ill-prepared for an equipment failure.
    C. overconfident in his own skills.
    D. an incompetent novice.

GO ON TO THE NEXT PAGE.

Passage V (Questions 77–83)

The latest prominent principle of criminal sentencing is that of "selective incapacitation." Selective incapacitation, like general incapacitation, involves sentencing with the goal of protecting the community from the crimes that an offender would commit if he were on the street. It differs from general incapacitation in its attempt to replace bluntness with selectivity. Under a strategy of selective incapacitation, probation and short terms of incarceration are given to convicted offenders who are identified as being less likely to commit frequent and serious crimes, and longer terms of incarceration are given to those identified as more crime prone.

An attractive aspect of the selective incapacitation concept is its potential for bringing about a reduction in crime without an increase in prison populations. This reduction could be substantial. . . .

Is selective incapacitation truly an effective and appropriate proposal, an "idea whose time has come," or is it . . . a proposal that carries with it a potential for injustice? . . .

Reserving prison and jail space for the most criminally active offenders may in some instances conflict not only with other norms of legal justice, but with norms of social justice as well. Repeat offenders fall basically into two categories: those who are prone to violence and those who are not. If we reserve the sanction of incarceration only for the dangerous repeat offender, excluding the white-collar offender and certain other criminals who pose no serious threat of physical injury to others, we may end up permitting harmful people from the middle class to evade a sanction that less privileged offenders cannot. Some white-collar offenders, after all, impose greater costs on society than many dangerous street offenders, and it is clearly unjust to allow the former to pay a smaller price for their crimes than the latter must pay. . . .

One of the most pervasive criticisms of selective incapacitation is that it is based on the statistical prediction of dangerousness; because such predictions are often erroneous, according to this point of view, they should not be used by the court. This criticism is related to both the nature of the errors and to the use of certain information for predicting a defendant's dangerousness.

Let's first consider the nature of errors in prediction. Prediction usually results in some successes and in two kinds of errors: predicting that a phenomenon such as recidivism will occur when in fact it does not ("false positives") and predicting that it will not occur when in fact it does ("false negatives"). The problem of false positives in sentencing is costly primarily to incarcerated defendants who are not really so dangerous, while false negative predictions impose costs primarily on the victims of subsequent crimes committed by released defendants. In predicting whether a defendant will recidivate or "go straight," the problem of false positives is widely regarded as especially serious, for many of the same reasons that it has been regarded in our society as better to release nine offenders than to convict one innocent person. . . .

A tempting alternative is to reject prediction altogether; obviously, if we do not predict, then no errors of prediction are possible. A flaw in this logic is that, whether we like it or not, criminal justice decisions are now, and surely always will be, based on predictions, and imperfect ones, at that. Attempts to discourage prediction in sentencing may in fact produce the worst of both worlds: the deceit of predictive sentencing disguised as something more tasteful, and inferior prediction as well.

If we are to reserve at least some prison and jail space for the most criminally active offenders, then the prediction of criminal activity is an inescapable task . . . .

GO ON TO THE NEXT PAGE

77. Suppose the number of dangerous criminals who would be imprisoned under selective incapacitation but otherwise set free is greater than the number of harmless criminals who would be set free under selective incapacitation but otherwise imprisoned. How would this information be relevant to the passage?

    A. It weakens the claim that the goal of selective incapacitation is to protect the community.
    B. It strengthens the claim that there are more violent than nonviolent criminals.
    C. It weakens the claim that selective incapacitation would not increase prison populations.
    D. It strengthens the claim that white-collar criminals unfairly receive shorter sentences.

78. Implicit in the author's discussion of the idea of rejecting statistical prediction is the idea that

    A. statistical prediction will always be imperfect.
    B. a judge may well make more errors than a flawed statistical formula would.
    C. prediction will never attain widespread acceptance in the criminal justice system.
    D. sentencing should not take into account a criminal's future behavior.

79. Which of the following would the author advocate LEAST as a defense of the idea that we should employ statistical prediction in sentencing?

    A. Prediction always has been used in sentencing.
    B. Prediction will reduce the overcrowding in prisons.
    C. Rejecting statistical prediction leaves us with no predictive basis for sentencing.
    D. Making some predictive errors is better than not predicting at all.

80. The author's statement that selective incapacitation may "end up permitting harmful people from the middle class to evade a sanction that less privileged offenders cannot" (paragraph 4) assumes that

    A. there are more offenders in the lower class than in the middle-class.
    B. the dangerous repeat offenders are lower class and not middle-class.
    C. harmful middle-class people can use their money to avoid prison.
    D. lower-class offenders do not deserve to suffer incarceration.

81. Based on the information in the passage, if one's goal is to protect the community, one would employ a predictive formula that

    A. maximized the number of "false positives" and "false negatives."
    B. minimized the number of "false negatives."
    C. minimized the number of "false positives."
    D. minimized the number of "false positives" and maximized the number of "false negatives."

82. Based on the passage, which of the following would most likely be cited by an opponent of statistical prediction of dangerousness as the reason that prediction should be abandoned?

    A. The possibility of letting a dangerous criminal loose is too great.
    B. The possibility of imprisoning someone who should be allowed to go free is too great.
    C. The court makes more accurate decisions when statistics is employed.
    D. Dangerousness has yet to be adequately defined as a legal concept.

GO ON TO THE NEXT PAGE.

83. Which of the following is a claim made by the author but NOT supported in the passage by evidence, explanation, or example?

    A. Selective incapacitation may conflict with norms of social justice.
    B. The criticism of statistical dangerousness is related to the nature of predictive errors.
    C. Under selective incapacitation, first-time offenders would get short terms of incarceration.
    D. Some white-collar offenders impose greater costs on society than many dangerous street offenders.

GO ON TO THE NEXT PAGE.

Passage VI (Questions 84–87)

The tsetse fly, belonging to any of approximately twenty species composing the genus *Glossina,* is indigenous to Africa and is found primarily in forests and savannas south of the Tropic of Cancer. Dependent on vertebrate blood for nourishment, the tsetse fly is equipped with a long proboscis which is sharp enough to penetrate most animal skins and powerful enough to enable the tsetse to drink quantities of blood up to three times its own body weight. Measuring less than half an inch in length, this tiny pest has emerged at the center of health and environmental controversies.

At the same time that the tsetse drains blood, it can also transmit a variety of dangerous diseases. A bite from a tsetse fly can induce African sleeping sickness in human beings and nagana, a similar ailment, in domestic livestock. The agent of these diseases is the *trypanosome,* a unicellular, flagellated parasite which feeds primarily on the blood of vertebrates and is generally transmitted by an intermediary leech or insect host, such as the tsetse fly. In humans, the *trypanosome* causes damage to the brain and spinal cord, leading to extreme lethargy and, ultimately, death; in livestock, *trypanosomes* destroy red blood cells, causing fatal anemia.

The immune system is ill-equipped to counter *trypanosomes.* As the immune system attempts to counter disease, antibodies are produced to attack microbes whose antigens, surface proteins, are foreign to the body. Various antibodies are specific for particular antigens. However, the *trypanosome* is capable of disguising itself by altering its genetic code, thereby changing its antigen coating in resistance to each new antibody that evolves. This "quick change" has confounded pathologists and made the development of effective vaccines elusive.

Since the protozoan cannot be conquered through antibodies or vaccines, scientists have begun efforts to prevent the transmission of the *trypanosome* parasite by eliminating the tsetse. Attempts to eradicate the tsetse fly, however, have met with little success. Rhodesia used to combat tsetse by extensive brush cleaning, game shooting, and chemical attack, yet the fly persisted. Aerial pesticide treatments have produced inconclusive results. The reproductive cycle of the tsetse fly is such that a larva pupates underground for several weeks before it emerges as an adult fly. This makes repetitive chemical sweeping at intermittent periods an inconvenient necessity. A third method, called the "soft approach," makes use of the tsetse's attraction to the odors of carbon dioxide, acetone, and octenol. Open bottles of these compounds are hung behind black screens and nets permeated with insecticides. Massive numbers of flies, attracted to the chemicals from great distances, are lured into the nets where they are poisoned and die. All of these methods, however, share the weakness of dependence on harmful chemicals, such as DDT, which threaten both the health of the humans who handle them and the environment in which their toxic residues amass.

Thus, a controversy has been sparked between proponents of the elimination of the tsetse fly and African environmentalists. Those in favor of eradication feel that in addition to reducing disease, the removal of the tsetse fly will open immense tracts of land to cattle breeding. This, however, is precisely what the opposition fears. Environmentalists and conservationists dread the day when cattle and livestock, permitted to roam and graze freely, will uncontrollably devour plush African grasslands, converting them into barren desert. They argue that the tsetse fly must remain for the sake of the land.

With efforts to eradicate the tsetse fly largely unsuccessful, a compromise between tsetse control and tsetse elimination need not be forced. As elimination of the tsetse seems unlikely and may be impossible, control of the tsetse population offers the only available option for the interests of both health and environment.

GO ON TO THE NEXT PAGE.

84. All of the following statements correctly describe the relationship between the tsetse fly, the *trypanosome*, and vertebrates EXCEPT

  A. vertebrate blood provides the nourishment for the transport of *trypanosomes*.
  B. the "bite" of a tsetse fly can kill vertebrates since it often injects a deadly chemical.
  C. both the tsetse fly and the *trypanosome* utilize vertebrate blood for nourishment.
  D. vertebrates may die after *trypanosome* contamination via a tsetse proboscis.

85. Which of the following is NOT identified in the passage as a characteristic of the tsetse fly?

  A. Dependence upon vertebrate blood
  B. Ability to transmit a fatal parasite to livestock and humans
  C. Ability to alter its genetic code
  D. Ability to influence the African cattle population

86. The passage implies that the tsetse fly must be controlled for all of the following reasons EXCEPT

  A. to prevent the spread of disease throughout the African continent.
  B. because many human and animal lives are threatened by *trypanosomes*.
  C. because cattle in Africa are reproducing at an alarming rate.
  D. because *trypanosomes* cannot be overcome by vaccine.

87. In many warm climates, locusts feed on agricultural crops, and lizards feed on locusts. Which of the following is most analogous to the effect that eradicating the tsetse fly would have on African grasslands?

  A. Locusts transmit a deadly parasite from the agricultural crops to the lizards.
  B. Lizards are dependent upon both the locusts and the grasslands for nourishment.
  C. Elimination of the locusts results in bumper wheat crops.
  D. Elimination of lizards results in locust infestation and devastation of agricultural crops.

GO ON TO THE NEXT PAGE.

Passage VII (Questions 88–92)

Traditional science and philosophy have been built on an argument spiritual and scientific in equal measure. Philosophers have argued that there is a complete and unbridgeable separation between the nature of divinity and the nature of the creations springing from that divinity. There is, they argue, division between soul and matter, and between the thought of an object and the actual object itself. This dualistic argument has been held in roughly equal balance by opposing sides that are in turn philosophical and empirical. In one era it leans to the side of experience and solidity, and in another to the less tangible and immeasurable essences of the mind and the spiritual essence of the being that seeks to comprehend the object. On one side stands Immanuel Kant with his claim that the intangible soul is the cornerstone of existence, elevating the ego to a position of privilege over the material. On the other side are the Socratics with their claim that the only acceptable intangible is that the mind can know nothing on its own but must rely upon what it sees. Both extremes assume, however, the same idea of two essences, the material and the spiritual.

A great number of philosophers past and present contend that the understanding of an object is separate from the object itself. They argue that it would be wrong to claim that the image of a fountain one has in mind is the same thing as the fountain itself, or that the idea of "fountain" that the mind builds up after seeing thousands of fountains can be linked to any fountain existing in actual reality. This Platonic argument would suggest that there must be a gap between what is real and what is perceived.

Some would object, however, that this difference in fundamental essences is not an actual difference at all, but is rather a flaw in the method of perception itself. The philosopher William James in his Essays in Radical Empiricism champions this materialist view and argues that the very idea of consciousness, of the ability to perceive a certain thing, is a useful but immaterial concept. James regards it as an arbitrary creation that must be recognized as a model rather than an entity in and of itself before the broader problem of dualistic philosophies can be addressed.

James argues from the supposition that rather than two types of matter, one from which springs the spiritual, and one the material, there is only one type of substance that explains the same actions dualism explains but with more efficiency. If there is only one substance from which everything springs, the philosopher argues, that realm of experience called consciousness by dualistic philosophers can be explained simply as an interaction between the objects perceived and the one perceiving. When someone pushes an object from one place to another, for example, one does not regard the act of pushing as separate from either the person doing the pushing or the object being pushed. Rather, it is a junction between the two objects. It is a description of the two materials' behaviors in relation to one another, with no need to call in a separate type of existence to explain the action. James argues that the same is true of consciousness: It is the interaction of the individual and what he perceives rather than a separate and distinct entity unto itself.

Critics of James, however, raise at least two fundamental objections to his argument. First, James seems to engage in circular reasoning when he argues from the starting point that only one type of matter exists. Secondly, those challenging James' approach will point to the possibility that the interaction of two different objects may in and of themselves create something new and entirely different.

GO ON TO THE NEXT PAGE.

88. Which of the following is a claim made in the passage but NOT supported by evidence, explanation, or example?

    A. Interaction between objects of the same material may result in the creation of something with a different nature

    B. The understanding of a physical object can be separated from the object that is being understood.

    C. James presents arguments that may be open to valid challenge on logical grounds.

    D. What is known as "consciousness" can be explained by interactions between individuals and physical objects.

89. The author of the passage would be most likely to agree with which of the following statements?

    A. The universe can be clearly delineated into two categories of existence.

    B. The idea of consciousness is an outdated concept that should be removed from modern philosophy.

    C. Abstract ideas can provide insight into actual human practice.

    D. Philosophies of existence can only be challenged with practical example.

90. Which of the following statements, if true, would most challenge the argument set forth by William James as described in the passage?

    A. Children's concepts of right and wrong can be altered by exposure to some computer games.

    B. A theory of consciousness that does not involve a spiritual element is more complicated than one that separates consciousness and objects.

    C. Individuals can lose self-awareness if certain areas of the brain are surgically removed.

    D. Actions cannot be separated from the objects that they involve.

91. Suppose that a certain surgery is discovered to eliminate the sense of right and wrong while retaining self-consciousness. Based on the information in the passage, this discovery would:

    A. support James' theory.
    B. support the dualistic theory.
    C. support both theories.
    D. support neither theory.

92. The author most probably cites the Socratics in the first paragraph in order to:

    A. support the materialist view that there is no spiritual element.

    B. demonstrate the disparity between modern and ancient philosophies.

    C. provide an example of a dualistic philosophy.

    D. counter James' theory of a single essence.

STOP.
IF YOU FINISH BEFORE TIME HAS EXPIRED, CHECK YOUR WORK.
YOU MAY GO BACK TO ANY QUESTION IN THIS PART ONLY.

Biological Sciences Test

Time: 70 minutes—Questions 93–144

DIRECTIONS: Most of the questions in the following Biological Sciences test are organized into groups, with a descriptive passage preceding each group of questions. Study the passage, then select the single best answer to each question in the group. Some of the questions are not based on a descriptive passage; you must also select the best answer to these questions. If you are unsure of the best answer, eliminate the choices that you know are incorrect, then select an answer from the choices that remain. A periodic table is provided below for your use with the questions.

A Periodic Table of the Elements

1 H 1.0																	2 He 4.0
3 Li 6.9	4 Be 9.0											5 B 10.8	6 C 12.0	7 N 14.0	8 O 16.0	9 F 19.0	10 Ne 20.2
11 Na 23.0	12 Mg 24.3											13 Al 27.0	14 Si 28.1	15 P 31.0	16 S 32.1	17 Cl 35.5	18 Ar 39.9
19 K 39.1	20 Ca 40.1	21 Sc 45.0	22 Ti 47.9	23 V 50.9	24 Cr 52.0	25 Mn 54.9	26 Fe 55.8	27 Co 58.9	28 Ni 58.7	29 Cu 63.5	30 Zn 65.4	31 Ga 69.7	32 Ge 72.6	33 As 74.9	34 Se 79.0	35 Br 79.9	36 Kr 83.8
37 Rb 85.5	38 Sr 87.6	39 Y 88.9	40 Zr 91.2	41 Nb 92.9	42 Mo 95.9	43 Tc (98)	44 Ru 101.1	45 Rh 102.9	46 Pd 106.4	47 Ag 107.9	48 Cd 112.4	49 In 114.8	50 Sn 118.7	51 Sb 121.8	52 Te 127.6	53 I 126.9	54 Xe 131.3
55 Cs 132.9	56 Ba 137.3	57 La * 138.9	72 Hf 178.5	73 Ta 180.9	74 W 183.9	75 Re 186.2	76 Os 190.2	77 Ir 192.2	78 Pt 195.1	79 Au 197.0	80 Hg 200.6	81 Tl 204.4	82 Pb 207.2	83 Bi 209.0	84 Po (209)	85 At (210)	86 Rn (222)
87 Fr (223)	88 Ra 226.0	89 Ac † 227.0	104 Rf (261)	105 Db (262)	106 Sg (263)	107 Bh (264)	108 Hs (269)	109 Mt (268)	110 Ds (269)	111 Rg (272)	112 Uub (277)	113 Uut (284)	114 Uuq (289)	115 Uup (288)	116 Uuh (292)	117 Uus (291)	118 Uuo (293)

	58 Ce 140.1	59 Pr 140.9	60 Nd 144.2	61 Pm (145)	62 Sm 150.4	63 Eu 152.0	64 Gd 157.3	65 Tb 158.9	66 Dy 162.5	67 Ho 164.9	68 Er 167.3	69 Tm 168.9	70 Yb 173.0	71 Lu 175.0
*														
†	90 Th 232.0	91 Pa (231)	92 U 238.0	93 Np (237)	94 Pu (244)	95 Am (243)	96 Cm (247)	97 Bk (247)	98 Cf (251)	99 Es (252)	100 Fm (257)	101 Md (258)	102 No (259)	103 Lr (260)

GO ON TO THE NEXT PAGE.

Passage 1 (Questions 93–99)

A common disease that afflicts the digestive system is *peptic ulcer disease*. In humans, this condition occurs when the concentration of gastric juice overwhelms the protection provided by the mucous lining of the stomach and the neutralizing secretions of the pancreas. This acidity damages the stomach walls, causing pain, bleeding, or laceration of the digestive tract. The most frequent site of peptic ulcers is the first few centimeters of the duodenum.

Parietal cells in the stomach secrete HCl. HCl secretion is stimulated by gastrin, acetylcholine (ACh), and histamine. There are two negative feedback mechanisms that regulate acid secretion. First, excess HCl in the duodenum stimulates the secretion of the hormone secretin, which increases the rate and volume at which pancreatic juice containing bicarbonate ion is secreted. Second, gastrin inhibits HCl secretion when the stomach pH reaches a certain minimum.

93. All of the following structures secrete digestive juices EXCEPT the

    A. oral cavity.
    B. esophagus.
    C. stomach.
    D. small intestine.

94. It has recently been hypothesized that the triggering event for some ulcers is bacterial infection. If this is true, which of the following would be the most effective method to eliminate the ulcer?

    A. Stimulate ACh release.
    B. Inhibit the formation of formylmethionyl-tRNA, which is the initiator aminoacyl-tRNA found in prokaryotes only.
    C. Administer puromycin, which is an aminoacyl-tRNA analog in both prokaryotes and eukaryotes.
    D. Inject excess clotting factors to reduce bleeding.

95. Based on information in the passage, which of the following is NOT a plausible cause of peptic ulcer disease?

    A. Excessive gastrin production
    B. Weakness in mucosal barriers
    C. Decrease in parietal cell sensitivity to histamine
    D. Abnormally high density of parietal cells in the stomach

96. Which of the following treatments would most likely NOT alleviate peptic ulcer disease?

    A. Surgical removal of part of the stomach
    B. Administration of a drug that neutralizes stomach acid
    C. Coating the stomach lining with an exogenous substance
    D. Increasing stomach acidity to stimulate the negative feedback mechanism

GO ON TO THE NEXT PAGE.

97. Which of the following organs is involved in neutralizing gastric acidity?

    A. Pancreas
    B. Large intestine
    C. Stomach
    D. Liver

98. Which of the following best explains why gastric pH must be precisely controlled?

    A. Gastric enzymes are most active at a low pH.
    B. High gastric pH stimulates the release of pancreatic secretions.
    C. Low intracellular pH is necessary for proper parietal cell function.
    D. Gastric juices create the optimal environment for nutrient absorption in the large intestine.

99. Which of the following is implied by the term *negative feedback mechanism* as used in the passage?

    A. An increase in acid secretion decreases the rate at which bicarbonate ion is secreted into the duodenum.
    B. A decrease in acid secretion increases the rate at which bicarbonate ion is secreted into the duodenum.
    C. An increase in gastric pH increases acid secretion.
    D. A decrease in gastric pH increases acid secretion.

GO ON TO THE NEXT PAGE.

Questions 100 through 104 are NOT
based on a descriptive passage.

100. Differentiation of the ectoderm in a developing mammalian embryo eventually gives the animal the ability to

   A. produce urine.
   B. digest food.
   C. respond to stimuli.
   D. breathe.

101. If an endothelial cell were placed in distilled water, the cell would most likely

   A. shrivel.
   B. divide.
   C. remain the same size.
   D. lyse.

102. Which of the following compounds has the most stable structure?

   A. Cyclopropane
   B. Cyclohexane
   C. Cyclononane
   D. Cyclodecane

103. Why is carbon monoxide poisonous to humans?

   A. It decreases the total hemoglobin concentration of the blood.
   B. It destroys lung tissue.
   C. It blocks the electron transport chain.
   D. Hemoglobin has a greater affinity for carbon monoxide than for molecular oxygen.

104. Which of the following is true of anomers?

   A. They are achiral.
   B. They are mirror images.
   C. They differ in the configuration of the first carbon.
   D. They differ in the configuration of the second carbon.

GO ON TO THE NEXT PAGE.

Passage II (Questions 105–109)

P elements are a type of *transposable element* found in fruit flies. Transposable elements are self-replicating DNA sequences that are able to insert themselves in random locations within a host's genome. P elements were discovered after scientists noticed that crossing certain strains of flies produced offspring with an unusually high incidence of mutation. This syndrome, known as *P-M hybrid dysgenesis,* occurs only if the inherited P elements are activated. P elements are activated in all offspring when males from strains containing P elements, called P (paternal contributing) strains, are crossed with females from strains lacking P elements, called M (maternal contributing) strains. P elements produce an increased mutation rate by several different mechanisms: 1) Insertion of a P element into the coding region of a gene deactivates that gene; and 2) recombination between P elements on different chromosomes or in different regions of a single chromosome can produce inversions, translocations, deletions, or duplications. This high level of mutation produces sterile offspring.

Geneticists have noted that strains of flies descended from wild flies caught at least 30 years ago are almost always M strains, whereas strains descended from flies caught fewer than 10 years ago are usually P strains. Two hypotheses have been proposed to account for this observation.

Hypothesis 1

P elements arose in wild fruit fly populations during the last 10–30 years and subsequently spread throughout the species. P elements may have originated as viruses. Consequently, only strains derived from recently captured flies possess P elements.

Hypothesis 2

P elements have long existed in wild fruit fly populations but have a finite probability of being lost from the genome during each generation. Therefore, strains that have been cultured for many generations are likely to have lost their P elements over the course of time.

105. A researcher puts 9 M-strain flies and 1 P-strain fly into a culture box and grows them for 800 days (100 generations). She finds that most of their descendants are P flies. This observation supports

    A. Hypothesis 1, because the flies with P elements leave more offspring than M-strain flies.
    B. Hypothesis 1, because the incidence of P elements in the population has increased.
    C. Hypothesis 2, because the P elements have been lost during lab culture.
    D. Hypothesis 2, because the flies have been cultured for many generations.

106. If P elements arose by viral infection, as suggested by Hypothesis 1, the virus in question would have been

    A. lytic.
    B. lysogenic.
    C. a bacteriophage.
    D. attenuated.

GO ON TO THE NEXT PAGE.

107. Which of the following would NOT be a plausible mechanism whereby P elements might be "lost" from a fruit fly's DNA, as suggested by Hypothesis 2?

   A. Genetic drift
   B. Recombination between P elements on a single chromosome, leading to deletion
   C. Recombination between P elements on separate chromosomes, leading to translocation
   D. Natural selection

108. Which of the following is a potential consequence of P elements in a population?

   A. Increased likelihood of speciation
   B. Increased viability of offspring
   C. Decreased mutation rate
   D. Decreased genetic drift

109. Dysgenesis will be seen in the offspring from a cross between which of the following?

   I. A P-strain female and an M-strain male
   II. A P-strain male and a female offspring from a cross between a P-strain male and an M-strain female
   III. Two offspring from a cross between an M-strain male and a P-strain female
   IV. A male from a cross between two P-strain flies and a female from a cross between two M-strain flies

   A. I and III only
   B. IV only
   C. II and IV only
   D. II, III, and IV only

GO ON TO THE NEXT PAGE

Passage III (Questions 110–114)

Blood pressure is the force per unit area that blood exerts on the walls of the vessels it travels through. An instrument called a *sphygmomanometer* is used to measure blood pressure in an artery in the arm. A sphygmomanometer is an inflatable cuff attached to a pressure gauge; it is wrapped around the upper arm and inflated with air until blood flow to the artery is completely cut off. The cuff is then gradually deflated until blood begins to flow through the artery again. The initial sounds heard with the stethoscope are those produced when the blood pressure exceeds the pressure exerted by the cuff, and the pressure measured at this point corresponds to the pressure during ventricular contraction (systole). As the cuff is further deflated such that blood flow through the artery is normal, the pressure recorded corresponds to the residual pressure between contractions (diastole). Blood pressure is recorded as systole/diastole. Another measurement often taken is *cardiac output.* Cardiac output is defined as the volume of blood pumped by the left ventricle into systemic circulation per minute. Cardiac output is computed by multiplying heart rate (the number of beats per minute) and stroke volume (the volume of blood pumped by the left ventricle per contraction).

A trained athlete and a nonathlete both perform strenuous exercise (running up and down a flight of stairs) for 1 minute. Diastolic pressure and systolic pressure were measured four times: at rest, immediately following the exercise, 2.5 minutes following the exercise, and 6 minutes following the exercise (see Figure 1).

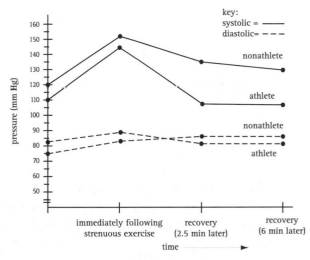

Figure 1

110. What is the athlete's blood pressure at rest (in mmHg)?

   A. 108/83
   B. 83/108
   C. 120/83
   D. 83/120

111. If, during exercise, the nonathlete and the athlete have the same heart rate but the athlete's cardiac output is greater, then

   A. the athlete's pulse is greater than the nonathlete's.
   B. the nonathlete's pulse is greater than the athlete's.
   C. the athlete's stroke volume is greater than the nonathlete's.
   D. the nonathlete's stroke volume is greater than the athlete's.

GO ON TO THE NEXT PAGE.

112. If a woman's pulse is 20 beats per 15 seconds and her stroke volume is 70 mL per beat, what is her cardiac output?

   A. 1.4 L/min
   B. 1.4 beats/min
   C. 5.6 beats/min
   D. 5.6 L/min

113. Both immediately before and during exercise, there is increased sympathetic activity. As revealed by the slopes of the lines in Figure 1, there is a rise in both systolic and diastolic pressure during exercise. Which of the following best accounts for this observation?

   A. Vasoconstriction of all blood vessels in active muscle
   B. Vasoconstriction of systemic blood vessels except for those in active muscle
   C. Vasodilation of systemic blood vessels except for those in active muscle
   D. Buildup of lactic acid

114. If the athlete normally has a greater cardiac output than the nonathlete, which of the following would most likely occur during strenuous exercise?

   A. The athlete would have a higher systolic pressure than the nonathlete.
   B. The nonathlete would have a higher diastolic pressure than the athlete.
   C. The nonathlete would have a greater buildup of lactic acid in muscle cells than the athlete.
   D. The athlete would have a higher rate of glucose catabolism than the nonathlete.

GO ON TO THE NEXT PAGE

Questions 115 through 118 are NOT based on a descriptive passage

115. Which of the following has the lowest boiling point?

  A. n-pentane
  B. isopentane
  C. 2-methylbut-2-ene
  D. pent-2-yne

116. If a researcher needed to distinguish between catechol and 2-hydroxymuconic semialdehyde, which of the following types of spectroscopy would be useful?

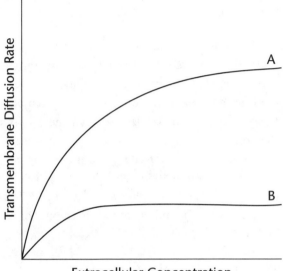

catechol

2-hydroxymuconic semialdehyde

  I. Mass spectroscopy
  II. NMR spectroscopy
  III. Infrared spectroscopy

  A. I only
  B. I and II only
  C. II and III only
  D. I, II, and III

117. Which of the following is NOT true regarding the relationship of insulin and glucagon?

  A. They are secreted by the pancreas
  B. They are secreted in response to high blood glucose
  C. They work to regulate blood glucose levels
  D. They are secreted in response to amino acids in the blood

118. The graph below plots the transmembrane diffusion rates for Compound A and Compound B as a function of their extracellular concentrations. Given that both compounds are approximately the same size, and there are no facilitated diffusion sites, it can most likely be inferred that:

  A. Compound A is polar and Compound B is nonpolar.
  B. Compound A is nonpolar and Compound B is polar.
  C. Compound A is polar and Compound B is polar.
  D. Compound A is nonpolar and Compound B is nonpolar.

GO ON TO THE NEXT PAGE.

Passage IV (Questions 119–122)

The different conformations of cyclic alkanes vary significantly in energy, and these energy differences often affect behavior. In cyclohexane, for example, the higher energy conformations are transitory except at high temperatures; the molecule spends most of its time in the lower-energy states.

In cyclic compounds that contain substituents other than hydrogen atoms, the energy differences between conformations are often larger. In some cases, these differences are large enough that even at room temperature, the molecules are permanently fixed in the conformation with the lowest possible energy. In such cases, this lowest-energy conformation may be studied, and information about its energy values may be obtained. The table below shows energy differences between the axial and equatorial positions for several different substituent groups.

Table 1

Name	Group	Energy difference (Axial/equatorial)
Bromide	$-Br$	0.50 kcal/mol
Hydroxyl	$-OH$	0.95 kcal/mol
Amino	$-NH_2$	1.40 kcal/mol
Methyl	$-CH_3$	1.74 kcal/mol
Isopropyl	$-CH(CH_3)_2$	2.15 kcal/mol
t-Butyl	$-C(CH_3)_3$	5.00 kcal/mol

119. What is the correct name for the following compound?

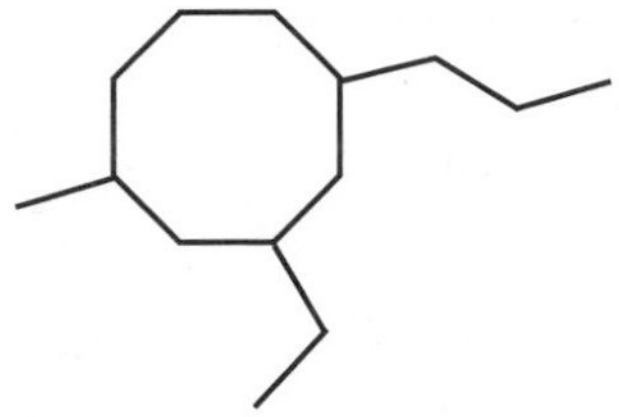

A. 1-ethyl-3-methyl-7-propylcyclooctane
B. 1-methyl-3-ethyl-5-methylcyclooctane
C. 1-methyl-3-ethyl-5-propylcyclooctane
D. 3-ethyl-1-methyl-5-propylcyclooctane

120. What is the energy difference between the two conformations of 1-methyl-4-bromocyclohexane shown below?

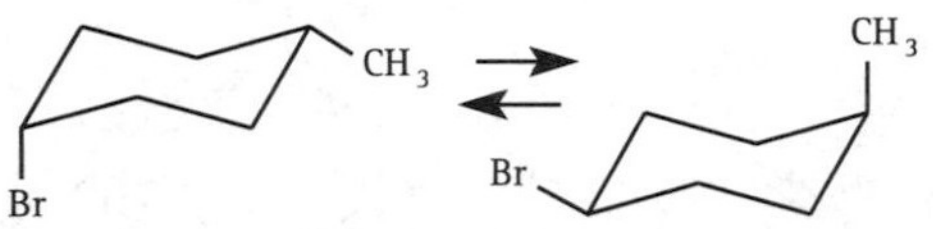

A. 0.50 kcal/mol
B. 1.24 kcal/mol
C. 1.74 kcal/mol
D. 2.24 kcal/mol

GO ON TO THE NEXT PAGE

121. Which of the following structures is the most stable?

A.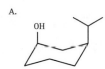

C.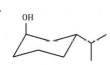

B.

HO

D.

HO

122. Which of the following structures is NOT in its lowest energy conformation?

A.

C.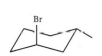

Br

B.

NH₂

CH₃

D.

NH₂

OH

Passage V (Questions 123–128)

Antibodies are proteins produced by animal immune systems in response to foreign agents, called antigens. The active site of an antibody is called the antigen-binding site; this antigen-binding site "recognizes" the antigen and binds to it, thereby rendering it inactive. Each antibody is specific to a particular antigen; it recognizes this antigen and occasionally closely related ones. Two theories attempt to explain antibody recognition and binding.

Theory 1

An antibody recognizes its antigen by means of the antigen's chemical composition via chemical interactions between the antibody's antigen-binding site and the antigen. The specific amino acids in the antigen-binding site are what enable the antibody to interact with the antigen. Thus, the chemical composition of the antigen is the crucial factor determining whether binding between antibody and antigen occurs. The physical configuration of the antigen does not affect this interaction.

Theory 2

An antibody recognizes its antigen by means of the antigen's physical configuration. The chemical composition of the antigen is of lesser importance. The antigen-binding site on the antibody is a "pocket" of characteristic shape into which the antigen fits and binds. The antigen must have the correct configuration, regardless of chemical composition, to be able to fit into and bind to the antigen-binding site of the antibody.

123. If Theory 1 were correct, which of the following structures would be recognized by an antibody produced against *p*-aminophenole-α-glucoside (shown below)?

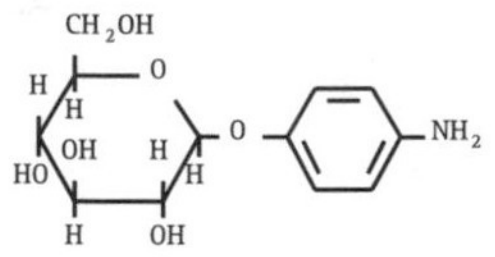

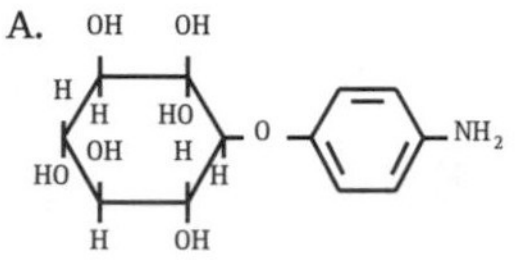

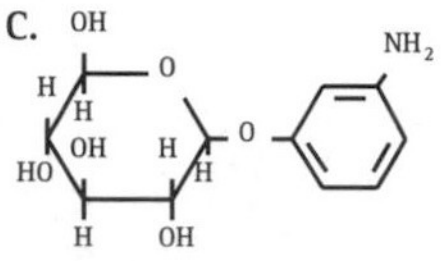

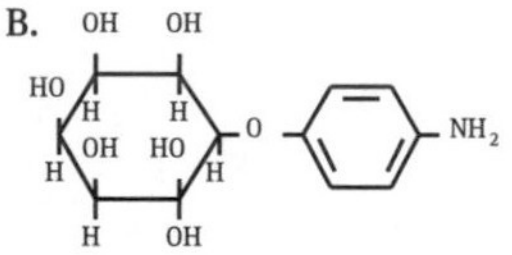

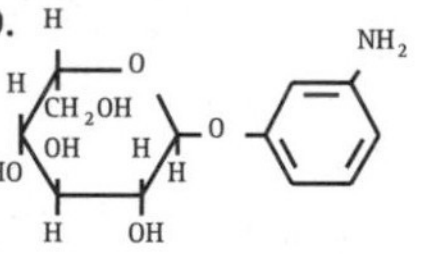

124. Which of the following statements supports Theory 2?

I. The antibody to *p*-aminobenzenesulfonic acid does not interact with *m*-aminobenzenesulfonic acid.
II. The antibody to *p*-aminobenzenesulfonic acid interacts with *p*-aminohydroxybenzene.
III. The antibody to *p*-aminobenzenesulfonic acid does not interact with *m*-aminohydroxybenzene.

A. II only
B. I and II only
C. II and III only
D. I, II, and III

GO ON TO THE NEXT PAGE

125. In an experiment, benzenesulfonic acid is chlorinated and an antibody is produced against it. According to Theory 2, which of the following structures will interact with this antibody?

A. 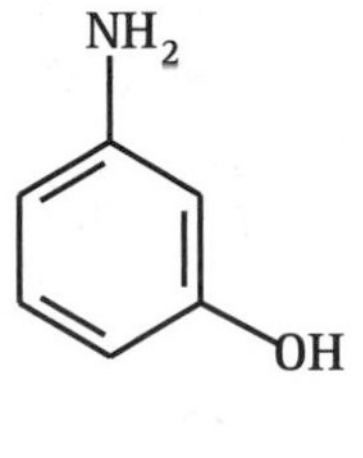
NH$_2$

OH

C. 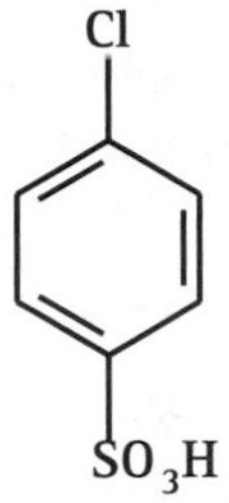
Cl

SO$_3$H

B. 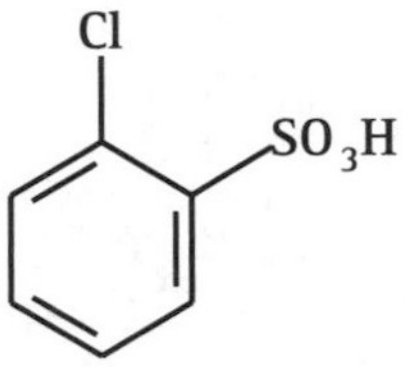
Cl

SO$_3$H

D. 
NH$_2$

SO$_3$H

126. Which of the following statements is FALSE?

A. The fact that two conformational isomers were recognized by the same antibody supports Theory 1 over Theory 2.

B. The fact that two enantiomers were recognized by the same antibody supports Theory 1 over Theory 2.

C. The fact that two structural isomers were recognized by the same antibody supports Theory 2 over Theory 1.

D. The fact that two geometric isomers were not recognized by the same antibody supports Theory 2 over Theory 1.

127. A mouse is injected with *m*-aminobenzenesulfonic acid, and the antibodies that it produces in response are extracted and tested for their ability to bind to different organic compounds. The resulting data are shown below.

Antigen	Response to Antibody
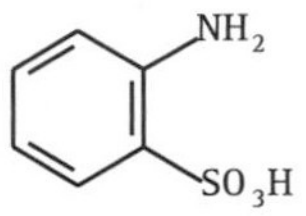 NH$_2$ SO$_3$H	No
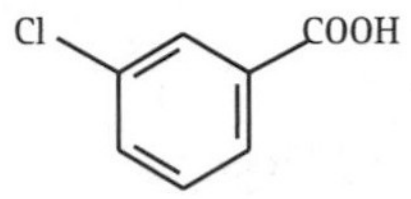 Cl COOH	Yes
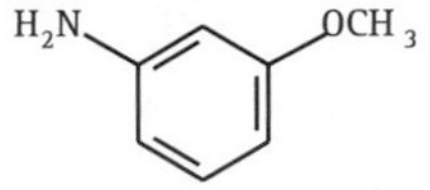 H$_2$N OCH$_3$	Yes
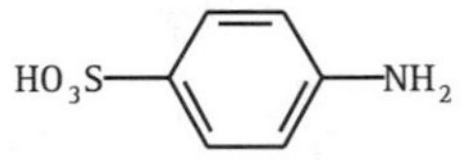 HO$_3$S NH$_2$	No

Which of the following statements best describes these results?

A. The antibody recognizes the chemical composition of the antigens, supporting Theory 1.

B. The antibody recognizes the physical configuration of the antigens, supporting Theory 2.

C. The antibody recognizes the chemical composition of the antigens, supporting Theory 2.

D. The antibody recognizes the physical configuration of the antigens, supporting Theory 1.

GO ON TO THE NEXT PAGE.

128. The antigen-binding site of an antibody

    A. is nonpolar.
    B. cannot contain disulfide bonds.
    C. cannot be denatured.
    D. represents the antibody's tertiary structure.

Questions 129 through 132 are NOT based on a descriptive passage.

129. *In vitro*, intracellular glucose concentration in muscle cells varies as a function of the composition of the growth media. Based on the graph below, which of the following conclusions can be drawn?

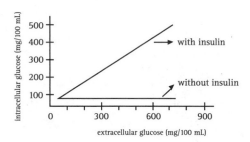

    A. Insulin decreases intracellular glucose concentration in muscle cells.
    B. Muscle cell membranes are practically impermeable to glucose.
    C. Glucose transport across muscle cell membranes requires ATP.
    D. Insulin stimulates the conversion of glucose into glycogen in almost all body tissues.

130. A patient with insufficient ADH secretion would most likely exhibit an

    A. increased urinary volume.
    B. increased urinary osmolarity.
    C. increased water reabsorption in the kidneys.
    D. increased filtration rate in the kidneys.

GO ON TO THE NEXT PAGE

131. In the male, a Leydig cell tumor would cause:

    A. feminization due to increased binding of androgens by androgen-binding proteins.
    B. virilization due to excessive androgen production.
    C. infertility due to inadequate androgen production.
    D. an increase in luteinizing hormone (LH) levels due to lack of negative inhibition on the posterior pituitary.

132. The importance of micelles is that they:

    A. allow for easy transport of fats across the sodium dependent co-transport.
    B. have a hydrophobic core and hydrophilic exterior to assist the absorption of fat.
    C. break down protein and move it through the sodium dependent co-transport.
    D. have a hydrophilic core and hydrophobic exterior to digest fats.

GO ON TO THE NEXT PAGE.

Passage VI (Questions 133–137)

Duchenne muscular dystrophy (DMD) is an X-linked recessive degenerative disorder of the muscle. By comparing the ability of X-linked DNA probes to hybridize with DNA from DMD patients and with DNA from normal individuals, cloned fragments were obtained that correspond to the region of DNA that contains the deletions characteristic of DMD. The deletions occur at different locations in each patient, suggesting that they occurred *de novo*. Analysis of this region of DNA obtained from numerous patients identified large deletions, extending in either direction. The most revealing deletion is located in the center of the isolated region. The sequence of this segment was determined to be the following:

5'-GCCATAGAGCGA-3'

The normal gene codes for a protein of approximately 500 kD, which has been named *dystrophin*. It is a component of muscle, present in rather low amounts. All patients with DMD have deletions at this locus and either lack dystrophin or synthesize defective dystrophin.

133. Which of the following sequences of DNA is complementary to the one given in the passage?

   A. 5'-TCGCTCTATGGC-3'
   B. 5'-CGGTATCTCGCT-3'
   C. 5'-CGGUAUCUCGCU-3'
   D. 5'-CGGUUUCUCGCU-3'

134. Based on the chart of the genetic code below and the DNA sequence provided in the passage, what is the missing sequence of dystrophin amino acids in DMD patients with this particular deletion?

second letter

	U	C	A	G	
U	UUU UUC } Phe UUA UUG } Leu	UCU UCC UCA UCG } Ser	UAU UAC } Tyr UAA Stop UAG Stop	UGU UGC } Cys UGA Stop UGG Trp	U C A G
C	CUU CUC CUA CUG } Leu	CCU CCC CCA CCG } Pro	CAU CAC } His CAA CCA } Gin	CGU CGC CGA CGA } Arg	U C A G
A	AUU AUC } Ile AUA AUG Start/Met	ACU ACC ACA ACG } Thr	AAU AAC } Asn AAA AAG } Lys	AGU AGC } Ser AGA AGG } Arg	U C A G
G	GUU GUC GUA GUG } Val	GCU GCC GCA GCG } Ala	GAU GAC } Asp GAA GAG } Glu	GGU GGC GGA GGG } Gly	U C A G

(first letter / third letter)

   A. Ser-Glu-Ile-Pro
   B. Met-Ala-Ile-Glu
   C. Arg-Tyr-Leu-Ala
   D. Ser-Leu-Tyr-Gly

135. Which of the following is the site of transcription in eukaryotic organisms?

   A. Ribosome
   B. Nucleus
   C. Centromere
   D. Cytoplasm

GO ON TO THE NEXT PAGE

136. If a normal woman whose father had DMD married a normal man, what is the probability that they will have two children with DMD?

    A. 6.25%
    B. 12.5%
    C. 25%
    D. 50%

137. Based on the information in the passage, which of the following can be inferred about the ability of the X-linked DNA probes to hybridize with the DNA from DMD patients as compared to the DNA from normal individuals?

    A. The probes have a greater degree of complementarity with DMD DNA.
    B. The probes have a greater degree of complementarity with normal DNA.
    C. The probes have an equal degree of complementarity with both DMD DNA and normal DNA.
    D. The probes hybridized with the DMD DNA of female patients only.

GO ON TO THE NEXT PAGE.

Passage VII (Questions 138–144)

Three pairs of electrons may be transferred among atoms of a phenyl ether by forming an intermediate that facilitates movement of these electrons through a sigmatropic process known as the Claisen rearrangement. A *sigmatropic rearrangement* is a reaction in which an allylic *s* bond at one end of a ≠-electron system appears to migrate to the other end of the ≠-electron system. An example of a reaction involving the Claisen rearrangement follows:

allyl phenyl ether   unstable intermediate   2-allylphenol

In this example, rearrangement occurs by a sigmatropic shift of the allylic group to give an *ortho* dienone, before forming the stable product. However, if the *ortho* position is occupied in an aromatic ring system, migration will primarily occur at the *para* position of the aromatic ring system. This type of rearrangement is not limited to phenyl ethers. A similar reaction can take place with aliphatic unsaturated ethers as well as unsaturated hydrocarbons. With aliphatic unsaturated ethers, the reaction usually stops at the intermediate stage (prior to enolization).

The Cope rearrangement is also a sigmatropic reactions, which can be used as a synthetic tool to produce seven- and eight-membered unsaturated rings systems from 1,2 divinylalkanes.

1,2-divinylcyclopropane   cyclohepta-1,4-diene

In other reactions involving the Cope rearrangement, 1,5-dienes are rearranged to produce their 1,5-diene isomers. This transformation occurs with the addition of heat. The Cope/Claisen rearrangement is often visualized as the interaction of two allylic systems, a carbocation and a carbanion.

X = carbon for Cope rearrangement
X = oxygen for Claisen rearrangement

The Cope rearrangement is reversible so that the thermodynamically favorable isomer predominates. Evidence that an isomerization occurs is determined from the configuration of the end product. For example, among *meso*-3,4-dimethylhexa-1,5-diene, the diene formed almost exclusively is *cis, trans*-octa-2,6-diene with the addition of heat. A look at the chair and boat configurations of the reaction and intermediate transition geometries gives insight as to why the *cis, trans*-isomer predominates for the *meso* compound. During the transition state, the allylic group is delocalized to provide overlap between the *p orbitals*, and a new bond is formed between carbons 1 and 6.

meso-3,4-dimethylhexa-1,5-diene   *cis, trans*-octa-2,6-diene

Both the Cope and Claisen rearrangements are cyclic, concerted, intramolecular reactions that are thermally induced and classified under the [3,3] sigmatropic shift. Depending on steric constraints, the transition states of both rearrangements prefer the chair conformation. Upon analysis of the stereochemical properties of the rearranged product, one may be able to discern which transition state conformation (chair or boat) was favored. While the Cope rearrangement is often used to give stereochemical products different from the starting material, a given molecule may undergo the rearrangement to form a product indistinguishable from the starting material.

GO ON TO THE NEXT PAGE.

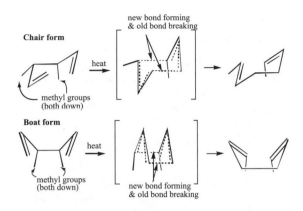

Figure 1. Chair and boat structures during the transition state of the Cope rearrangement of *meso*-3,4-dimethylhexa-1,5-diene.

138. List the following structures in order of increasing stability.

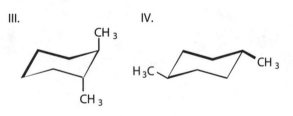

A. II < IV < III < I
B. IV < II < III < I
C. I < II < III < IV
D. I < III < II < IV

139. What is the product of a Claisen rearrangement of the following allyl vinyl ether?

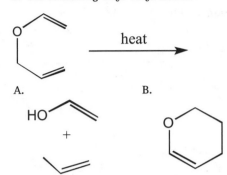

GO ON TO THE NEXT PAGE.

140. Which of the following is the MOST LIKELY intermediate of the following "oxyCope" rearrangement?

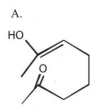

heat

unstable intermediate

A.

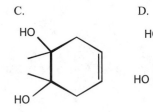

HO

B.

O

HO

C.

HO

HO

D.

HO

HO

141. What is the MOST LIKELY product of the following reaction?

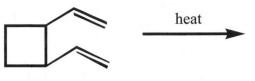

heat

A. B.

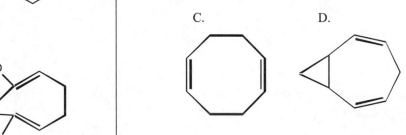

C. D.

GO ON TO THE NEXT PAGE.

142. What type of relationship exists between the intermediate of the Claisen rearrangement and the product of the allyl phenyl ether reaction?

    A. Keto-enol tautomerism
    B. β-keto Claisen condensation
    C. Conjugate addition
    D. Proton shift

143. What would be the MOST LIKELY product(s) for the Cope rearrangement of *racemic* 3,4-dimethylhexa-1,5-diene, assuming the transition state geometry favored the chair form?

    A. Trans, trans-hepta-2,6-diene *and* cis, cis-hepta-2,6-diene
    B. Trans, cis-hepta-2,6-diene *and* cis, trans-hepta-2,6-diene
    C. Cis, trans-octa-2,6-diene *and* trans, cis-octa-2,6-diene
    D. Cis, cis-octa-2,6-diene *and* trans, trans-octa-2,6-diene

144. Which of the following reactions would proceed via the boat transition state?

A.

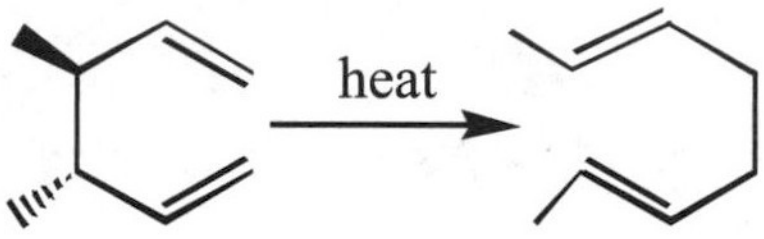

B.

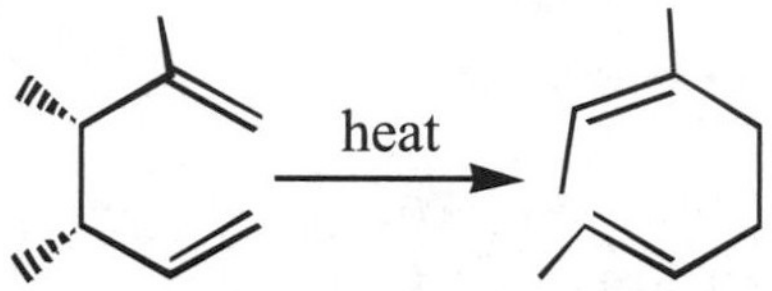

C.

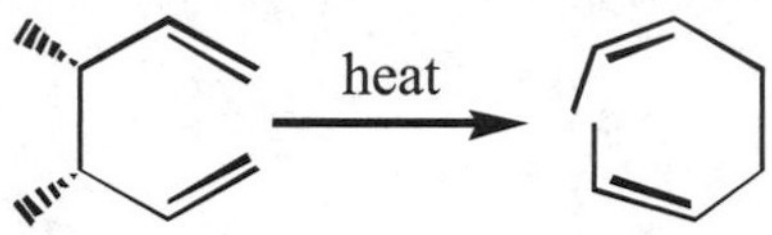

D.

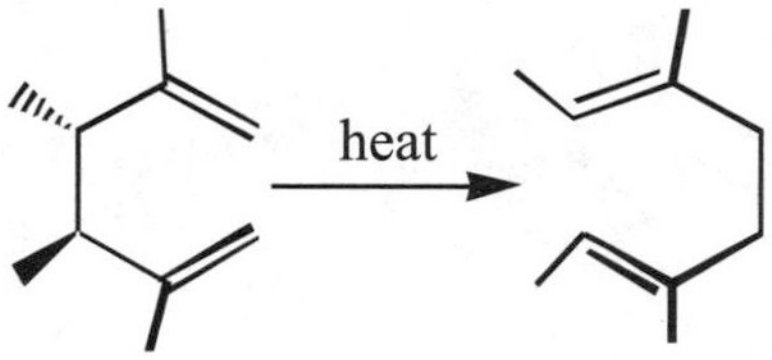

STOP.

IF YOU FINISH BEFORE TIME HAS EXPIRED, CHECK YOUR WORK.
YOU MAY GO BACK TO ANY QUESTION IN THIS PART ONLY.

Practice Test 1 Answer Key

Full-Length Practice MCAT

PHYSICAL SCIENCES

1. A	9. B	17. B	25. D	33. C	41. D	49. D
2. B	10. B	18. B	26. A	34. C	42. A	50. C
3. B	11. C	19. B	27. D	35. D	43. C	51. D
4. C	12. D	20. D	28. B	36. A	44. C	52. D
5. D	13. B	21. A	29. A	37. C	45. B	
6. D	14. C	22. B	30. C	38. C	46. A	
7. A	15. D	23. D	31. A	39. A	47. D	
8. B	16. A	24. B	32. B	40. B	48. C	

VERBAL REASONING

53. B	59. C	65. B	71. C	77. C	83. D	89. C
54. A	60. D	66. A	72. B	78. B	84. B	90. B
55. B	61. C	67. C	73. A	79. C	85. C	91. D
56. C	62. B	68. B	74. D	80. B	86. C	92. C
57. D	63. D	69. A	75. C	81. B	87. D	
58. B	64. B	70. B	76. B	82. B	88. A	

BIOLOGICAL SCIENCES

93. B	101. D	109. B	117. B	125. A	133. A	141. C
94. B	102. B	110. A	118. B	126. C	134. D	142. A
95. C	103. D	111. C	119. D	127. B	135. B	143. D
96. D	104. C	112. D	120. B	128. D	136. A	144. C
97. A	105. B	113. B	121. C	129. B	137. B	
98. A	106. B	114. C	122. D	130. A	138. D	
99. C	107. C	115. B	123. D	131. B	139. C	
100. C	108. A	116. D	124. B	132. B	140. D	

Score Conversion Chart

Full-Length Practice MCAT

Physical Science		Verbal Reasoning		Biological Science	
Raw Score*	Estimated Scaled Score*	Raw Score*	Estimated Scaled Score*	Raw Score*	Estimated Scaled Score*
0 to 10	1	0 to 16	1	0 to 13	1
11 to 12	2	17 to 18	2	14 to 16	2
13 to 15	3	19 to 20	3	17 to 19	3
16 to 17	4	21 to 22	4	20 to 22	4
18 to 19	5	23 to 24	5	23 to 25	5
20 to 21	6	25 to 27	6	26 to 28	6
22 to 24	7	28 to 29	7	29 to 31	7
25 to 26	8	30 to 32	8	32 to 34	8
27 to 28	9	33 to 34	9	35 to 37	9
29 to 31	10	35	10	38 to 39	10
32 to 34	11	36	11	40 to 42	11
35 to 36	12	37	12	43 to 45	12
37 to 39	13	38	13	46 to 48	13
40 to 42	14	39	14	49 to 51	14
43 to 52	15	40	15	52	15

*No test or score conversion chart can exactly predict actual Test Day performance.

Answers and Explanations

Physical Sciences

Passage 1 (Questions 1–5)

1. A

This is one of those questions that can be answered without using any information from the passage. All we need to know is the relationship between the index of refraction of a medium, the speed of light in a medium, and the speed of light in a vacuum. The definition of the index of refraction is $n = c/v$, where n is the index of refraction of the medium, c is the speed of light in a vacuum, and v is the speed of light in the medium. So if we can rearrange the equation to solve for v, we get $v = c/n$. The material with the lowest index of refraction will enable light to travel through it at the fastest speed. Therefore, **choice (A)** must be correct. It lists the media in order of increasing indices of refraction, so the speed of light in the media will be in decreasing order.

2. B

We are asked to determine the focal length of the eye's lens, so as to focus on an object 20 centimeters away. The equation that relates the focal length of a lens f to the image distance i and the object distance o is $1/f = 1/o + 1/i$. In the question, we are told that the object is 20 centimeters away, but we don't know what the image distance is. If you read the passage carefully and/or underlined the numbers in the passage, you would have easily found that the distance between the lens and the retina is 2 centimeters. This is essentially the image distance. Note that we haven't converted the distances from centimeters into meters. This is fine, as long as we use centimeters for *all* the distances. We would have a problem if we started mixing units, using centimeters for some things and meters for others. Substituting into the equation, we get that $1/f = 1/20 + 1/2$, or $11/20$. Taking the reciprocal of this, we find that the focal length $f = 20/11$. Of the answer choices, this is closest to 1.8 centimeters, which is **choice (B)**.

3. B

To answer this question, you must remember that for a multiple-lens system, the reciprocal of the total focal length is equal to the sum of the reciprocals of the focal lengths of the individual lenses. So for a two-lens system, this means that $1/f_t = 1/f_1 + 1/f_2$, where f_t is the total focal length and f_1 and f_2 are the individual focal lengths of the two lenses. Here we have two lenses, each with a focal length of 5 centimeters, so $1/f_t = 1/5 + 1/5$, which equals 2/5. Taking the reciprocal, we find that the focal length of the two-lens system equals 2.5 centimeters, which is answer **choice (B)**.

4. C

In the passage, we're told that myopia, or nearsightedness, is caused when the image of an object at infinity is brought into focus in front of the retina. In the question, we're told that a myopic person's eye has a relaxed focal length of 1.9 centimeters, and we're asked to determine the maximum distance from the eye at which this person can clearly see an object. This question essentially asks us to calculate the object distance, which is the distance from the eye's lens to the object. We know the focal length is 1.9 centimeters, but we don't know the image distance. In the passage, we are told that the distance from the lens to the retina is 2 centimeters. This is equal to the image distance because the image must be focused on the retina. As mentioned before, $1/f = 1/o + 1/i$. Rearranging this to get an equation in terms of the object distance, we find that $1/o = 1/f - 1/i$. Now, remember our sign conventions: For a converging lens, the focal length is positive. Substituting in, we get that $1/o = 1/1.9 - 1/2$, which works out to 1/38. Taking the reciprocal of this, we get that the object distance o is 38 centimeters.

That's the first part of our answer, and it narrows our choices down to **(B)** or **(C)**. The second part of the question asks us to calculate the magnification of the image. The equation for magnification m is $m = -i/o$, where i is the image distance and o is the object distance. Well, we just calculated that the object distance is 38 centimeters, and we know that the image distance is 2 centimeters. Putting these numbers into the equation, we find that the magnification m equals −2 over 38, or −1 over 19. (The fact that this value is much less than 1 tells us that the image is reduced, and the negative sign tells us that the image is inverted.) Therefore, the maximum distance from the eye that an object can be seen clearly is 38 centimeters, and the magnification of an object at this point is −1/19. **Choice (C) is correct.**

5. D

This question asks us which of the Roman numeral statements about the image formed in the eye is true. The first statement says that the image formed is real. In the passage, we are told that the lens of the eye is a converging lens, and you should remember that for a converging lens, the image is real, provided that the object is placed outside the focal length. Note that all objects clearly viewed by the eye are outside the focal length. We can figure this out from the information in the passage and a little reasoning. We are told that the focal length of the eye is only 2 centimeters, and we can reason that a young person with normal sight won't be able to focus on objects at a distance of less than 2 centimeters from the eye. Therefore, Statement I is true. So we can eliminate **choice (C)** because it doesn't contain Statement I.

Statement II says that the image is inverted. Remember that any real image formed by a converging lens is inverted, so this statement is also true. Now we can eliminate **choice (A)** because it doesn't contain Statement II.

Now we have to examine Statement III to choose between answer **choices (B)** and **(D)**. Statement III says that the image is reduced. To determine whether or not this is true, consider that the retina is about the size of a postage stamp, so for it to be possible to view an object that is larger than the retina of the eye, the image formed must be reduced. At this point, you might say, "Hang on; it is also possible for a converging lens to produce a virtual image." This is true, but only if the object itself is inside the focal length of the eye, and as already mentioned, this is not the case for objects seen by the eye. So Statement III is true, and the correct answer is **(D)**.

Passage II (Questions 6–11)

6. D

When two substances form a maximum-boiling azeotrope, the mixture has a higher boiling point than that corresponding to the vapor pressure predicted by Raoult's law. You should realize that this increase in boiling point results from a decrease in the vapor pressures of the constituent species. That means that **choice (D)** is correct. **Choice (C)**, an increase in the vapor pressure of the constituents, would result in a lower boiling point, which is characteristic of a minimum-boiling azeotrope. **Choices (A)** and **(B)** can be eliminated because the two species being mixed together do not change the characteristic specific heats of each other.

7. A

You're looking for a combination of molecules that would not be strongly attracted to each other. All the choices contain water, which is a highly polar substance. **Choice (A)** is the only one in which water is combined with a molecule that is mostly nonpolar and hydrophobic. In a mixture of water and chlorobenzene, the absence of dipole–dipole or hydrogen-bonding attractions would allow them both to escape into the vapor phase more easily than they could if they were in separate, pure solutions.

8. B

Answering this question is simply a matter of understanding boiling point elevation and what is meant by the percent solute by weight. For every mole of solute in a kilogram of solvent, the boiling point is raised by a certain amount. This means that the boiling point is proportional to the molality of a solution. However, molality does not increase linearly with the percent of solute in solution, so **choice (A)** is wrong. With that choice out of the way, the easiest way to answer this question is to simply reason your way though it. When the solution becomes 100 percent NaCl by weight, it will have a much higher boiling point than the pure water. Does this change come on gradually or quickly? When you add just a little salt, the boiling point won't change too much because there is very little salt interacting with the water. That eliminates **choice (C)**, since it has the greatest degree of boiling point change coming when there is very little salt added. So what happens as you add more and more salt? As the percent salt becomes greater, it takes less and less added salt to increase the solution's boiling point to the same degree. So the graph will show a steady curve upward. That is **choice (B)**, the correct answer. **Choice (D)** makes it seem like there is a critical point at about 50 percent salt where the slightest addition of salt kicks the boiling point of the solution up to the pure NaCl boiling point. This is the sort of thing we'd expect to see in a neutralization, not a steady increase in boiling point.

9. B

The key to answering this question is understanding the correct way to read Figure 1. On the x-axis are the mole fractions of A and B, while the y-axis indicates temperature. The lower line on the graph—the one that's concave upward—shows the boiling points of a mixture of A and B at various mole fractions. The two upper lines, the ones that are concave downward, show the mole fractions of A and B in the vapor at any given temperature. The two upper lines—the vapor lines—are the real issue in this question. The vapor that boils off from an azeotrope does not necessarily contain the same mole fraction of A and B that is found in the boiling liquid. In fact, the mole fractions in the vapor will always be different from the mole fractions in the liquid except at the single unique composition where the two curves meet. Since we're concerned with vapor in this question, we'll ignore the lower line completely. We want to know the mole fractions in the vapor at 40 degrees, not the mole fractions in the boiling liquid at 40 degrees. So all we have to do is read the points on the graph where the vapor curve crosses 40 degrees on the y-axis. There are actually two points that correspond to this temperature, so there are two possible compositions of the vapor at 40 degrees. One consists of a mole fraction of A equal to 0.60 and a mole fraction of B equal to 0.40. The other consists of a mole fraction of A equal to 0.80 and a mole fraction of B equal to 0.20. So 0.40 and 0.20 are the two mole fractions of B possible in the vapor at 40 degrees, and **choice (B)** is the correct answer. You could find the compositions of the solutions boiling at 40 degrees that produce these vapor ratios by seeing where the lower, liquid line matches up to 40 degrees. However, that would just be for a point of interest since it isn't part of the question.

10. B

The passage tells you that if you try to separate the components of an azeotrope by fractional distillation, the best you can do is get one pure component and the azeotrope. In the case of ethanol and water, the best you can get is a 95 percent solution of ethanol. But is the azeotrope minimum-boiling or maximum-boiling, and which species is more volatile? Well, the boiling point of the 95 percent ethanol solution is the temperature at which the azeotrope boils. Since the boiling point is lower than the boiling point of either pure component, this must be a minimum-boiling azeotrope, eliminating **choices (C)** and **(D)**. Now, think about the distillation. As the mixture is boiling, the vapor above it must have a greater percentage of ethanol than water, because when the vapor is condensed, the resulting solution had a greater percentage of ethanol than the original mixture. That means that ethanol is more likely to enter the gas phase and is, therefore, the more volatile of the two components. As said in the first paragraph of the passage, an ideal solution will always have a greater percentage of the more volatile component in the vapor. Since this mixture is not ideal, we can't make that assumption, but we can assume that the component that is more abundant in the critical composition is the more volatile of the two components. That makes **choice (B)** correct.

11. C

This is just a matter of remembering the boiling point elevation equation and the designations for molarity and molality. The K_b is called the molal boiling point elevation constant. Its value is different for each solvent. The increase in boiling point is found by multiplying this constant by the molality of the solution. Boiling point elevation, just like freezing point depression, does not depend so much on the identity of the solute as it does on its concentration. As discussed earlier, the change in boiling point is directly proportional to the molality of the solution. That means that **choices (B) and (D)** are out. Since the symbol for molarity, moles per liter solution, is a capital *M*, and the symbol for molality, moles per kilogram solvent, is a small *m*, the correct choice is **(C)**.

Passage III (Questions 12–17)

12. D

To answer this question, we need an equation that relates the electric field to the potential difference. This equation is $E = V/d$, where E is the electric field, V is the potential difference, and d is the separation of the plates. In the question stem, we are told that the potential difference between the plates V_{AB} is 20 volts, but we don't have a value for the separation of the plates. For this, we have to go back to the passage. In the first sentence of the second paragraph, we are told that the plates are separated by a distance of 1 centimeter, or 0.01 meters. Substituting into the equation $E = V/d$, we get that $E = 20/0.01$, which equals 2,000, or 2×10^3 volts per meter. This is answer choice (D).

13. B

When a drop is held motionless between the plates, there are two forces acting on the drop: the force of gravity acting downward, which equals mg, and an equal but opposite force acting upward, which is due to the electric field. The force due to the electric field is given by $F = qE$, where F is the force, q is the total charge on the drop, and E is the electric field. Both the force F and the electric field E are vector quantities; in other words, they have both magnitude and direction. Therefore, when we use this equation, we keep the sign of the charge. So for a negative charge, the force F is in the opposite direction to the electric field. Since the droplet is stationary, the force due to the electric field must be acting upward to counteract the force due to gravity. Therefore, the electric field must be in the opposite direction, which is downward, and choice (B) is correct.

14. C

In the question stem, we are told that the separation of the two parallel plates is reduced but the potential difference across the plates is kept constant. We are asked which of the Roman numeral statements is true. Let's go through each of them in turn. Statement I says that the electric field increases. We noted earlier that the electric field is given by the equation $E = V/d$, where E is the electric field, V is the potential difference, and d is the separation of the plates. Since the potential difference is kept constant, the electric field E is inversely proportional to the separation of the plates d. Therefore, as we decrease the separation of the plates, the electric field must increase proportionally. So Statement I must be true, and we can eliminate choice (D).

Statement II says that the magnetic field increases. Magnetic fields are created by moving charges, currents in wires, and permanent magnets. There is no current flow in our setup, no movement of charges, and therefore no magnetic field. Decreasing the separation of the plates will not change the situation. Therefore, Statement II is untrue.

It's either choice (A) or (C), so let's look at Statement III. This says that the capacitance increases. It's a little tricky, though; you might have ignored this statement since it has nothing to with the passage. However, two plates in parallel form a parallel-plate capacitor, with a capacitance C given by the equation $C = e_0\, A/d$, where e_0 is the permittivity of free space, A is the area of overlap of the two plates, and d is the separation of the plates. e_0 is a constant, and the area of overlap of the plates is kept constant, so the capacitance of the parallel plates must be inversely proportional to the separation of the plates. In other words, as the separation of the plates decreases, the capacitance must increase. Thus, Statements I and III are true, and the correct answer is (C).

15. D

The drop is stationary, so the force due to the weight of the drop acting downward is exactly balanced by the force due to the electric field directed upward. The force due to the weight of the drop is given by the equation $F_w = mg$, where m is the mass and g is the acceleration due to gravity. The force due to the electric field is given by the equation $Fe = neE$, where n is the total number of excess charges, e is the fundamental unit of charge—which we are told equals 1.6×10^{-19} coulombs—and E is the electric field. We know that $Fw = Fe$, so our force equation becomes $mg = neE$. We don't have a value for the mass of the oil drop, but we do know the volume of the drop, and we are given the density of oil at the end of the passage. So from the equation $\rho = m/V$, where ρ is the density, m is the mass, and V is the volume, we can determine the mass of the drop. Rearranging the equation, we get that $m = \rho V$. Substituting this into our force equation, we find that $\rho V g = neE$. We want to find the value of n. Rearranging the equation, we find that $n = \rho V g /(e E)$. Putting values in, we get that $n = (800 \times 4 \times 10^{-19} \times 9.8)/(0.6 \times 10^{-19} \times 490)$. Doing the math, we find that n equals 40, answer **choice (D)**.

16. A

This question is a two-step reasoning problem. We are told that an oil drop carrying a single electron charge falls between the two plates when the electric field is zero. The electric field is then increased from zero to 800 volts per meter, and we are asked to predict what happens to the oil drop. Initially the electric field is zero; the only force acting on the drop is the force due to the weight of the drop, and this force acts directly downward. So at the beginning, the drop will move downward under the influence of gravity. As the electric field increases from zero, there is an additional force due to the electric field. So there are now two forces acting on the drop: its weight acting downward and the force due to the electric field acting upward. The force due to the electric field increases gradually as the electric field increases, since the force is directly proportional to the electric field. We have to determine what the magnitude of the electric field would be at the point that the forces become equal and see whether this is larger than the maximum value of the electric field applied across the plates.

Well, at the point that the drop becomes stationary, the force due to the weight of the drop equals the force due to the electric field. So our force equation is $qE = mg$, or, in terms of E, $E = mg/q$. We can approximate g as 10 m/s^2. Substituting in, we get that $E = (5 \times 10^{-16} \times 10)/(8 \times 10^{-18})$, which equals 625 volts per meter. We are told in the question stem that the maximum value of the electric field is 800 volts per meter, which is greater than the field required to hold the drop stationary. So there will be a point when the forces become equal. But the field continues to increase; therefore, there will be a net upward force acting on the drop when the electric field is greater than 625 volts per meter increasing as the electric field increases. So the drop initially moves down, then stops and reverses direction, moving upward. Therefore, the correct answer is **choice (A)**.

17. B

This is a tricky question. We have two forces acting on the oil drop: the force due to its weight acting downward and the force due to the electric field acting upward. Our drop is accelerated toward the top plate, and this tells us that the force in the upward direction is greater than the force in the downward direction. In other words, the force due to the electric field is greater than the force due to the weight of the oil. Therefore, the resultant force acting on the oil drop $Fr = Fe - Fw$, where Fw is the force due to the weight of the drop and Fe is the force due to the electric field. Now, Fe is equal to qE, where q is the total charge and E is the electric field, and Fw is equal to mg, where m is the mass and g is the acceleration due to gravity. Putting this into the equation for the resultant force, we get that $Fr = qE - mg$. In the question stem, we are told that the charge on the drop is 3×10^{-18} coulombs, the electric field equals 4×10^3 volts per meter, and the mass of the drop is 5×10^{-16} kilograms. Substituting into the equation for the resultant force, we get that $Fr = 3 \times 10^{-18} \times 4 \times 10^3 - 5 \times 10^{-16} \times 9.8$. Doing the math, we get that $Fr = 7.1 \times 10^{-15}$ newtons.

Well, we have found the resultant force acting on the drop, but the question asks us to find the resultant *acceleration*. To do this, we must use Newton's second law, $F = ma$. Rearranging to get an equation in terms of a, we find that $a = F/m$, so putting our values in, we get that $a = (7.1 \times 10^{-15})/(5 \times 10^{-16})$, or 14.2 m/s². This is answer **choice (B)**.

Discrete Questions

18. B

The molality of a solution is defined as the number of moles of solute added to 1 kilogram of solvent (you should know that 1 kilogram of water has a volume of 1 liter at room temperature). Molarity is the number of moles of solute per liter of total solution. Since you are told that 1 mole of calcium chloride has been added to 1 liter of water, the total volume of the solution will be greater than 1 liter. Noticing this, you should know that molality is a far more convenient concentration unit; **choices (A)** and **(C)** can be eliminated. Since the question is asking for the calcium concentration and there is only 1 mole of calcium per mole of calcium chloride, the correct answer is **(B)**, one molal.

19. B

In the question stem, we are told that we have two blocks of equal density but different mass and, therefore, different volume. We're asked to determine the ratio of their apparent weights when they're completely submerged in water. Well, there are two forces acting on a block when it is completely submerged in water: its weight, mg, acting downward, and the buoyant force acting upward. The apparent weight in water is equal to the actual weight of the block in air, mg, minus the buoyant force.

The buoyant force exerted on a block when it is submerged in water is equal to the weight of water that the block displaces. The weight of water displaced is equal to mwg, where mw is the mass of the water displaced and g is the acceleration due to gravity. Using the equation $m = \rho V$, where m is the mass, ρ is the density, and V is the volume of the block (and therefore the volume of water displaced when the block is completely submerged), we can express the mass of water displaced as being $mw = \rho V$. We are given that the mass and volume of the first block are m and V, respectively. We are told that the second block has a mass of $2m$ and the same density as the first block. The density of the first block is just m/v, so m/v must equal the mass of the second block over the volume of the second block. The mass of the second block is $2m$, so the volume of the second block must equal $2V$. Thus, the second block displaces twice as much water, and the buoyant force on the second block is twice as great.

Now we can express the apparent weights of the two blocks when submerged in water. The block of mass m has an apparent weight of $mg - mwg$, and the block of mass $2m$ has an apparent weight of $2\ mg - 2mwg$. So the apparent weight of block one is one-half the apparent weight of block two. Therefore, the correct ratio is 1 to 2, which is answer **choice (B)**.

20. D

This question requires a good understanding of circuit laws. A key law to remember here is that charge is conserved and, as a result, the current that flows through the first parallel combination must also flow through the second parallel combination.

We're told that the reading on ammeter A_1 is 3 amps. You should remember that for resistors in parallel, the sum of the currents through each of the resistors is equal to the total current that enters the parallel combination. The current is split in the ratio of the resistance of the two resistors, and since the resistors in the first parallel combination are equal, the current traveling through each must be equal. We know that the current traveling through one of the resistors is 3 amps, so the current traveling through the other resistor must be 3 amps also. This means that the total current in the circuit equals $3 + 3$, or 6 amps. As we've already said, this 6-amp current also travels through the second parallel combination. This time, we have a $1R$ resistor in parallel with a $2R$ resistor, so the current will *not* be split equally between the two resistors. To find how much current goes through the $1R$ resistor, we must first calculate the resistance of the parallel combination. For two resistors in parallel, the reciprocal of the total resistance equals the sum of the reciprocals of the individual resistances. Substituting in, we get that one over the total resistance equals $1/(1R) + 1/(2R)$, which equals $3/(2R)$. Taking the reciprocal of this, we find that the total resistance equals $2R/3$.

Now, we can use Ohm's law to determine the voltage across the parallel combination. Ohm's law in equation form is $V = iR$, where V is the potential difference, i is the current, and R is the resistance. Substituting in, we get that $V = (6 \times 2R)/3$, or $4R$ volts. To find the current through the $1R$ resistor and, therefore, the current through ammeter A_2, we apply Ohm's law again. This time, we have the $4R$ volts across the $1R$ resistor, so substituting in, we get that $i = 4R/(1R)$, or 4 amps, which is answer **choice (D)**.

Passage IV (Questions 21–25)

21. A

From the passage, we know that a light bulb burns out because its filament is gradually vaporized by intense heat. If the filament is in a vacuum, it will vaporize at a faster rate than it would at normal atmospheric pressure. You can see this if you remember the shape of a phase diagram, which gives the relationship among temperature, pressure, and phase. If you think about the line separating the solid phase from the gaseous phase in that diagram, you'll remember that a reduction in pressure, at constant temperature, can cause a solid to sublimate to the gaseous form. Vacuum bulbs were originally used so as to exclude oxygen from the system so that they wouldn't oxidize the filament, but the vacuum greatly increases the sublimation rate, so it's not an optimal solution to the problem of oxidation. An inert gas won't cause oxidation, of course, but it does slow down the process of sublimation; thus, **choice (A)** is correct.

It's true that the presence of a gas removes some heat from the filament, as is stated in **choice (B)**, but this isn't the reason for putting gas into the light bulb. The heat of the filament could easily be decreased just by reducing the voltage through the filament or by using a filament with a lower resistance. But in fact, the filament is intentionally designed to become very hot so that it will produce an intense white light; a lower temperature would mean less intense, redder light. The ultimate purpose of the inert gas is actually to allow the filament to be made hotter without being destroyed too fast by vaporization. **Choice (C)** is wrong because the danger of implosion is not the reason for using inert gas in a light bulb. The end of the first paragraph of the passage tells us that the inert gas increases the life of the filament, so there's no reason to go off into speculation about implosion and all that. Of course, light bulbs do sometimes break when subject to vibration, but whether they implode or not when they break is hardly the issue here, since as you probably know, light bulbs burn out—that is, their filaments break—much more often than their bulbs break. Finally, **choice (D)** is wrong because the gas normally would absorb very little energy from the electrons, which are moving through the metal of the wire, not in the gas. Even if the gas did absorb energy, it wouldn't be helpful, since we want the energy from the voltage to go into producing heat in the wire, not be dissipated in the gas.

22. B

Exposure to light is known to improve people's moods, while long hours of darkness can cause depression. There is still some question as to whether the improvement in mood is caused simply by exposure to very bright light or whether exposure to certain wavelengths is also needed. So it's not clear whether some people get depressed in cloudy weather simply because there is less light or because they need more light of a certain wavelength. The advertiser in this question is claiming that short-wavelength light is needed and that incandescent lights are, therefore, inadequate to improve people's moods. You are asked which statement could be used as an argument against this claim, based on the information in the passage.

The first paragraph tells you that the visible light produced by an incandescent lamp is just the tip of the iceberg: Most of the radiation is produced in the infrared range. As a filament is heated, it becomes hot enough to radiate energy in the visible wavelengths, starting at the red end of the spectrum and then adding wavelengths of other colors. So incandescent light is stronger on the red side of the spectrum. Infrared radiation, or heat, has longer wavelengths and lower frequency than visible light, while ultraviolet light is of higher frequency and shorter wavelengths. So incandescent light is relatively more intense in the longer wavelengths and less intense in the shorter wavelengths, and **choice (A)** is wrong.

As for **choice (B)**, the passage states that the light on a sunny day is least intense in the short wavelengths, while light on a cloudy day is most intense on the blue end of the spectrum, which is the short-wavelength end. Thus, the light on a sunny day is most intense at the long wavelengths, while on a cloudy day the short wavelengths are most intense. So a person could argue that what we need in cloudy weather is more long-wavelength light and that incandescent lamps would be helpful for that purpose. This could be used as an argument against the advertiser's claim. On the other hand, we don't know if this is really true. On a cloudy day, all light is less intense, so it might turn out to be the short-wavelength light that we need more of after all. However, the advertiser here doesn't provide any evidence to support this position. Since long-wavelength light is most reduced in cloudy weather, judging by the information available in this passage, we can only conclude that people most likely need more light of longer, not shorter wavelengths, if wavelengths really do matter. **Choice (B)**, which says outdoor light is of longer wavelength on a sunny day than a cloudy day, is true. **Choice (C)**, which says the opposite, is false.

As for **choice (D)**, this says that the spectrum produced by an incandescent lamp is irrelevant since the intensity is too low. But that's a weaker argument than choice B, since the advertiser is arguing specifically about the wavelengths produced by incandescent lamps. Actually, D is false, since it's possible, though expensive, to produce very high-intensity light using incandescent lamps.

23. D

Since incandescent lamps produce mostly infrared radiation and the visible radiation they produce is most intense on the red end of the spectrum, they must produce comparatively little ultraviolet radiation. Fluorescent lamps do produce ultraviolet radiation, but this radiation is absorbed by the phosphorescent coating on the surface of the glass tube, and longer-wavelength visible radiation is emitted. Thus, neither kind of lamp will normally produce dangerous levels of ultraviolet radiation. It *is* possible to produce special lamps of both kinds that do produce ultraviolet—for instance, the lamps used in tanning salons. But ultraviolet radiation is not a danger from the kind of incandescent and fluorescent lamps that are commonly used in people's homes.

24. B

A lamp is an apparatus for converting electrical energy into light energy, so its efficiency is defined as how much visible light it puts out for a given input of electrical power. Like any other system, a lamp is somewhat inefficient. To figure out where that inefficiency enters into the process, you have to use information from the passage. Incandescent lamps produce a great deal of infrared—that is, heat—and only a comparatively small amount of light. Notice the fourth sentence in the first paragraph: This states that *almost all* of the radiation produced by incandescent lamps is in the infrared range. In a fluorescent lamp, on the other hand, all the radiation gets converted to light, although the final frequency of that light is lower than the original frequency, so some energy must be lost there. So fluorescent lamps lose some of their energy, but incandescent lamps lose almost all of theirs. Thus, the correct answer is **(B)**.

25. D

The passage tells you that the wavelengths of light emitted from a fluorescent lamp are controlled by the composition of the phosphor coating the inside of the glass tube. It also tells you that a "warm white" lamp produces more light at the red end of the spectrum than a "cool white" lamp. So if a manufacturer that made "warm white" lamps wanted to start making "cool white" lamps, all it would have to do is change the composition of the phosphor to produce more blue-violet light when it absorbed ultraviolet light from the mercury vapor. This is **choice (D)**.

Choice (A) is wrong because the phosphor will always emit the same wavelengths of light, regardless of the amount of ultraviolet light. **Choice (B)** is wrong because "warm white" and "cool white" lights are defined by the wavelengths of the light they emit, not by the angle at which they emit the light. **Choice (C)** is wrong because it is the identity of the phosphor that determines the wavelengths of visible light emitted, not the strength of the electric arc.

Passage V (Questions 26–30)

26. A

The passage mentions that metals have partially filled valence bands. This means that there are low-energy unoccupied atomic orbitals in metals through which electrons may move freely. Therefore, the valence band for metals is the conduction band, and consequently, there is no band gap. Metals, such as iron, are good conductors of electricity because of these unoccupied low-energy orbitals. (All of this information is contained in the passage and requires little or no background knowledge.)

Choice (B) is incorrect because metals, unlike semiconductors, do not have a band gap. Choice (C) is wrong because iron's $3d$ orbital is not filled; it has only 6 electrons, not 10. Choice (D) is true of many solids including metals, semiconductors, and insulators, but it does not answer the question and so is incorrect.

27. D

Statement I says that heat could be expected to reduce the frequency of collisions between moving electrons. This is not true: Heat increases the kinetic energy of electrons, thereby increasing, not decreasing, the frequency of collisions. Choice (A) and choice (C) can be eliminated.

Statement II says that heat breaks covalent bonds. This is true: Sufficient energy—in this case supplied by heat—will break covalent bonds. The passage doesn't tell you explicitly that heat breaks covalent bonds in semiconductors, but it is implied in the description of the semiconductive properties of silicon. In the first sentence of the second paragraph, you are told that silicon forms tetrahedral covalent bonds and that when heated, it will conduct. Since silicon is sp^3 hybridized—forming a filled valence band—bonds must be broken to promote electrons to the conduction band. Choice (B) can therefore be eliminated, making choice (D) the correct response.

The truth of Statement III should then be obvious: For the freed electrons to "jump" to the higher energy band gap, they must gain energy. Heat supplies the energy and permits this to happen.

28. B

The passage states that phosphorus atoms increase the conductivity of silicon because phosphorus provides the crystal with unbonded electrons, while boron atoms produce holes in the bonding structure. From the periodic table, it can be seen that boron has three valence electrons, silicon has four, and phosphorus has five. Since the bonds in the silicon crystal are tetrahedral, a phosphorus atom surrounded by silicon atoms will be able to form covalent bonds with only four of its valence electrons, leaving the fifth one unbonded. Boron has only three valence electrons, so a boron atom surrounded by silicon atoms will only be able to form three covalent bonds, leaving a hole in the bonding structure of silicon. It is the presence of these unbonded electrons and holes that enhances the conductivity of phosphorus. Choice (B) is therefore the correct answer.

Choice (A) is wrong because the difference in electronegativity among boron, phosphorus, and silicon is quite small. Choice (C) is wrong for two reasons: Phosphorus isn't a semimetal; and even if these two elements were both semimetals and good semiconductors, this in itself wouldn't explain the enhancement of silicon's conductivity produced by doping silicon with some of these elements. Choice (D) is wrong because, like choice (C), it wouldn't explain the phenomenon the question asks about even if it were true.

29. A

Since the band gap is 1.1 eV, an applied voltage in excess of 1.1 V would give the electrons enough energy to cross the band gap and populate the conduction band. (You should know that an electron volt is equal to the energy required to move an electron through a potential difference of one volt.) Choice (A) is therefore the correct response.

Choice (B) is wrong because pure, undoped silicon doesn't have any holes. The passage states that holes are produced when the silicon is doped with boron. **Choice (C)** is wrong because no information in the passage suggests that the band gap is affected by an external potential. **Choice (D)** is wrong because the electrons do have enough energy to overcome the band gap and would move into the conduction band.

30. C

The passage provides almost all the necessary information to answer this question. The only piece of background information needed is that electrons flow from the negative terminal to the positive terminal. The passage states that phosphorus-doped silicon has more electrons than pure silicon and that boron-doped silicon has fewer electrons than pure silicon. In addition, it is stated that electrons flow more easily from a side with excess electrons—the phosphorus-doped silicon—to a side with fewer electrons—the boron-doped silicon. So if the semiconductor orientation were switched, electron flow would not be as easy as in the original configuration.

Discrete Questions

31. A

The equation you need to answer this question was derived by Neils Bohr. It predicts the frequency of light produced when an electron falls from one quantum level to another in a hydrogen atom, though it doesn't work for other kinds of atoms, since those have more complex subshells. The equation states that E equals $-A$ times the quantity $(1/n_i^2 - 1/n_f^2)$, where n_i is the first quantum number of the electron in its initial state and n_f is the first quantum number of the electron in its final state. A, which is a constant, is the amount of energy needed to remove an electron from the lowest energy level of a hydrogen atom to a point at an infinite distance away. The negative sign in front of the A is there because the electron in the question is falling *toward* the nucleus of the atom and, therefore, is giving off energy. So we have to multiply $-A$ by $1/3^2 - 1/2^2$. This comes to $-A \times -5/36$, which is equal to 0.14 A, **choice (A)**.

32. B

We're told that an airplane with a mass of 150,000 kilograms produces a thrust of 200,000 newtons to go from rest to a cruising speed of 720 kilometers per hour. So we're given a mass, force, and speed, and we're asked to find the time it takes to reach that speed. We need to find an equation that relates what we need to find to what we're given.

An equation that accomplishes this is the familiar kinematic equation $v = v_0 + a\,t$, where v is the final speed, v_0 is the initial speed, a is the acceleration (which is equal to the force over the mass) and t is the time. The plane starts from rest, so $v_0 = 0$. Solving for t, we find that $t = v/a$. We know $v = 720$ kilometers per hour, but what is the acceleration? As noted earlier, we can calculate the acceleration from Newton's second law, $F = m\,a$, where F is the force and m is the mass. We know that $F = 200,000$ newtons and $m = 150,000$ kilograms. So we can calculate a by dividing F by m. We get $a = 200,000$ over 150,000, or four-thirds. Now that we have a, we can calculate t from the equation $t = v/a$. But before we can substitute our numbers in, we must first convert the speed of the aircraft from kilometers per hour to meters per second. Multiplying the speed by the number of meters in a kilometer and dividing it by the number of seconds in an hour, we get that the speed equals $(720 \times 1,000)/3,600$, or 200 meters per second. Plugging that number into our equation, we find that the time t equals v over a, or 200 over four-thirds, or 150 seconds, which is answer choice (B).

You could also use the formula for impulse to answer this question. Impulse, J, is the product of the force, F, and the time over which the force acts, t. It also equals the change in momentum, Dp, which equals the final momentum minus the initial momentum. Therefore, we can say that $J = Dp = Ft$. Since momentum is the product of mass and speed and the aircraft is initially at rest, the initial momentum of the aircraft is zero. So the change in momentum Dp is simply the final momentum of the aircraft. Thus, our equation becomes $mv = Ft$, where m is the mass of the aircraft and v is the final speed of the aircraft. We are trying to find the time, so rearranging to get an equation in terms of the time t, we get that $t = mv$ over F. Plugging in the values for m and v, we get that $t = (150,000 \times 200)/200,000$, or 150 seconds.

33. C

There are two ways you could do this problem: an easy way if you have the Henderson-Hasselbach equation memorized and a longer way based on the definition of the acid dissociation constant, K_a, if you don't remember that equation. (If you don't, you'll have to decide if it's worth trying to memorize. It can potentially save you time on the exam, but on the other hand, if you try to memorize it, that's one more equation you could forget or get mixed up. If you understand how to figure out questions like this one based on pK_a, they may take longer, but you'll be less likely to forget how to do them.)

By definition, the pK_a of an acid solution is –log of the acid dissociation constant, or K_a. The acid dissociation constant, in turn, is equal to (the concentration of the hydrogen ion) × (the concentration of the anion, X⁻) ÷ (the concentration of the undissociated acid, HX). If the concentration of X⁻ and the concentration of HX are equal, they'll cancel each other out. This means that the concentration of hydrogen ion will be equal to the value of the acid constant. In that case, the pH, which is the *negative log* of the hydrogen ion concentration, will be equal to the negative log of the acid constant—that is, equal to the pK_a. So any time the pH is equal to the pK_a, the concentration of X⁻ must also be equal to the concentration of HX. In this example, the pH is not equal to the pK_a, so the concentrations of X⁻ and of HX will not be equal. But you can figure out what they will be just by remembering that the pK_a is the negative log of the acid constant. Since the pH is 6, the hydrogen ion concentration will be 1×10^{-6}. Since the pK_a is 5, the acid constant must be 1×10^{-5}. If you plug these values into the equation for the acid constant and then divide both sides of the equation by the hydrogen ion concentration, you find that the concentration of X⁻ divided by the concentration of HX is equal to 1×10^{-5} divided by 1×10^{-6}. This comes to 10^1, or 10. So the concentration of X⁻ must be 10 times the concentration of HX, and **choice (C)** is correct.

Now for the other method of answering this question. The Henderson-Hasselbach equation says that for a weak acid solution, the pH equals the pK_a plus the log of the ratio of the concentration of conjugate base to the concentration of acid. For an acid HX, the conjugate base is the X⁻ ion that's formed when the acid dissociates. Now, if the pK_a of an acid is 5, then for its pH to be 6, the log of that concentration ratio must be 1, or in other words, the ratio must be 10. This means that the concentration of conjugate base and, therefore, of dissociated acid, must be 10 times the concentration of acid.

34. C

We are told that a metal plate is *completely* illuminated by a monochromatic light source, and we are asked which of the Roman numeral statements would increase the number of electrons ejected from the surface of the metal.

Statement 1 says that increasing the intensity of the light source would increase the number of electrons ejected. Light may be thought of as being made of particles. These light particles, more commonly known as photons, have an energy given by the equation $E = hf$, where E is the energy, h is Planck's constant, and f is the frequency of the light. The intensity of a light source is the number of photons produced per unit time. Therefore, when we increase the intensity of the light source, we increase the number of photons striking the metal plate, resulting in more electrons being ejected from the metal. Thus Statement 1 is true, so we can eliminate answer **choice (D)**.

Statement II says that increasing the frequency of the light source would increase the number of electrons ejected. From the equation $E = hf$, we see that by increasing the frequency of the light, we increase the energy of the incident photons. This means that a photon that strikes the metal will eject an electron with a higher kinetic energy. However, it will not increase the number of electrons ejected, since the number of electrons ejected is proportional to the number of incident photons. Therefore, Statement II is false, and we can eliminate answer **choice (B)**. This leaves us with answer **choices (A)** and **(C)**.

The final statement says that increasing the surface area of the metal plate would increase the number of electrons ejected. The key point to remember here is that the metal plate is completely illuminated by the light source. Therefore, by increasing the area of the metal plate, we increase the area on which the light source is incident. This means that more photons will strike the plate, resulting in an increase in the number of electrons ejected. Since Statements I and III are true, the correct answer must be **choice (C)**.

35. D

There are two things you need to know to answer this question. First, in a chemical cell, the flow of electricity through the wire—and thus the flow of electrons—always runs from the anode to the cathode. This is true both in galvanic cells such as this one, where the reaction itself is the source of power, and in electrolytic cells that are powered by an external power source. Thus the cathode receives the electric current, which subsequently runs down into the solution. This means that we can eliminate **choices (A)** and **(C)**, since both of these talk about the electrons moving toward the anode. Second, the cell voltage is measured with a voltmeter, not an ammeter, so **choice (B)** is wrong. Again, the direction of the current is from the anode to the voltmeter to the cathode, and thus **choice (D)** is correct.

Passage VI (Questions 36–41)

36. A

We're told that the "energy of the clusters" can be derived from the minimum frequency of light required to break down a cluster. The frequency of a photon of light is related to its energy, and clearly if light is required to break down a cluster, energy must be absorbed when the cluster breaks down. That means **choice (D)** is wrong.

None of the choices describes the energy absorbed when the cluster breaks down, so to answer the question, we have to look for a choice that's equivalent to that value. Clusters are held together by intermolecular forces; therefore, formation of a cluster represents an increase in stability compared to the overall stability of the original component molecules when they existed independently. That's why energy must be added to break down a cluster. Likewise, when a cluster forms, an identical amount of energy will be released. Thus, **choice (A)** is correct.

Choice (B) is wrong because once the cluster forms, the energy is gone—it's not in the cluster at all—so it's simply wrong to say that it's shared among the cluster molecules. And the bond energy of the molecules in the cluster, **choice (C)**, is the energy needed to break the intramolecular bonds that hold the individual molecules together; this is definitely not related to the energy released when the cluster is formed.

37. C

To solve this question, you have to remember the relative energies of different parts of the electromagnetic spectrum. In the electromagnetic spectrum, energy increases along the following sequence: radio waves, microwaves, far-infrared, near-infrared, red light, the rest of the visible spectrum, and finally ultraviolet light. The passage states that the energy required to break a chemical bond is tens of thousands of wavenumbers, or wavelengths per centimeter, while the energy of the strongest cluster bond is on the order of a couple thousand wavenumbers. Since a few thousand wavenumbers correspond to the near-infrared region of the spectrum, it follows that the energy required to break a chemical bond will be considerably higher than the near-infrared. The narrow spectral region of red light is only slightly higher in energy than the near-infrared. Therefore, the only possibility is the choice with the highest energy, the ultraviolet region of the spectrum, choice (C).

38. C

Both water and methanol possess dipole moments, since the electronegative oxygen atoms attract electron density from the hydrogen atoms, and both molecules are asymmetrical. They're also both capable of forming hydrogen bonds. Since hydrogen bonding is the strongest form of dipole–dipole interaction, it will be the primary attractive force between these two molecules, so answer choice (C) is correct.

Hydrogen bonds are a type of dipole–dipole interaction, choice A, but remember we're always looking for the *best* answer. Since choice (C) describes the interaction more precisely, it's a better answer. As for choices (B) and (D), both of these types of forces will also occur, but they will have much weaker effects, and since you're looking for the strongest interaction, those answers are also wrong.

39. A

Like all the noble gases, neon is often considered an ideal gas, meaning that neon atoms don't interact with each other at all; however, in reality, even neon atoms are weakly attracted to each other. To be exact, neon atoms are subject to dispersion forces, as Statement 1 describes. Dispersion forces, also called London forces, are temporary dipoles caused by momentary unevenness in the electron distribution around atoms. If you didn't know off the top of your head that even noble gases are subject to dispersion forces, you should have been able to guess it from the table, which shows that atoms of argon, another noble gas, are subject to dispersion forces. However, as described in Question 34, noble gas molecules can't have permanent dipole moments, and so Statements II and III are both out. The correct answer choice is therefore (A).

40. B

The easiest way to answer this is by a process of elimination. Since sulfur dioxide is shown as being involved in dipole-dipole interactions, the sulfur dioxide must have a net dipole moment, and that means it must be asymmetrical. This rules out choice (A), linear, and choice D, trigonal planar, both of which are symmetrical shapes. This leaves **choices (B)** and **(C)**. A T-shaped molecule, **choice (C)**, requires four atoms, so sulfur dioxide, which is only triatomic, can't be T-shaped, because it doesn't have enough atoms; this rules out C. The sulfur dioxide molecule must be bent. Therefore, **choice (B)** is the correct answer.

41. D

To answer this question, you need to know the expression for electromagnetic energy, which states that the energy of a photon is equal to h, Planck's constant, times nu, the frequency of the radiation. Since nu is equal to c, the speed of light, divided by l, the wavelength of the radiation, the equation can be rewritten as E equals h times c over l. Here we're given the wave number, which is the inverse of the wavelength, or the number of wavelengths per centimeter. So we can say that E is h times c times the wavenumber. But be careful here: Since the wavenumber is given per centimeter, you have to express the speed of light, 3×10^8 meters per second, as 3×10^{10} centimeters per second. Then multiplying, you should get $(6.6 \times 10^{-34}) \times (3 \times 10^{10}) \times 1,000$, or 2×10^{-20} Joules. This corresponds to answer **choice (D)**.

Passage VII (Questions 42–47)

42. A

The energy of a process is always the sum of the final energies minus the sum of the initial energies:

$$\Delta E = \Sigma(\Delta E_f) - \Sigma(\Delta E_i)$$

The balanced combustion reaction for benzophenone (as for all oxygenated hydrocarbons) is

$$(C_6H_5)2CO + 15O_2 \rightarrow 13CO_2 + 5H_2O$$

The energy of combustion is then the sum of the products' energies of formation minus the sum of the reactants' energies of formation. We incorporate the stoichiometric coefficients in

$$\Delta E_{comb} = 13\Delta E_{f,CO2} + 5\Delta E_{f,H2O} - \Delta E_{f,benzophenone} - 15\Delta E_{f,O2}$$

Recall that the energy of formation of an element in its standard state is 0. Therefore we can remove the term with oxygen:

$$\Delta E_{comb} = 13\Delta E_{f,CO2} + 5\Delta E_{f,H2O} - \Delta E_{f,benzophenone}$$

This is **choice (A)**.

43. C

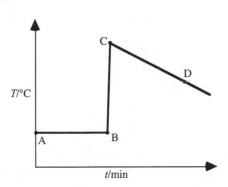

The experiment starts at point B, with ignition. Therefore, we can eliminate point A from contention. Point B is the initial temperature, T_i, so it cannot be the final temperature T_f, and **choice (B)** is incorrect. Point C is the final temperature T_f after combustion of products. Point D is incorrect, for it is an arbitrary point somewhere along the cooling curve as the calorimeter cools back to room temperature.

44. C

Let us convert grams of benzophenone to moles:

$13 \times C = 13 \times 12$ g/mol
$10 \times H = 10 \times 1$ g/mol
$1 \times O = 1 \times 16$ g/mol
Total benzophenone = 182 g/mol

1 mol/182 g $\times$ 1.3916 g benzophenone can be simplified to 1 mol/200 g $\times$ 1.5 g benzophenone = 0.005 mol/g $\times$ 1.5 g benzophenone = 0.0075 mol benzophenone.

From stoichiometry, we set up a proportion of oxygen gas to benzophenone:

? mol O_2/0.0075 mol benzophenone = 15 mol O_2/1 mol benzophenone

We solve the proportion to get 0.1 mol oxygen, which is **choice (C)**.

45. B

We use Equation II:

$$C_{calorimeter} = -\Delta E/\Delta T$$

and solve for the energy required, ΔE:

$$\Delta E = -C_{calorimeter}\Delta T$$

$$= -(2,417 \text{ cal/}°C)(4.92 \text{ }°C)$$

$$= -12,000 \text{ J}$$

The negative value indicates energy added to the system. We convert our answer into kJ to match the choices and end up with 12 kJ, **choice (B)**.

46. A

We assume the system is adiabatic; that is, no energy enters or leaves the system. Then any temperature rise in the system is due solely to that caused by combustion of the sample and iron wire. The other assumption, that pressure is constant, is false, because the bomb is sealed. Thus product gases are created and raise the pressure inside the bomb. **Choice (A) is correct.**

47. D

In general, any process for heat exchange uses the relation ΔE = amount $\times$ heat capacity.

We can find the molar heat capacity for iron (the heat capacity for 1 mol Fe) by converting from mass to moles:

$$C_{Fe} \text{ (cal/g)} \times \text{molar mass (g/mol)} = C_{mol}, \text{Fe (cal/mol)}$$

When we susbstitute in numbers,

1,400 cal/g $\times$ 56 g/mol = C_{mol},Fe

Simplifying gives

1,500 cal/g $\times$ 60 g/mol = 90,000 cal/mol

The closest answer is 78 kcal/mol, or 78,000 cal/mol, which is **choice (D)**.

Discrete Questions

48. C

Convection is the process of energy transfer through mass movement of heated material. Clearly, this cannot occur in a vacuum, since by definition there are no particles with mass in a vacuum. Likewise, the process of conduction requires vibrations of molecules and, hence, requires molecules. Conduction, then, can't proceed in a vacuum. Radiation, however, is the transfer of energy via electromagnetic waves, and certainly electromagnetic waves propagate through a vacuum.

49. D

We're given that the half-life of the radioactive isotope $^{204}_{84}$Po is 3.8 hours. This means that in a time of 3.8 hours, half of the original nuclei will undergo α-decay. In a time of 7.6 hours (two half-lives), only one-quarter of the original nuclei will not have undergone decay. This also means that after 7.6 hours, three-quarters of the original nuclei will have undergone decay. Every α-decay results in the emission of an a particle. Recall that an a particle is a helium nucleus. Thus, the reduction with mass over time is due to the emission of the α-particles.

To determine the total reduction in mass, we need to find the mass of the α particles emitted. We're given an initial quantity of two moles of $^{204}_{84}$Po, and we've determined that three-quarters of these two moles undergo decay. Thus, the quantity decayed is 3/2 moles. Since every decay produces one α-particle, we know that 3/2 moles of α-particles are produced. An α-particle is a helium nucleus, containing two protons and two neutrons, so its mass number is 4. The production of 3/2 moles of helium nuclei means a mass of (4)(3/2) = 6 grams. Thus, 6 grams of the original substance has been emitted in the form of α-particles. The original 2 moles correspond to a mass of (2)(204) = 408 grams. A loss of 6 grams then gives a final mass of 402 grams.

50. C

To solve this problem, we'll need to use the Doppler effect equation for sound. The equation is: $f_1 = f(v \pm V_D)/(v \pm V_S)$, where f is the frequency of the sound wave when the source and the detector are both at rest, f_1 is the frequency of the sound wave when either the source or detector is in motion, v is the speed of sound in the medium, V_D is the speed of the detector relative to the medium, and V_S is the speed of the source relative to the medium. In the current problem, the detector (observer) is stationary, so $V_D = 0$.

As far as the plus and minus signs in the equation are concerned, you can try and remember them or just use what you know qualitatively about the Doppler effect. Since $V_D = 0$, we only have to worry about the signs in the denominator. We know that when the source is moving away from the observer, the perceived frequency is lower than f, which implies using the + sign. When the source is moving toward the observer, the perceived frequency is greater than f, so we'll need to use the – sign.

When the source is moving away from the observer (observer behind source), the equation becomes $f_{behind} = 1,000v/(10,000 + 2,000)$. When the source is moving toward the observer (observer in front of source), the equation becomes $f_{in front} = 1,000v/(10,000 - 2,000)$. We're interested in the ratio of the wavelengths and not the frequencies. Recall that wavelength and frequency are related via $v = \lambda f$, so $\lambda = v/f$. Thus, we have $\lambda_{behind} = 12,000/1,000$, and $\lambda_{in front} = 8,000/1,000$. So, finally, we have the ratio $\lambda_{behind}/\lambda_{in front} = 12,000/8,000 = 3/2$.

51. D

This potential gas law problem can be solved faster through reasoning than through calculations. First, if the temperature is higher while the pressure and number of moles are the same, it follows that gas A must occupy a larger volume than does gas B, so **choices (A)** and **(B)** can be removed. Secondly, since 30°C is only slightly higher than 20°C when we convert to the (mandatory!) Kelvin scale by adding 273, it follows that the volume of gas A will be only slightly larger than that of gas B. **Choice (D)** is thus the only sensible answer. (Note in particular that **choice (C)** is provided for those who forget that gas law problems must always be done with temperature on the Kelvin scale.)

To use the gas law, PV = nRT, to solve this problem through calculation, we can rearrange to solve for each of the volumes, V_A and V_B, then set up the desired ratio as follows:

$V_A = \dfrac{n_A R T_A}{P_A}.=$ and $V_B \dfrac{n_B R T_B}{P_B}$. We know that $n_A = n_B$ = 1 mol, $P_A = P_B$ = 1 and R is a constant.

Therefore, $V_A : V_B = \dfrac{\frac{n_A R T_B}{P_A}}{\frac{n_B R T_B}{P_B}}$. The pressures, moles, and

Rs all cancel, leaving $V_A : V_B = \dfrac{T_A}{T_B} = \dfrac{(30+273)}{(20+273)} = \dfrac{303}{293}$.

52. D

This problem is best answered based on atomic properties and periodic trends. In general, a cation is smaller than a neutral atom of the same element, because the removal of electrons decreases the electrostatic repulsion between the remaining electrons, thereby allowing the nucleus to pull them closer and decreasing the ionic radius. Conversely, anions are generally larger than the corresponding neutral atoms because of an increased number of electrons that repel one another. Thus, the question can be translated into "Which of the following elements is most likely to form an anion?"

This revised stem can be answered on the basis of periodic trends, in particular the trend in electronegativity, which increases toward the upper right corner of the table. Chlorine, Cl, is the most electronegative of the elements listed; it would thus be expected to have the greatest electron affinity and is most likely to take on an electron and become anionic. The three elements in the incorrect choices are all more likely to form cations than anions; their ionic radii will thus be smaller than their atomic radii.

Verbal Reasoning

Passage 1 (Questions 53–58)

53. B

In paragraph 4, the author mentions that American unions employ more militant tactics than foreign unions. Thus, American unions would be more likely to use violence during a strike, **choice (B)**. **Choice (A)** is the opposite of the correct answer. As for **choices (C)** and **(D)**, the author never says whether American or foreign unions are more likely to bargain during a strike.

54. A

American society emphasizes individual achievement over class solidarity. So Statement I is false. Statements II and III, however, are true. The author says that American unions tend to be less concerned with nonunion issues than foreign unions, and the author notes that both American business and religious organizations reflect basic American values.

55. B

It would contradict the author's view: Again, the author contends that American unions tend to be "narrowly self-interested" in comparison to foreign unions. An American union that encouraged its members to get involved in nonunion issues like national politics would be inconsistent with this view. **Choices (A)** and **(C)** are logically eliminated by **choice (B)**. **Choice (D)** would contradict the author's view.

56. C

The phrase *strong materialistic bent* appears in the context of a discussion of basic American values, one of which is the acquisition of wealth. **Choices (A)** and **(D)** are beyond the scope of the passage. There is no mention of what European socialists think of aristocrats **(A)**, nor is there any religious criticism of secular values **(D)**. **Choice (B)** distorts information in paragraph one.

57. D

The author compares American and foreign labor movements but doesn't suggest that foreign labor movements have influenced the American labor movement. **Choices (A)** and **(B)** are mentioned as influences in paragraph 2, while **choice (C)** is mentioned as an influence in paragraph 3.

58. B

The "traditional value system" refers to those basic values that are reflected in America's institutions. Individual achievement, according to paragraph 1, is one of those values. As for **choice (A)**, the author contends that class solidarity isn't part of the American value system. **Choices (C)** and **(D)** play on details in the passage that have nothing to do with the American value system.

Passage II (Questions 59–64)

59. C

Paragraph 1 states that algal photosynthesis maintains the high level of oxygen saturation in the reef environment. **Choices (A), (B), and (D)** are all "subjects of scientific puzzlement" discussed in the passage.

60. D

Paragraph 3 states that *Scleractinia,* the coral producers, account for only 10 percent of the average community.

As for **choice (A)**, to the contrary, the author proposes in the last sentence of paragraph 3 that this is the reason for the name "coral reef." **Choice (B)** is wrong because paragraph 1 indicates that the coral portion of the reef plays a large role in reef formation as well as reef "renewability." And **(C)** is a true statement and would not contribute to a misnomer.

61. C

Opponents of Darwin's theory believe that the "end of the Ice Age" had more to do with the development of reefs than did the "submergence of volcanic islands." **Choice (A)** is a belief held by scientists in general. **(B)** is a commonly accepted view concerning reefs. And as for **choice (D)**, the crux of the theory held by Darwin's opponents is that the Ice Age played a major role in reef development.

62. B

The theory about reef development is one of transformation; therefore, the reefs would not have developed independently of one another.

As for **choice (A)**, the passage suggests that each theory may contribute to explaining how reefs develop. With **choice (C)**, paragraph 3 states that corals that "lack an algal presence" exist throughout the world. **Choice (D)** is wrong because paragraph 1 demonstrates that multiple factors contribute to a reef's "amazing renewability."

63. D

Paragraph 2 contrasts Darwin's theory to that of its opponents by discussing his focus on the submergence of volcanic islands.

As for **choice (A)**: To the contrary, Darwin's theory is more persuasive due to recent discoveries at the Eniwetak atoll. **Choice (B)** is wrong because according to the passage, reefs develop through transformation rather than through separate, distinct processes. With **(C)**, the passage implies in paragraph 2 that both theories of reef development are only "partially correct."

64. B

The last sentence of paragraph 1 states that scientists are puzzled by the mechanism through which the symbionts stimulate the secretion of calcium carbonate in one another. If a chemical stimulus could be isolated, then the symbiotic relationship would be more clearly understood.

Choice (A) is wrong because paragraph 1 states that algal photosynthesis is responsible for the high level of oxygen saturation. **(C)** is wrong because the components of the reef's protective layer are already known. As for **choice (D)**, scientists know that the coral produces the colors and formations seen in reefs.

Passage III (Questions 65–69)

65. B

How could scientists hold onto the view that *Archaeopteryx lithographica* represented a "transitionary" species between reptiles and birds if a bird capable of flight already existed before it? **Choices (A)** and **(C)** are logically eliminated by **(B)**, and **(D)** focuses on an irrelevant passage detail.

66. A

The passage points out the many differences in skeletal structure between *Archaeopteryx lithographica* and modern birds.

For **choice (B)**, paragraph 4 reveals that *Archaeopteryx lithographica's* tail played a larger role in its daily life than the essentially vestigial tail of a modern bird plays in its daily life. For **choice (C)**, paragraphs 1 and 5 make this point. And paragraph 4 raises the point made in **choice (D)**.

67. C

The phrase *wealth of information* appears in the context of a remark about what scientists have learned about birds' ability to fly by studying the fossil remains of *Archaeopteryx lithographica.*

Choice (A) is wrong because no "recent research projects" are mentioned in the passage. As for **(B)**, the passage provides a lot of detail on *Archaeopteryx lithographica's* skeletal structure, but the phrase in question doesn't pertain to this information. And **choice (D)** is beyond the scope of the passage. There's no mention of any fossil discoveries in central Germany. The passage says only that *Archaeopteryx lithographica* lived near that area.

68. B

The passage mentions that *Archaeopteryx lithographica* had wings but couldn't fly. Since modern birds have wings and can fly, it can be inferred that the wings of *Archaeopteryx lithographica* and those of modern birds serve different purposes.

Choice (A) is contrary to the passage: *Archaeopteryx lithographica* had a much better developed tail than modern birds. **Choices (C)** and **(D)** are beyond the scope of the passage. The author never compares the intelligence **(C)** or the size **(D)** of *Archaeopteryx lithographica* and modern birds.

69. A

Paragraphs 1 and 5 state that the *Archaeopteryx* did indeed possess "birdlike feathers." **Choices (B) and (C)** are both described in paragraph 2, while **choice (D)** is described in paragraph 3.

Passage IV (Questions 70–76)

70. B

In the first paragraph, the author states that each "lighthouse is as unique as the landscape that surrounds it," and uses the rest of the passage to prove that point with specific examples. The correct answer here is (B).

Choice (A) is incorrect because the only functions of a lighthouse mentioned are the fact that it acts as a beacon at night and a landmark by day, both terms too general to be described as specific. The only real opinion offered in the passage is found in the last sentence, so (C) is incorrect. The passage does enumerate many lighthouse facts, but these facts function as support of the primary purpose, which is to make the author's point; (D) is incorrect.

71. C

This is a tough question that asks you to choose the one answer that could not possibly be inferred from details in the passage. Here, that one answer is (C). The first sentence of the second paragraph states that there is not one arbitrary feature about a lighthouse, which directly contradicts the statement that a "period" is randomly assigned from a list.

It is easy to infer from the passage's opening sentence that (A) is probably true, so it can be excluded. It is also not a stretch to assume that a structure that serves as a navigational beacon and landmark for mariners would be considered strategically important to a navy during a war, so (B) can be excluded as well. Lines 38–40 of the passage state that lighthouses built after the introduction of the Fresnel lens were much taller than their predecessors, so it can be inferred that (D) is true, too. Again, (C) is the correct answer.

72. B

The answer is not stated directly in the passage, so you are required to infer it from the author's other statements. The U.S. Coast Guard publishes a document called a light list, which covers the different daymarks and nightmarks. It can be inferred, then, that daymarks and nightmarks are a specialized or esoteric language that only a small population, sailors, can read and understand. Choice (B) is the correct answer.

From reading the passage, it is clear that daymarks are equally as relevant as nightmarks in helping sailors distinguish their location, so answer choice (A) is incorrect. You can eliminate answer choice (C) because daymarks and nightmarks are not merely decorative; they are extremely functional and utilitarian. Answer choice (D) is also incorrect because even when lighthouses have installed a catadioptric system, lighthouses still use daymarks.

73. A

According to the passage the earliest modern lighthouses employed a catoptric light system and the Fresnel lens, associated with the dioptric system, was not invented until 1822, so Statement I is true. Eliminate (B). The passage also states that by 1860, every existing lighthouse in the United States had a Fresnel lens, so Statement III is false. You can then exclude **choice (D)** as well. Finally, paragraph 3 states that it was the dioptric system that used refraction, not the catoptric system, which was based on reflection, so Statement II is false as well. You can eliminate (C), which leaves (A) as your answer.

74. D

It's very easy to get hung up on worrying about differences in the two optical systems and make this question much harder than it actually is. The important thing to recognize is that although one system reflects light and the other refracts it, they both accomplish the same thing: They concentrate a light into a powerful beam. The only choice that does not project a concentrated beam of light is (D), a lantern, and that's your answer. As stated in paragraph 4, a lantern can be used in an optical system, but it does not utilize an optical system itself.

Choice (A) uses a dioptric optical system. **Choices (B) and (C)** use catoptric systems.

75. C

The only choice supported by details from the passage is (C). Paragraph 2 states that no two daymarks are alike, and paragraph 5 states that each lighthouse's "period" (i.e., nightmark) is unique.

This last statement proves (A) to be incorrect. **Choice (B)** can be excluded on those same grounds; though it is mentioned that lighthouses were built taller after the introduction of the Fresnel lenses, no specific height requirement is detailed. **Choice (D)** is the trickiest of the choices because paragraph 4 states that that all lighthouses were converted to Fresnel lenses and therefore, dioptric systems, but it is not specifically stated that every lighthouse was later changed to catadioptric.

76. B

In the final sentence, the author refers to sailors who still understand the value of lighthouses as "smart" and then contrasts the modern navigational devices, radios and radar, to lighthouses with the adjectives "fragile" and "stalwart." In other words, the author believes that technology is not infallible and if one were to solely rely upon it for navigating, one would be ill prepared if that technology failed. Therefore, (B) is your answer.

Choices (A) and (C) are incorrect because the author offers nothing in the passage to suggest he would describe that sailor as "typical" or "overconfident." **Choice (D)**—though the closest of the remaining choices to being correct—is too extreme a statement to fit the bill.

Passage V (Questions 77–83)

77. C

If more criminals are going in than are coming out of prison under selective incapacitation, prison populations are going to increase.

Choice (A) is wrong because if anything, the information in the stem strengthens this claim. You can eliminate choice (B) because it represents a claim that is never made. And (D) is a claim that is never made as well; what the author says is that white-collar criminals may unfairly receive shorter sentences under selective incapacitation.

78. B

This is the point of the next-to-last paragraph. Judges make predictions now when they are sentencing criminals, and a judge's judgment is flawed—even more flawed than statistical prediction, according to the author. Choices (A) and (C) are far too extreme to be correct. Choice (D) contradicts everything the author argues for.

79. C

The author would not agree with this because the author thinks that all sentencing has a predictive basis. Choices (A) and (D) can be found in the next-to-last paragraph, and choice (B) comes from the second paragraph.

80. B

If less privileged offenders cannot evade sanction, this means they must be dangerous repeat offenders, since dangerous repeat offenders are the ones imprisoned under selective incapacitation.

Choice (A) does not follow from the author's statement. Choice (C) misses the point that harmful middle-class people who commit white-collar crimes would go free under selective incapacitation; no money is involved. And choice (D) distorts the real point, that some middle-class offenders will go free but deserve incarceration.

81. B

The idea is to minimize all error, but that is not a choice here. (B) is correct because if you minimize the "false negatives," you minimize the number of crimes committed by mistakenly released criminals.

82. B

This is a paraphrase of the end of paragraph 6. As for choice (A), some people may not like this, but according to the author, more people are worried about "false positives" than about "false negatives." Choice (C) is an argument for statistical prediction. And choice (D) is way outside the scope of the passage.

83. D

The author makes this claim but never backs it up with solid evidence. Choices (A) and (B) are claims that the author makes and then explains in detail. (C) is not a claim made in the passage; as far as we know, first-time offenders could get probation.

Passage VI (Questions 84–87)

84. B

The tsetse fly transmits a deadly parasite, not a chemical.

Choice (A) is wrong because paragraph 2 states that *trypanosomes* depend on vertebrate blood for nourishment. For choice (C), paragraph 1 states that the tsetse uses vertebrate blood for nourishment, while paragraph 2 states that the *trypanosome* does as well. Choice (D) is definitely true, according to the passage.

85. C

The passage discusses the *trypanosome's* ability to alter its genetic code, not the tsetse fly's. Choices (A), (B), and (D) are all mentioned in the passage.

86. C

Choice (C) is exactly what environmentalists fear would happen if the tsetse fly were controlled to the point of elimination.

You can infer choice (A) from the passage, since diseases spread by *trypanosomes* can't be controlled by antibodies or vaccines. Choice (B) is mentioned in paragraph 2, while choice (D) is directly stated in the first sentence of paragraph 4.

87. D

Choice (D) directly follows the logic of the environmentalists, argument in paragraph 5. The lizard represents the tsetse fly, the locust represents the cattle, and the agricultural crops represent the African grasslands.

Choices (A) and (B) both misconstrue the analogy presented in the question stem. Choice (C) is a nonsense answer.

88. A

A shortcut to answer these rare question types is to look for answer choices that fall at the end of paragraphs or the end of the passage, like **Choice (A)**. Very often the item that has no support will be at the end of a thought before the author segues into something different. This will often allow the answer choices to be narrowed down quickly even if it does not immediately yield the correct answer.

Choice (B) is a summary of the second paragraph supported by the example of the fountain. **Choice (C)** is the premise of the last paragraph and is elaborated on with specific examples of possible challenges. **Choice (D)** is a paraphrase of James' argument and is supported by the example immediately following.

89. C

This question is primarily a logic question that tests the structure rather than the content of the passage. The author argues that two divergent and abstract philosophies compete to explain human consciousness. These questions are particularly vulnerable to the denial test: if an answer looks tempting, deny it and investigate whether the author's argument is hurt. If it is, the author must rely on the idea behind the statement and it is a correct answer choice. In this case, if the author believes that abstract ideas cannot lend insight into human behavior, both philosophies are irrelevant. Each of the following wrong answer choices, if denied, won't devastate any part of the author's argument and so are less attractive than **Choice (C)**.

Choice (A) supports the dualistic theory, which the author does not endorse. **Choice (B)** is an extreme answer choice mentioned nowhere in the passage. **Choice (D)** is out of scope, as challenging philosophies of existence with practical examples is never mentioned in the passage.

90. B

The primary claim to superiority of James' theory mentioned in the fourth paragraph is its "efficiency" (paragraph 4), that it is simpler, or more economic than a dualistic philosophy. If this is proven false, James' theory is stripped of its primary advantage.

Choice (A) is out of scope; it involves concepts of morality. **Choices (C)** and **(D)** lend support to James' theory, rather than challenge it.

91. D

Application questions are common on abstract passages, and will require you to apply the ideas in the passage to specific situations. The key is to identify what relevance the situation has to what part of the passage. In this instance, an action is performed on an object, removing the moral sense while leaving consciousness intact. Since self-awareness is unchanged, neither philosophy is supported or hurt by the experiment, thereby leading to **Choice (D)**.

92. C

Logic questions are answered easily if a good map has been created beforehand. The first paragraph presents the dualistic view and gives examples of sub-philosophies on opposite ends of that same philosophy, which matches **Choice (C)**.

Choices (A) and **(D)** cannot be correct, as neither of those philosophies had yet been brought up in the first paragraph, when the Socratics are mentioned. **Choice (B)** is a faulty use of detail: a disparity between a modern and ancient philosophy is presented, but Socrates is not introduced into the passage for that reason.

Biological Sciences

Passage 1 (Questions 93–99)

93. B

This is one of those outside-knowledge questions. Choice (A), the oral cavity, contains the salivary glands, which begin chemical digestion with the secretion of salivary amylase, or ptyalin. This enzyme hydrolyzes starch to maltose, so choice (A) is wrong.

The esophagus, choice (B), is simply a conduit through which a food bolus passes from the pharynx to the stomach. The bolus is propelled forward by peristalsis, which is the involuntary rhythmic contraction of smooth muscle in the digestive tract. Peristalsis is controlled by the autonomic nervous system. The esophagus has two sphincters prevent the movement of food in the wrong direction. The lower esophageal sphincter prevents the stomach's acidic juices from entering the esophagus. There are no glands that secrete into the esophageal lumen, so choice (B) is the right answer. The esophagus is lined by squamous epithelium, which is aglandular tissue.

The stomach, choice (C), contains numerous glandular cells, such as the parietal cells, which secrete hydrochloric acid; the chief cells, which secrete pepsin; and neuroendocrine cells that secrete gastrin. You should have ruled out the stomach immediately since the passage discusses the secretions of the stomach.

The duodenum has mucosal glands, called Brunner's glands, which secrete mucus to protect the small intestine from the acidity of gastric juices. The rest of the small intestine contains pits known as crypts of Lieberkuhn, which also have mucus-secreting glandular cells. In addition, the intestinal glands secrete aminopeptidase and dipeptidases—enzymes that hydrolyze peptide bonds and enterokinase, which converts trypsinogen to trypsin. So choice (D) is incorrect.

94. B

If the ulcer is triggered by bacterial infection, as you are told in the question stem, then the easiest way to eliminate the ulcer would be to eliminate the bacteria. Look for the answer choice that would most effectively eliminate the bacteria without harming the patient.

Increasing acetylcholine secretion will stimulate HCl secretion, which we know from the passage is a symptom of ulcers. This would only aggravate the symptoms; thus, choice (A) is incorrect.

Choice (B) suggests that we inhibit formation of the initiator aminoacyl-tRNA molecule, which is found only in prokaryotes. First of all, from the word *tRNA*, you should have realized that this choice deals with the process of translation, which is the means by which the genetic information in mRNA is translated into a sequence of amino acids during protein synthesis. Translation occurs at the ribosome, which is comprised of two subunits, one large and one small. Ribosomes attach to the 5' end of mRNA. tRNA is an adapter molecule that transports the correct amino acid to the growing chain. When a tRNA is charged with an amino acid, it is called an aminoacyl-tRNA. Each tRNA carries the specific amino acid called for by the mRNA codon to which the tRNA pairs. So as each tRNA molecule base pairs with an mRNA codon, the amino acid chain grows by one residue. This occurs until a termination codon is present in the mRNA. If the initiator aminoacyl-tRNA of prokaryotic protein synthesis cannot be formed, then translation cannot start, no proteins can be made, and the bacteria will die. Since formylmethionyl-tRNA is the initiator of protein synthesis in prokaryotes only, eukaryotic cells will not be affected. Thus, this seems like it would effectively eliminate the ulcer and not harm the patient. Therefore, choice (B) is correct.

According to **choice (C)**, puromycin is an aminoacyl-tRNA analog. This means that it looks like an aminoacyl-tRNA molecule, but it's not. You don't have to know the function of the analog, because you're told that it operates on both prokaryotes and eukaryotes. That means that whatever this thing does, it will do it to both the bacterial cells and the patient's cells. Therefore, it will not be the most effective treatment.

As for **choice (D)**, alleviating one of the symptoms of ulcers—internal bleeding—will not eliminate the bacteria causing the ulcer.

95. C

Peptic ulcers develop when the concentration of gastric juice overwhelms the mucoprotective surface of the digestive tract and the neutralizing secretions of the pancreas. Therefore, anything that increases the production of hydrochloric acid, decreases the protective lining, or decreases these pancreatic secretions would contribute to peptic ulcer disease. Which of the choices does *not* do this?

Choice (A), excessive gastrin production, is a plausible cause of peptic ulcer disease, since gastrin, which is the hormone secreted by the pyloric glands of the stomach, stimulates the parietal cells to secrete more HCl, especially in response to high stomach pH. In fact, an excess of gastrin is a common cause of ulcers in the disease known as Zollinger-Ellison syndrome. So **choice (A)** is wrong.

Weakness in mucosal barriers, **choice (B)**, is also a possible cause of peptic ulcer disease. If mucus secretions are abnormal or diminished in some way, then there is a predisposition to peptic ulcer disease. So **choice (B)** is also wrong.

Choice (D), an abnormally high density of parietal cells, might also predispose an individual to peptic ulcer disease. While the negative feedback system of stomach pH helps to protect against this, a correlation does exist between ulcer development and excessive parietal cells. **choice (D)** is plausible and therefore, incorrect.

As stated in the passage, parietal cells release hydrochloric acid in response to gastrin, acetylcholine, and histamine. Histamine stimulates HCl secretion by acting on specific histamine receptors on the outer membrane of parietal cells. If the parietal cell's sensitivity to histamine was decreased, as in **choice (C)**, then less acid would be released. Therefore, this is *not* a cause of ulcers. In fact, one of the most common drug therapies for ulcer disease is histamine receptor blockers. **choice (C)** is the only one that is *not* a plausible cause of peptic ulcer disease and is, therefore, the correct answer.

96. D

The portion of the stomach that contains the majority of the parietal cells is the antrum. A common treatment for severe peptic ulcer disease, after medical therapy has failed, is an antrectomy. Removal of the antrum decreases the amount of acid produced by the stomach and, therefore, decreases the occurrence of ulcers. **Choice (A)** would alleviate peptic ulcer disease, and is therefore incorrect.

Choice (B) describes your common, over-the-counter antacid. These are alkaline substances that act within the stomach to neutralize the acid before it can cause cellular damage. So **choice (B)** is also a viable treatment and is therefore, incorrect.

Another oral drug acts to reinforce the stomach's mucosal barrier by coating it with a gel-like substance. If a weakened mucosal barrier is responsible for the peptic ulcer disease, then administration of such a drug is also a possible treatment; **choice (C)** is wrong, too.

Choice (D), however, is *not* a possible therapy for peptic ulcer disease. Increasing stomach acidity might very well decrease the release of acid via a negative feedback mechanism that is responsive to stomach pH. However, the very nature of this acidity would by itself cause more injury to a digestive tract lining already afflicted with peptic ulcer disease.

97. A

You can find the answer to this question in the passage.

The pancreas, **choice (A)**, releases negatively charged bicarbonate ion into the duodenum. This neutralizes the incoming acid and protects the duodenal lining. The pancreas secretes sodium bicarbonate, which combines with the hydrochloric acid to form carbonic acid and sodium chloride. The carbonic acid dissociates into water and carbon dioxide, the carbon dioxide is absorbed into body fluids, and the remaining solution of sodium chloride is neutral. So **choice (A)** is correct.

The stomach has a special mucoprotective surface to combat its acidic environment. The walls of the stomach consist of a continuous layer of mucous cells which secrete a one-millimeter-thick layer of viscous mucus. This mucus both protects the stomach from its acidic environment and lubricates food. So the stomach does not rely on neutralization to protect itself; it couldn't possibly do this since its enzymes work best at a very acidic pH. Therefore, **choice (C)** is wrong.

Choice (B), the large intestine, is also wrong. By the time the chyme reaches the large intestine, it is fully neutralized.

The liver, **choice (D)**, synthesizes bile, which emulsifies fats. The liver also detoxifies the poisons of cellular metabolism. In addition, one of the main functions of the liver is the regulation of blood glucose concentration. Though the liver has many other functions as well, not one of them is involved in the neutralization of gastric acidity. Therefore, **choice (D)** is incorrect.

98. A

Gastric ·enzymes, such as pepsin, have optimum activity in an environment with a pH between 2 and 3. Enzymes are proteins; they rely on the appropriate ionic state of their primary amino acid structure for proper function. For example, if the substrate-binding site of pepsin is altered by a change in electrical charge, then pepsin would not be able to hydrolyze those peptide bonds for which it is specific. The inherent nature of gastric enzymes makes them most effective in an acidic environment. Extreme acidity, however, can cause denaturation of proteins, which is why there is that complex negative feedback system that maintains a narrow pH range within the stomach. So **choice (A)** is the correct answer.

Choice (B) is incorrect because low pH, not high, stimulates the release of pancreatic secretions. When acidic chyme enters the duodenum, it stimulates the release of secretin from intestinal mucosa. Secretin enters the bloodstream and acts on the pancreas, causing it to secrete large amounts of pancreatic juice with a high concentration of bicarbonate ion. Secretin is secreted any time the pH in the duodenum falls below 4.5.

Choice (C) is also incorrect. As previously stated, many proteins are denatured by acidity. A low intracellular pH would impair cellular function, not to mention protein function. It is the lumenal pH of the stomach that must be kept low.

Choice (D) is incorrect. First of all, the acidity of the chyme entering the small intestine is neutralized by the bicarbonate ion in the duodenum; by the time it reaches the large intestine, the chyme is no longer acidic. Secondly, nutrient absorption occurs in the small intestine, not the large intestine. The large intestine is involved in the absorption of salts and water.

99. C

To answer this question, you have to understand the concept of a negative feedback mechanism. A negative feedback mechanism is one of the primary methods by which homeostasis is maintained; a change in a physiological variable, such as the pH of the gastric juices or the presence of acidic fluid in the duodenum, triggers a physiological response that counteracts the initial change.

Two such mechanisms are described for you in the passage. When excess HCl enters the duodenum, the mucosal glands of the small intestine are stimulated to secrete the hormone secretin, which acts on the pancreas to increase its secretion of fluid high in bicarbonate ion. And bicarbonate ion neutralizes the acidity in the duodenum, thereby protecting the small intestine from the harsh effects of acid. The second mechanism discussed is this: When HCl secretion in the stomach becomes so high that pH drops below the minimum of optimal activity for the stomach's enzymes, there is a negative feedback loop involving the hormone gastrin that turns off HCl secretion. This raises the pH of the stomach back to its optimum.

Based on this discussion, **choices (A)** and **(B)** are both wrong because they have their "decreases" and "increases" mixed up. An increase in acid secretion *increases* the rate at which bicarbonate ion is secreted into the duodenum. Likewise, **choice (D)** is wrong because a decrease in gastric pH *decreases* acid secretion.

Choice (C) is correct because an increase in gastric pH—that is, the pH becoming more alkaline—would stimulate an increase in acid secretion until the gastric pH return to its optimum for peptic enzyme function, which is approximately 2.5.

Discrete Questions

100. C

This is your basic endoderm, ectoderm, mesoderm question; that is, a question about the three primary germ layers in a developing mammalian embryo. It's just worded a little differently than you're probably used to seeing. You're simply being asked to determine which of the physiological systems described in the answer choices is derived from ectoderm. Ectoderm gives rise to the epidermis, the lens of the eye, the inner ear, the adrenal medulla, and the nervous system. And since responding to stimuli is a function of the nervous system, **choice (C)** is the correct answer. Mesoderm gives rise to the musculoskeletal system, the circulatory system, the excretory system, the gonads, the kidneys, the lining of the body cavity, and the dermis. Endoderm gives rise to the lining of the digestive tract, the lining of the respiratory system, and the liver and pancreas.

101. D

This question tests your understanding of osmosis, which is the passive diffusion of water from regions of low solute concentration to regions of high solute concentration until solute concentration is the same between the two regions. An endothelial cell, like most other eukaryotic cells, is surrounded by a water-permeable lipid bilayer membrane and contains a nucleus, mitochondria, endoplasmic reticulum, Golgi apparatus, lysosomes, cytoplasm, and other cellular structures and organelles. Cytosol, the fluid component of cytoplasm, consists of an aqueous solution with proteins, nutrients, ions, and other solutes dissolved in it. Distilled water has nothing dissolved in it; it has a solution concentration of 0. Therefore, an endothelial cell is said to be hypertonic to a medium of distilled water—that is, it has a higher solute concentration than its surroundings. Furthermore, because of this difference in solute concentration, water will flow into the cell, from a region of low to high solute concentration. The cell eventually lyses because its membrane cannot withstand the great volume of water entering it.

An endothelial cell would shrivel if it were placed in a medium to which it was hypotonic; in this instance, water would rush out of the cell into the medium. So **choice (A)** is wrong. **Choice (C)** is wrong because the cell would remain the same size only if it were placed in a medium to which it was isotonic—say, for instance, if it were placed in a medium of free cytoplasm. **Choice (B)** is wrong because cell division has nothing whatsoever to do with osmosis and solute concentration; it is irrelevant to the question.

102. B

Cyclohexane is the most stable structure since there is almost no angle, torsional, or Van der Waals strain. The bond angle of a tetrahedral carbon atom, which is the structure of a carbon with four single bonds, is $109.5°$, and the closer the actual bond angle is to this number, the more stable the ring. The bond angle in cyclohexane is just about $109.5°$, so angle strain is minimized. Also, none of the hydrogens in the ring are eclipsed—the chair conformation ensures that they are all staggered with respect to each other—so torsional strain is avoided. In addition, the hydrogens don't compete for the same position in space, which eliminates any Van der Waals strain.

On the other hand, cyclopropane has a carbon–carbon bond angle that's less than $109.5°$ and so is subjected to more angle strain. Moreover, the hydrogens are eclipsed, so the molecule undergoes a great deal of torsional strain. As a result, **choice (A)** is incorrect.

Choices (C) and (D)—cyclononane and cyclodecane—can assume a number of conformations, none of which can minimize all three types of strain. For instance, a conformation that minimizes torsional strain results in an increase in angle strain.

103. D

Carbon monoxide is poisonous to humans because it binds more readily to hemoglobin than does oxygen; that is, hemoglobin has a greater affinity for carbon monoxide than for oxygen. Carbon monoxide is a gas formed by the incomplete combustion of carbon, and it's toxic because it readily forms carbonmonoxyhemoglobin, or COHb. COHb cannot bind to oxygen. In fact, hemoglobin's affinity for carbon monoxide is 210 times greater than its affinity for oxygen. Therefore, when carbon monoxide enters the bloodstream and binds to hemoglobin, the amount of hemoglobin capable of carrying oxygen decreases.

However, the total concentration of hemoglobin in the blood remains unaffected, so **choice (A)** is wrong. But carbon monoxide does decrease the amount of oxygen that is released to the tissues, causing anemic hypoxia. Anemic hypoxia is a condition where the arterial partial pressure of oxygen remains the same but the amount of hemoglobin available for binding oxygen is reduced. Since the arterial partial pressure of oxygen remains the same, the chemoreceptors in the carotid arteries and aorta do not become stimulated and, hence, do not stimulate an increase in respiration. **Choices (B)** and **(C)** are wrong, because carbon monoxide does not destroy lung tissue, nor does it block the electron transport chain, thereby preventing ATP formation.

104. C

You should know that a monosaccharide in an aqueous solution will form two isomeric cyclic hemiacetals, or anomers. The difference between the two hemiacetals is the orientation of the substituents around the first carbon. In the α-anomer, the hydroxyl substituent on C1 is oriented down from the plane of the molecule, *trans* to the substituent on C5; in the β-anomer, it is oriented up, *cis* to the functionality on C5. The point is that anomers are diastereomers that differ only in their configuration around the first carbon, so **choice (C)** is correct.

Choice (A) is wrong because most of the other carbons in a carbohydrate, besides the one in the carbonyl group, are chiral, so anomers are usually chiral. **Choice (B)** is wrong because mirror images have opposite configurations around *all* their chiral carbons, not just around one. Finally, open-chain monosaccharides that differ in configuration around the *second* carbon are called epimers, not anomers, so **choice (D)** is also incorrect.

Passage II (Questions 105–109)

105. B

Choice (A) says the experiment supports Hypothesis 1 because the flies with P elements leave more offspring than the flies without P elements. This is a natural selection argument. That is, it says that the P-strain flies have a selective advantage and reproduce more than the M-strain flies. Is this true? There's no evidence for it. This is really a trick question. Normally, if you found that the frequency of a trait increased over time, you might assume that it was evolutionarily favorable. But that's not the only way it could happen—for instance, it could also be due to migration or selective mating. In any case, we're told that the offspring of these crosses have a lot of mutations and as a result are often sterile. And if many P-strain flies are sterile, then they certainly wouldn't be expected to leave more offspring then M-strain flies. So it doesn't sound like P elements should be favored evolutionarily. As a matter of fact, they're not: The reason the P elements spread is that they're really good at spreading—much better than your average gene—because they can self-replicate and insert themselves all over a fly's DNA. So choice (A) is wrong.

Choice (B) says Hypothesis 1 is supported because the incidence of P elements has increased. The incidence *has* increased and that does support Hypothesis 1, because that hypothesis requires the P elements to spread. So this looks like the correct answer. But check the other two choices anyway, in case one of them is better. (Persuasive argument passages tend to have a lot of questions about the reasoning of the theories they discuss that can sometimes seem pretty subjective; you need to be particularly careful in choosing your answers and checking all the choices.)

Choice (C) says that the observation that after 100 generations, almost all of the flies are P-strain flies supports Hypothesis 2 because P elements are lost during culture. However, we can see that P elements aren't lost during culture; they are gained, so choice (C) must be wrong.

Finally, choice (D) says that Hypothesis 2 is supported because the flies have been cultured for many generations. It's true that in the experiment, the flies were cultured for many decades. However, since P strains have been around for decades, a long culture time doesn't necessarily disprove Hypothesis 1. And according to Hypothesis 2, strains cultured for many generations are expected to lose their P elements, which, as already said, does not happen in this instance. So choice (D) is wrong as well. Choice (B) is indeed the correct answer.

106. B

The question asks what type of virus could possibly have been the original form of P elements, assuming that Hypothesis 1 is correct and P elements recently arose from viral infection. A lysogenic virus, Choice B, is one that infects a cell, integrates itself into its DNA, and then sits there for some amount of time before it does anything; that is, before it re-emerges and takes over the host cell's genetic and protein-synthesizing machinery. This ability to integrate itself into the cell's DNA is a property that P elements share, which is our clue that this is the correct answer.

How about the other choices? A lytic virus, choice (A), is one that infects a cell, immediately takes over the cell's "machinery" to replicate more viruses, and then kills the cell by lysing it so that the new viruses get released. A bacteriophage, choice (C), is a virus that attacks only bacteria—but this hypothetical virus must have been able to infect fruit flies, not bacteria, so choice (C) must also be wrong. Finally, an attenuated virus, choice (D), is a virus that has somehow been weakened—by mutation, for instance—to make it safe to inject it into someone as a vaccine. Since we're not talking about vaccines, choice (D) must be wrong. It's probably just thrown in here because it's a term that you might associate with viruses and might be inclined to pick if you were in a hurry.

107. C

Here you have to figure out the different ways whereby P elements might be "lost" from a fruit fly's DNA and which answer choice is *not* a plausible mechanism for this loss.

Choice (A), genetic drift, is a shift in gene frequency due to chance. That is, if you start out with a 50–50 frequency of two alleles for a particular gene, in the next generation, just by chance, there might wind up being a 49–51 distribution, and then in the next generation 48–52, and so on, until finally you might lose one of the alleles altogether. Genetic drift becomes noticeable only in small populations over periods of many generations. But here we're talking about lab populations, which are pretty small compared to a wild population, and we're talking about 30 years, which is a lot of generations for a fruit fly. So it is plausible that genetic drift could take place. And this *could* lead to the loss of P elements, just like any other genes. Because P elements tend to be present in multiple copies in an organism's genome, they are less likely to be lost to genetic drift, but it could still happen.

Now look at **choice (B)**. This says P elements might be lost through recombination within a chromosome, which could lead to a deletion. This was mentioned in the passage, so you know that it's a plausible mechanism. If recombination occurred between two P elements on the same chromosome, part of each P element would be lost, or deleted, along with any DNA between them. So **choice (B)** is also incorrect.

Choice (C) says that P elements might be lost due to recombination between separate chromosomes that causes a translocation. Translocation is when a chromosomal fragment joins up with a nonhomologous chromosome, resulting in a hybrid chromosome that contain parts of the two original ones. Translocation doesn't involve loss of DNA, just reassortment, so this *wouldn't* cause a loss of P elements. **(C)** is, therefore, the correct answer.

Finally, **choice (D)**, natural selection, refers to the selective reproduction rates in individuals within a population that have traits that confer an advantage on that individual. Since P elements often cause mutations, including inviability and sterility, the reproduction rates would most likely be lower in P strains. Therefore, over many generations, the strain may be selected against. This means that fewer and fewer P elements are found in the population, until they disappear entirely. So **choice (D)** does explain how P elements can be lost from a population.

108. A

P strains of fruit flies have a higher mutation rate, and a higher mutation rate should lead to more genetic variation and, therefore, to an increased likelihood of speciation; that is, the evolution of genetically distinct species. In fact, though you weren't told this in the passage, there is difficulty interbreeding P-strain flies and M-strain flies, which will tend to increase the chance of genetic divergence within the whole *Drosophila melanogaster* species. This also increases the likelihood that it will undergo radiation into multiple species.

Choice (B) is wrong because most mutations that have a significant effect are bad for the organism, which means that they will *decrease,* not increase, offspring viability. And besides, we're told that decreased viability is one of the consequences of having P elements. **Choice (C)** is wrong because, as we're told, P elements increase the mutation rate. **Choice (D)** is wrong because genetic drift doesn't have anything to do with the appearance of new mutations, which is the main effect of P elements. It acts on all alleles, old and new, so the P elements shouldn't affect genetic drift.

109. B

The first thing that you should notice about this question is that it is a Roman numeral question. These are more difficult in that more than one choice can be correct, and you need to pick out all the choices that apply. To solve these types of questions, you need to examine each choice and decide whether it is correct or not. Often times, after you have identified one correct item, it is possible to eliminate several choices by crossing out those that do not contain the item that you have just identified as correct.

All you need to do to answer this question is decide in which crosses the offspring will have dysgenesis. From the passage, you know that P–M hybrid dysgenesis only occurs if the inherited P elements are activated. And that activation can occur *only* if a P strain male is crossed with an M-strain female. Look at the choices with this in mind.

Roman numeral I crosses a P-strain female and an M-strain male. This does not cause dysgenesis, so Roman numeral I is incorrect and any choices that contain this item can be eliminated. Therefore, **choice (A)** is incorrect.

In Roman numeral II, the cross is between a P-strain male and a female from a cross between a P-strain male and an M-strain female. This female offspring will have dysgenesis and, thus, be sterile. Therefore, no offspring can be produced from the cross in item II, and no dysgenesis can occur. So item II is incorrect. From this piece of information, we can eliminate **choices (C)** and **(D)**. Therefore, **choice (B)** must be the correct answer.

Let's look at items III and IV. In item III, a cross between an M-strain male and a P-strain female will produce P offspring with inactivated P elements and, thus, no dysgenesis. So when these two P offspring are crossed, their offspring will also be P-strain flies with inactivated P elements and thus, no dysgenesis. Therefore, Roman numeral III is incorrect. In Roman numeral IV, two P-strain flies will produce another P-strain fly, and two M-strain flies will produce another M-strain fly. So the cross of these offspring is simply a P-strain male crossed with an M-strain female, which you know will cause dysgenesis. Therefore, Roman numeral IV is a correct response, and **choice (B)** is the correct answer.

Passage III (Questions 110–114)

110. A

As you're told in the passage, blood pressure is the measure of the hydrostatic force that the blood exerts on the walls of blood vessels, and it is recorded as systole over diastole in millimeters of mercury. Systole is the pressure exerted during contraction of the ventricles, and diastole is the pressure exerted during the period between successive contractions. To determine the athlete's blood pressure at rest, which is what you're asked to do, you simply need to read Figure 1, first for systolic pressure, then for diastolic pressure. Systolic pressure for the athlete at rest is approximately 108 mmHg, and diastolic pressure is approximately 83 mmHg. Since blood pressure is expressed as systole over diastole, the correct answer is 108/83, which is **choice (A)**.

111. C

To solve this question, all you need to do is plug the values into the equation for cardiac output that is given to you in the passage. As we're told, the heart rate, or pulse, is the number of heartbeats per minute. Stroke volume is defined as the volume of blood pumped out of the left ventricle per contraction. Cardiac output is defined as the total volume of blood that the left ventricle pumps out of the heart per minute and can be determined by multiplying the heart rate by the stroke volume. The only thing that's just a little bit tricky about this question is that **choices (A) and (B)** use the word *pulse* instead of *heart rate*, but you still should have gotten the right answer from the equation itself.

Choices (A) and (B) must be wrong because the question tells us that pulse, or heart rate, is the same for both the athlete and the nonathlete. Thus, if the athlete and the nonathlete have the same heart rate, but the athlete's cardiac output is the greater of the two, then the athlete's stroke volume must be greater than the nonathlete's stroke volume, which is **choice (C)**.

112. D

As discussed in the previous explanation, cardiac output is defined as the total volume of blood pumped by the left ventricle per minute and can be calculated by multiplying the heart rate, which is the pulse, with the stroke volume, which is the volume of blood pumped out of the left ventricle per contraction. We're told that the woman's pulse is 20 beats per 15 seconds and that her stroke volume is 70 mL per beat. We cannot simply multiply these two numbers to get the cardiac output because cardiac output is measured in units of L/min. Hence, we must first convert 20 beats/15 seconds into minutes; we simply multiply this number by 60 sec/min, which yields 80 beats/min. Likewise, 70 mL equals 0.070 L. So cardiac output equals 80 beats/min × 0.070 L/beat, which equals 5.6 L/minute, which is **choice (D)**.

113. B

This question requires you to apply your outside knowledge of the sympathetic division of the autonomic nervous system in accounting for the phenomenon described in the question stem. As revealed by the upward slopes of all four lines in Figure 1 during exercise, there is an increase in arterial pressure immediately before and during exercise. This is caused by sympathetic nervous stimulation. When the body is readying itself for action, the sympathetic division of the autonomic nervous system takes over. It stimulates the heart to increase its heart rate and pumping strength so that it can supply the active skeletal muscle with more blood and, hence, with more oxygen. To increase the blood supply to active muscle during exercise, the blood vessels in the muscles themselves become dilated, while the blood vessels elsewhere in the body are constricted. Vasodilation increases the blood flow through those vessels supplying the active muscle, and vasoconstriction of other systemic blood vessels diverts blood to the tissue that needs it most. For example, vessels that supply blood to the digestive tract are constricted during activity. Thus, **choice (B)** is correct, and **choices (A) and (C)** are incorrect.

Choice (D), the buildup of lactic acid, occurs during the initial stages of strenuous exercise, when glucose metabolism and ATP production outpace the oxygen supply delivered to muscle. When this occurs, the cells switch from aerobic respiration to anaerobic respiration. Lactic acid is one of the waste products of anaerobic respiration and can build up in muscle cells, causing fatigue. The buildup occurs because the conversion of lactic acid to pyruvic acid requires oxygen.

114. C

The question stem tells us that the athlete normally has a higher cardiac output than the nonathlete. From the passage you know that cardiac output is defined as the volume of blood pumped by the left ventricle into systemic circulation per minute. This means that the athlete is pumping more blood and, hence, delivering more oxygen per minute to the muscles than the nonathlete.

Since the athlete normally has a higher cardiac output, we can look at Figure 1 for choices (A) and (B). It reveals that during exercise, the athlete has a lower systolic pressure than the nonathlete and a higher diastolic pressure than the nonathlete. Since choices (A) and (B) state the opposite, they are both incorrect.

Recall that the athlete's muscles are receiving more oxygen per minute than the nonathlete's. This means that the athlete's muscle cells will be able to produce more energy by aerobic respiration than the nonathlete's per given time. The nonathlete will have to resort to anaerobic respiration more than the athlete. From introductory biology, you should remember that the end product of anaerobic respiration in eukaryotic cells is lactic acid. Therefore, you would expect the nonathlete to have a higher concentration of lactic acid in the muscles than the athlete, since the nonathlete is using anaerobic respiration more than the athlete. Therefore, choice (C) is the correct answer.

Choice (D) is incorrect because the nonathlete would have to have a higher rate of glucose catabolism than the athlete, because the only source of energy during anaerobic respiration is through the catabolism of glucose. Remember that catabolism is the breakdown of glucose to pyruvic acid via glycolysis.

115. B

Boiling requires that the molecules of a compound in the liquid phase overcome the intermolecular attractive forces and escape into the gas phase: the stronger these interactions are, the more thermal energy one will have to put in to pull the molecules apart, and hence the higher the boiling point. The rule to follow here is that compounds have a lower boiling point with increased branching, since branching disrupts the spatial packing of molecules in the condensed phase and hence compromises intermolecular attractions. Choice (B), the most branched of the saturated compounds without hydrogen bonding, is the correct choice.

Choices (A) and (D) have no branching, so they are incorrect. And unsaturated compounds, such as choice (C), have an inherent (albeit small) dipole moment that raises their boiling point compared with their saturated counterparts.

116. D

The main piece of information produced by mass spectroscopy, method 1, is the molecular weight of the compounds involved. Since 2-hydroxymuconic semialdehyde contains two more oxygen atoms and one less hydrogen atom than does catechol, the mass spectrum of the two compounds would be clearly different. Moreover, the one showing the larger molecular weight would belong to the semialdehyde, and the one with the smaller molecular weight would belong to catechol. So the correct answer choice has to include method 1, which means you can eliminate choice (C).

Method 11, NMR, or nuclear magnetic resonance spectroscopy, reveals the carbon skeleton of a compound. Specifically, it shows how many different, nonequivalent hydrogen atoms the compound has and how the carbon atoms they're attached to are connected. Catechol is an achiral molecule, so it has three sets of equivalent hydrogens and the compound should produce three different peaks. 2-Hydroxymuconic semialdehyde is asymmetric and

would produce a lot more different signals. Thus, even without getting into the specific structures of the two molecules and figuring out exactly what those peaks would look like, you'd be able to tell from looking at the spectrum that one was much simpler than the other. Method 11 also has to be in the correct answer, so you can eliminate choice (A).

Finally, in Method 111, infrared spectroscopy, the spectra will indicate the functional groups in each compound. The spectrum of 2-hydroxymuconic semialdehyde would have an aldehyde peak, whereas the spectrum of catechol would not. This means that the answer has to include choice 111 as well, making choice (D) correct.

117. B

This question requires outside knowledge of insulin and glucagon. Choice (B) is correct because only insulin is secreted in response to high blood glucose; glucagon is secreted in response to low blood glucose.

Choices (A), (C), and (D) are all true. Both insulin and glucagon are secreted by the pancreatic islets (insulin from the beta cells and glucagon from the alpha cells), so choice (A) is true. Both insulin and glucagon respond to blood glucose levels and work to keep those levels within a tight range, so choice (C) is true. And both insulin and glucagon are secreted in response to elevated blood amino acid levels, so choice (D) is true. Insulin promotes the uptake of amino acids by tissues while glucagon promotes the conversion of excess amino acids to glucose.

118. B

The most important factors determining the rate at which a compound diffuses through a membrane are the compound's size and its polarity, assuming there is no facilitated diffusion. Since Compound A and Compound B are the same size, and since there is no facilitated diffusion occurring, only polarity needs to be considered. Cell membranes are nearly impermeable to polar compounds because polar compounds are insoluble in the membrane's hydrophobic lipid bilayer. In contrast, nonpolar compounds (e.g., O_2) diffuse easily through the cell membrane. This implies that the transmembrane diffusion rate of a polar compound is likely to be fairly low and essentially independent of its concentration, which corresponds to the rate depicted by curve B. Likewise, the transmembrane diffusion rate of a nonpolar compound is likely to be fairly high and strongly dependent on its concentration, which corresponds to the rate depicted by curve A. Thus, Compound A is most likely a nonpolar compound and Compound B is most likely a polar compound, so **choice (B)** is correct.

Passage IV (Questions 119–122)

119. D

This question is about how to name cyclic hydrocarbons, so you have to know the rules of the IUPAC system. This is a cyclic alkane with eight carbon atoms in the ring, so it's a cyclooctane. All three of its substituents are alkyl groups, so none of them will automatically take precedence over the other in the numbering. This means we have to list the substituent groups in alphabetical order, but their numbers must add up to the lowest possible sum. The three groups are listed alphabetically as ethyl, methyl, then propyl. This means **choices (B)** and **(C)** can be eliminated. Finally, the numbers in **choice (A)** add up to a larger sum than the numbers in **choice (D)**, so **choice (D)** is the correct response.

120. B

To answer this question, we have to use the table of energy differences that's given in the passage. The two compounds have two substituents, a bromide group and a methyl group. If we consider the transition between the left and right configurations, the bromide group goes from being axial to being equatorial, and the methyl group goes from being equatorial to being axial. If we look up the differences for both of these groups, we see that it's 0.5 kilocalories per mole for the bromide group and 1.74 kilocalories per mole for the methyl group. Now we have to remember a key fact: The axial position is of higher energy than the equatorial position. So the change in the position of bromide represents a *loss* of 0.5 kilocalories per mole, and the change in the position of methyl represents a *gain* of 1.74 kilocalories per mole. Since we're told to assume that these values are additive, the overall difference between the two conformations is minus 0.5 kilocalories per mole plus 1.74 kilocalories per mole, or 1.24 kilocalories per mole, which corresponds to **choice (B)**, the correct answer.

121. C

The most stable conformation for a substituted cyclohexane is a chair conformation in which all of the substituents are oriented equatorially. None of the choices here has that sort of conformation, but in comparing the stability of the choices, it's useful to remember that the closer a structure is to that state, the lower its energy.

Choice (B) can be eliminated right away because it's a boat conformation, and there's a big energy difference between the chair and boat conformations. The other three choices are all chair positions. Choice (A) has both its substituents in axial positions, whereas choices (C) and (D) each have one substituent that's axial and one that's equatorial; thus, choice (A) will be less stable than either (C) or (D) and can also be eliminated. As for the difference between (C) and (D), look at the table of energy differences. The energy difference between conformations for a hydroxyl group is 0.95 kilocalories per mole, and for an isopropyl group it's 2.15 kilocalories per mole. So there's more stability to be gained by having the isopropyl group equatorial than in having the hydroxyl group equatorial. Thus, choice (C) will be more stable than choice (D), making (C) the correct answer.

122. D

Choice (A) has an isopropyl group and a tertiary butyl group. Looking at the table, we see that the energy difference between conformations is higher for the tertiary butyl group than for the isopropyl group, so the more stable conformation should have *tert*-butyl in an equatorial position. Choice (A) has that conformation, so it is in its lowest energy conformation and is an incorrect choice. Likewise, choice (B) has an amino group and a methyl group; the energy difference is greatest for methyl, so it should be equatorial. So choice (B) is also in its most stable conformation, making it an incorrect response. In choice (C), the energy difference for methyl is greater than for bromide but the methyl group is equatorial, so (C) is also wrong.

Finally, choice (D) has an amino group and a hydroxyl group. The energy difference for the amino group is greater than for hydroxyl; however, the amino group is axial, so this is not the compound's lowest energy conformation, making choice (D) the correct answer.

Passage V (Questions 123–128)

123. D

This question assumes that Theory 1 is valid, and based on that assumption, we have to find the structure that would most likely bind to the antibody produced against *para*-aminophenol-alpha-glycoside.

Theory 1 states that an antibody recognizes an antigen based on chemical composition, so we have to find a compound with the same chemical composition, and the only one is **choice (D)**. All of the other choices are lacking the methyl alcohol group, so they're all incorrect.

124. B

This question requires us to understand the basic concepts of the second theory, which states that antigen recognition is based on the physical configuration of the antibody.

Statement 1 gives two noninteracting compounds— *para*-aminobenzenesulfonic acid and *meta*-aminobenzenesulfonic acid—which have the same functional groups but different structures. This contradicts Theory 1 and supports Theory 2; therefore, Statement 1 must be part of the correct answer, and we can eliminate **choices (A)** and **(C)**.

Statement 11 gives the compounds *para*-aminobenzenesulfonic acid and *para*-aminohydroxybenzene. These have similar structures but different substituent groups. The statement says that these antibodies interact with each other, which also supports Theory 2; therefore, Statement 11 should also be part of the correct answer.

Finally, let's look at Statement 111. This gives two non-interacting compounds—*para*-aminobenzenesulfonic acid and *meta*-aminohydroxybenzene—which are different in both structure and chemical composition. This statement doesn't help distinguish between the two theories at all, since it would be predicted by either theory, so it's incorrect. Since only Statements 1 and 11 are true, the correct answer is **choice (B)**.

125. A

The first thing we need to figure out here is what the product will be when benzenesulfonic acid is chlorinated. The $-SO_3H$ group is a deactivating *meta* director, so the main product will be *meta*-chlorobenzenesulfonic acid. According to Theory 2, if two antigens have the same physical configuration, an antibody produced against one will be able to bind to the other, regardless of the chemical compositions. So the correct choice should be another *meta* compound. Since **choice (A)** is the only compound among the choices that has a *meta* configuration, it's the correct answer.

Choices (B) and **(C)** are wrong because they have the same chemical composition as *meta*-chlorobenzenesulfonic acid but different structures. **Choice (D)** differs from *meta*-chlorobenzenesulfonic acid in both chemical composition and in structure, so it's also wrong.

126. C

Structural isomers are compounds that have the same formulas but different atomic connectivities. Since structural isomers are different in their connectivity, the fact that they were recognized by the same antibody would support Theory 1, not Theory 2. Remember: Theory 1 states that "the physical configuration of the antigen does not effect this interaction." Therefore, **choice (C)** is false, making it the correct response.

All of the other answer choices are true. Conformational isomers and enantiomers both describe pairs of compounds that differ in the spatial arrangement of their atoms. So if one antibody recognized two conformational isomers or two enantiomers, it would support Theory 1 over Theory 2. Geometric isomers differ in the arrangement of atoms about a double bond, so if they were *not* recognized by the same antibody, that certainly would support Theory 2 over Theory 1.

127. B

To begin with, we can eliminate two choices right away. **Choice (C)** says that Theory 2 is about chemical composition, and **choice (D)** says that Theory 1 is about physical configuration. Both of these assertions are false, so we can eliminate them immediately.

Then to evaluate the other two choices, we have to look at the data from the experiment. We're told that an antibody is produced to an antigen, *meta*-aminobenzenesulfonic acid, and that this antibody is then tested for reactivity with other antigens. The first antigen tested, *ortho*-aminobenzenesulfonic acid, and the fourth antigen tested, *para*-aminobenzenesulfonic acid, both have the same chemical composition as but a different physical configuration than the original antigen; neither one produced any response. The second one, *meta*-chlorobenzoic acid, and the third one, *meta*-aminomethoxybenzene, have different chemical compositions but the same physical configurations; these both *do* produce responses. Thus, the antibody responds to physical configuration and not chemical composition, supporting Theory 2. **Choice (A)** is incorrect, and **choice (B)** is the correct answer.

128. D

This question asks about the antigen-binding site of an antibody, but what it's mainly about is protein structure. As the beginning of the passage says, antibodies are proteins, and all of the answer choices relate to the characteristics of proteins.

The amino acids in the active site of an antibody, which is its antigen-binding site, interact chemically with the antigen. Antibodies that bind different sorts of antigens will have different amino acids in their binding sites. For instance, we might expect nonpolar antigens to bind to antibodies that have lots of nonpolar amino acids in their antigen-binding sites,

and likewise highly polar antigens would probably bind to antibodies that have lots of polar amino acids in their binding sites. Thus, there's no reason to suppose that the antigen-binding site of an antibody is always nonpolar, so **choice (A)** is wrong.

Choice (B) is wrong because, again, we would expect different antibodies to have different structures, so there's no reason to rule out the possibility that some of them might contain disulfide bonds. (Remember that disulfide bonds are formed between two cysteines, either on one protein chain or between protein chains, and contribute to the three-dimensional structure of the protein.)

Choice (C) says the antigen-binding site cannot be denatured. Denaturation is the disruption of a protein's three-dimensional structure due to heat, leading to loss of function; all proteins can be denatured, so **choice (C)** is incorrect.

Finally, **choice (D)** says that the antigen-binding site represents the tertiary structure of the antibody. The tertiary structure of a protein is its three-dimensional shape, which is determined by interactions among its constituent amino acids, including hydrogen bonds, disulfide bonds, and various van der Waals forces. This three-dimensional structure, in turn, determines a protein's ability to interact with its environment and with its substrate, which in the case of an antibody means its ability to interact with its antigen. Thus, the three-dimensional structure of an antibody gives it its ability to bind antigens, and **choice (D)** is correct.

Discrete Questions

129. B

You're asked to draw a conclusion based on the experimental results depicted in the graph when muscle cells are grown in various glucose concentrations in the absence and presence of insulin. So first, let's look at the graph. Extracellular glucose concentration is plotted on the x-axis, and intracellular glucose concentration is plotted on the y-axis. In the absence of insulin, the intracellular glucose concentration does not change at all, despite high extracellular concentrations. Practically no glucose enters the cell, even though its concentration gradient favors the movement of glucose into the cell. In the presence of insulin, there is an increase in intracellular glucose concentration, up to 500 mg/100 mL. The glucose moves into the muscle cell in the presence of insulin. In fact, there is a directly proportional relationship between the extracellular glucose concentration and the intracellular glucose concentration in the presence of insulin; that is, as one increases, so does the other. So what we've basically determined from the graph is, first of all, no insulin equals no increase in intracellular glucose; and secondly, insulin equals increase in intracellular glucose.

Choice (A) says that insulin decreases intracellular glucose concentration in muscle cells. Well, that contradicts what we've just determined from the graph; insulin *increases,* not decreases, intracellular glucose. So **choice (A)** is incorrect. **Choice (B)** says that muscle cell membranes are practically impermeable to glucose. Do our data support this conclusion? Yes, they do; the control experiment supports it. Despite being grown in media of increasingly higher glucose concentration, intracellular glucose remained unchanged, indicating that although the glucose gradient favored the movement of glucose into the cell, glucose was somehow being prevented from entering it. And if glucose cannot freely cross a cell membrane, then the membrane is said to be impermeable to glucose. **Choice (B)** looks like our right answer, but let's look through the remaining two for good measure.

Choice (C) says that glucose transport across muscle cell membranes requires ATP. When glucose transport across the cell membrane does occur, which is in the presence of insulin, transport occurs along glucose's concentration gradient; you don't find glucose leaving the cell, which would be transport *against* its gradient. Energy, or ATP, is required only to move substances against their concentration gradient, so **choice (C)** cannot be concluded based on the experimental data. In fact, it is known that insulin causes the facilitated diffusion of glucose across muscle cell membranes. Facilitated diffusion is when a carrier molecule facilitates the diffusion of a substance across a membrane *along* the substance's concentration gradient, not *against* it.

Finally, **choice (D)** says that insulin stimulates the conversion of glucose into glycogen in almost all body tissues. This is, in fact, a true statement. Insulin is secreted by the pancreas in response to high blood glucose and stimulates the uptake of glucose and its conversion into glycogen in most body tissues, especially muscle, liver, and fat tissue. However, this cannot be concluded from the graph. The graph does not deal with what happens to the glucose after insulin stimulates its transport into muscle cells. You might know what happens after the glucose enters the cell, but the question asks you to draw a conclusion based solely on the information given in the graph. So **choice (D)** is also incorrect.

130. A

ADH, or antidiuretic hormone, also known as vasopressin, is secreted by the posterior pituitary gland in response to high plasma osmolarity. ADH acts on the kidneys to increase their water reabsorption, thereby decreasing the plasma's solute concentration by diluting it with water. Increasing water reabsorption in the kidneys decreases the volume of urine excreted and increases urine osmolarity. A person with insufficient ADH production would, therefore, be expected to suffer from the opposite effects—decreased water reabsorption in the kidneys, leading to an increase in urinary volume, a decrease in urine osmolarity, and an increase in plasma osmolarity.

Looking at the answer choices, we see that choice (A), increased urinary volume, is one of the effects we've just listed, while choices (B) and (C) are the effects of normal ADH secretion. Choice (D), increased filtration rate in the kidneys, is a function of blood pressure; it is not under direct hormonal control. So choice (A) is the correct answer.

131. B

The Leydig cells (the interstitial cells of the testes) are stimulated by LH to secrete androgens. A Leydig cell tumor would result in uncontrolled production of androgens, leading to virilization (excess body hair, acne).

It is Sertoli cells that produce androgen binding proteins, so Sertoli cell tumors, not Leydig cell tumors, would cause the results of choice (A). Choice (C) is wrong because androgen production will be excessive, not inadequate, in a Leydig cell tumor. Choice (D) is also incorrect: first of all, LH (luteinizing hormone) is produced by the anterior pituitary, and secondly, the excess androgens should suppress LH release by the anterior pituitary to cause decreased levels if negative inhibition were taking place.

132. B

Micelles assist in the digestion of fats by emulsifying them so they, can be absorbed from the small intestine. The micelles' structure of a hydrophobic core and hydrophilic exterior allow them to do this.

Choice (A) is a distortion: it is glucose and amino acids that are transported by sodium dependent co-transport, not fats. Choice (C) is incorrect because micelles are involved in the breakdown of fats, not proteins. And choice (D) has exactly reversed the characteristics of the core and exterior of micelles.

Passage VI (Questions 133–137)

133. A

There are two things that you need to remember to determine the sequence of the DNA that is complementary to the segment of DNA given in the passage. The first is that DNA strands are situated antiparallel to one another in a DNA helix, meaning that the 3′ end of one strand is paired with the 5′ end of the other strand. The next important point is that in DNA, there is complementary pairing of the nitrogenous bases; that is, adenine always pairs with thymine, and cytosine always pairs with guanine.

Taking this information into account, we can start from the 3′ end of the given strand, which will correspond to the 5′end of the complementary strand, and match up the bases with their complements. Therefore, the complementary DNA strand will be TCGCTCTATGGC in the 5′ to 3′ direction. So choice (A) is the right answer.

Choice (B) is wrong because it has the wrong polarity though the right sequence. By the way, you should have immediately ruled out choices (C) and (D) because they both contain uracil, which is found only in RNA.

134. D

To answer this question, you have to have an understanding of both transcription and translation. Transcription is the process by which mRNA is synthesized from a DNA template. The mRNA is thus complementary in sequence to this segment of DNA. A key thing to remember is that, as in DNA synthesis, mRNA synthesis occurs in the 5′ to 3′ direction only.

First, let's determine the mRNA strand that's transcribed: Starting at the 3′end of the DNA segment given in the passage, the resulting mRNA would be 5′-UCGCUCUAUGGC-3′, considering that in RNA, uracil, rather than thymine, pairs with adenine: (RNA does not contain thymine.)

Next, this strand must be translated from a sequence of bases into a sequence of amino acids. The bases are arranged in a series of triplets, known as codons, and each codon specifies a single amino acid. There are 64 possible codons, three of which are noncoding and signal termination, and one, AUG, that both signals for the start of synthesis and codes for the amino acid methionine. Synthesis begins at this codon only. But since we're told in the passage that this is only a fragment of the DNA coding for the protein dystrophin that is missing in DMD patients, we can assume that the initiation codon AUG is found somewhere else in the gene. So we can just start translating from left to right, beginning to end.

So looking at our strand of mRNA, we see that the codons are UCG, CUC, UAU, and GGC. Now, look at the list of mRNA codons in the chart of the genetic code to determine which amino acids they code for. The first codon, UCG, corresponds to serine. The second codon, CUC, corresponds to leucine. The third codon is UAU, which corresponds to tyrosine. And the fourth codon is GGC, which codes for glycine. Thus, the resulting polypeptide is Ser-Leu-Tyr-Gly, or choice (D).

135. B

This is one of those questions that could have been answered without even reading the passage. As previously discussed, transcription is the process whereby the information coded in the base sequence of DNA is transcribed onto a strand of mRNA. Since transcription directly involves the DNA, it must take place where the DNA is located—in the nucleus—so **choice (B)** is the right answer.

After the mRNA is processed inside the nucleus, it exits through pores in the nuclear membrane and goes to a ribosome—the site of translation. So **choice (A)** is incorrect. A centromere is the specialized site that joins two sister chromatids together during mitosis and meiosis; thus, **choice (C)** is wrong. **Choice (D)**, cytoplasm, is wrong because translation, not transcription, occurs in the cytoplasm. Be careful not to confuse transcription with translation!

136. A

This is your basic genetics question. From the passage, you know that DMD is an X-linked recessive disorder. This means that the gene for DMD, which we'll call D, is found on the X chromosome. Remember that men have one X chromosome and one Y chromosome, while women have two X chromosomes. From the question stem, you know that the woman is normal but her father had DMD. This means that her genotype must be X^DX. Why? Because she inherited one X chromosome from her mother and one from her father. Since you know that her father had DMD, his genotype must have been X^DY. So the only X chromosome he could have passed on to his daughter contained the gene for DMD. And because the woman is normal, the X chromosome from her mother must have been normal. From the question stem, you also know that the man is normal. This means that his genotype is XY. So crossing the X^DX woman with the XY male yields four possibilities: X^DX, XX, X^DY, and XY. So there is a 25 percent chance that this couple will have a child with DMD.

But the question stem asks for the probability of this couple having two children with the disease. How do you figure this out? Multiply the probability of having a DMD child with the probability of having a DMD child. This is the same way you would figure out the probability of getting two heads in a row when you toss a coin. In other words, 0.25×0.25, which is 0.0625. Thus, there is a 6.25 percent chance that this couple will have two children with DMD. Therefore, **choice (A)** is the correct answer.

137. B

From the passage, you know that one of the initial steps in isolating the gene for DMD was comparing the ability of X-linked DNA probes to hybridize with DNA from DMD patients and with DNA from normal individuals. From this comparison, cloned fragments were obtained that correspond to the region of DNA that contains the deletions characteristic of DMD. This means that DMD DNA contains fewer bases than normal DNA due to these deletions. So a probe will not be able to bind as well to DMD DNA as it can to normal DNA, because normal DNA contains more bases that are complementary to the sequence of bases in the probes. This means that the probes have a *greater* degree of complementarity with normal DNA than with DMD DNA. Thus, **choices (A)** and **(C)** are incorrect, and **choice (B)** is the correct answer. **Choice (D)** is wrong because both males and females have an X chromosome to which the probe could hybridize.

Passage VII (Questions 138–144)

138. D

When discerning the stability of substituent groups on a six-membered cyclic chair conformation, it is necessary to look at the position of the substituent group. There are two groups on each carbon atom in the ring, and the geometry of the substituent group can be axial or equatorial.

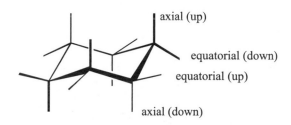

axial (up)

equatorial (down)

equatorial (up)

axial (down)

The axial position is more sterically hindered and has greater repulsion with the other axial groups than the equatorial group. The equatorial position allows for least repulsion of the larger substituent group. The structure 1,1-dimethylcyclohexane (I) will have the most steric hindrance because the substituent groups are on the same carbon atom. The 1,2-dimethyl cyclohexane structure (III) will be less stable than the other 1,2-dimethylcyclohexame (II) because structure (III) has both methyl groups in the axial position, which is higher in energy than the equatorial groups of structure (II). The 1,4-dimethylcyclohexane (IV) will be most stable because both methyl groups are in the equatorial position and they are separated by three bonds. So the order of increasing stability is I (least stable) < III < II < IV (most stable).

139. C

Three pairs of electrons are transferred among the atoms shown below. This is a Claisen rearrangement (as described in the latter part of the first paragraph, addressing the reaction with aliphatic unsaturated ethers) to form the aldehyde (carbonyl group) and alkene shown in the product of the rearrangement of the allyl vinyl ether. The reaction stops here prior to enolization. Enolization occurs in the example given in the passage because the phenol (enol) form is aromatic and more stable than the corresponding carbonyl form (ketone). Most carbonyl compounds are considerably more stable than their corresponding enols.

140. D

An "oxyCope" reaction is a sigmatropic variant of the Cope rearrangement. It reacts just as a Cope rearrangement, but it has an oxy group that forms an unstable enol. Upon the addition of heat, three electrons are transferred, as shown in the reaction, and a dienol is formed, which is unstable and readily undergoes tautomerization to the carbonyl (ketone) compound.

141. C

Three pairs of electrons are transferred as shown with 1,2-divinylcyclopropane, to form *cis, cis*-cyclohepta-1,4-diene. 1,2-divinylcyclobutane forms an eight-membered cyclodiene. The asterisk denotes the relative position of the carbon atom compared to the position of the double bonds during the rearrangement.

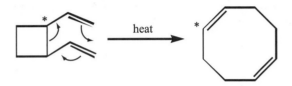

142. A

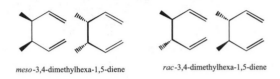

Tautomers are structural isomers that are conceptually related by the shift of a hydrogen and one or more π bonds.

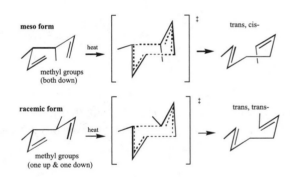

enolization (tautomers)

The enol form of the tautomer is generally not as stable as the carbonyl compound. However, the enol form of the tautomer of 2-allylphenol is more stable because an aromatic ring is formed during enolization. Phenol is an enol and it is aromatic. The β-keto Claisen condensation involves the enolate ions of esters. Conjugate addition is a type of reaction of conjugated dienes, including the Diels-Alder reaction.

143. D

A *meso* compound is an achiral compound with asymmetric atoms. It has an internal plane of symmetry if you divide the molecule in half, and both halves are structurally identical. A racemic mixture contains equal amounts of two enantiomers.

meso-3,4-dimethylhexa-1,5-diene   *rac*-3,4-dimethylhexa-1,5-diene

According to the chair transition state in Figure 1 of the passage, the *meso* compounds (when both methyl groups are either both up or both down) form *cis, trans*-octa-2,6-diene or *trans, cis*-octa-2,6-diene. The racemic mixture (when one methyl group is up and the other methyl group is down) would rearrange to form the *cis, cis*-isomer or the *trans, trans*-isomer.

meso form

methyl groups (both down)   heat   trans, cis-

racemic form

methyl groups (one up & one down)   heat   trans, trans-

144.　C

To determine the answer to this question, the reader will have to visualize or draw out each of the following reactions using the boat reaction shown in Figure 1. Reaction A would proceed via the chair transition state, as shown in Figure 1. Reaction B would also use the chair conformation during the transition state to form a *cis, trans*-product. Reaction C can be visualized as having both methyl groups down and according to the passage, it would form the *cis, cis*-isomer if the boat transition state utilized during the reaction. Reaction D results in a *trans, trans*-isomer and could only be formed using the chair transition state.

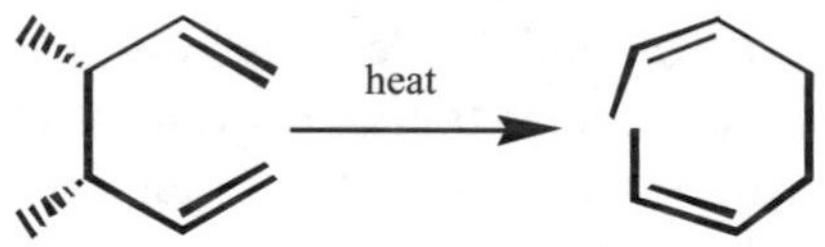

Reaction C

both methyl groups down

cis, cis-isomer

If reaction A were to utilize the boat transition state, the answer would be as shown below, which is not the *trans, trans*- product shown.

Reaction A (if it reacted via boat)

one down and one up

cis, trans-isomer

If reaction B utilized the boat transition state, the answer would be a *cis, trans*-isomer but not the one shown as the product of the reaction.

Reaction B (if it reacted via boat)

both methyls down

cis, trans-isomer

If reaction D were to utilize the boat transition state, the answer would be a *trans, cis*-isomer, not the *trans, trans*- product shown in the reaction.

Reaction D (if it reacted via boat)

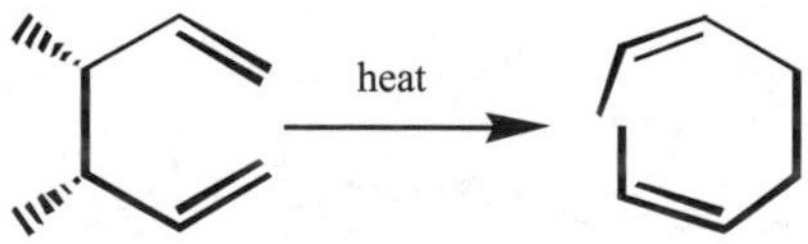

heat

Full-Length
Practice Test 11

MCAT Overview

PHYSICAL SCIENCES

Time   70 minutes
Format   52 multiple-choice questions:
            7 passages with 4–7 questions each;
            13 discrete questions (not passage-based)

VERBAL REASONING

Time   60 minutes
Format   40 multiple-choice questions:
            7 passages with 4–7 questions each

BIOLOGICAL SCIENCES

Time   70 minutes
Format   52 multiple-choice questions
            7 passages with 4–7 questions each
            13 discrete questions (not passage-based)

INSTRUCTIONS FOR TAKING THE FULL-LENGTH PRACTICE TEST

Before taking this Full-Length Practice Test, find a quiet place where you can work uninterrupted.

Use the answer grid on the following page to record your answers. Time yourself according to the time limits shown at the beginning of each section. Keep in mind that you'll be taking the real test on the computer.

You'll find the answer key, the score converter, and detailed answer explanations following the test.

Good luck.

#					#					#					#				
1	Ⓐ	Ⓑ	Ⓒ	Ⓓ	41	Ⓐ	Ⓑ	Ⓒ	Ⓓ	81	Ⓐ	Ⓑ	Ⓒ	Ⓓ	121	Ⓐ	Ⓑ	Ⓒ	Ⓓ
2	Ⓐ	Ⓑ	Ⓒ	Ⓓ	42	Ⓐ	Ⓑ	Ⓒ	Ⓓ	82	Ⓐ	Ⓑ	Ⓒ	Ⓓ	122	Ⓐ	Ⓑ	Ⓒ	Ⓓ
3	Ⓐ	Ⓑ	Ⓒ	Ⓓ	43	Ⓐ	Ⓑ	Ⓒ	Ⓓ	83	Ⓐ	Ⓑ	Ⓒ	Ⓓ	123	Ⓐ	Ⓑ	Ⓒ	Ⓓ
4	Ⓐ	Ⓑ	Ⓒ	Ⓓ	44	Ⓐ	Ⓑ	Ⓒ	Ⓓ	84	Ⓐ	Ⓑ	Ⓒ	Ⓓ	124	Ⓐ	Ⓑ	Ⓒ	Ⓓ
5	Ⓐ	Ⓑ	Ⓒ	Ⓓ	45	Ⓐ	Ⓑ	Ⓒ	Ⓓ	85	Ⓐ	Ⓑ	Ⓒ	Ⓓ	125	Ⓐ	Ⓑ	Ⓒ	Ⓓ
6	Ⓐ	Ⓑ	Ⓒ	Ⓓ	46	Ⓐ	Ⓑ	Ⓒ	Ⓓ	86	Ⓐ	Ⓑ	Ⓒ	Ⓓ	126	Ⓐ	Ⓑ	Ⓒ	Ⓓ
7	Ⓐ	Ⓑ	Ⓒ	Ⓓ	47	Ⓐ	Ⓑ	Ⓒ	Ⓓ	87	Ⓐ	Ⓑ	Ⓒ	Ⓓ	127	Ⓐ	Ⓑ	Ⓒ	Ⓓ
8	Ⓐ	Ⓑ	Ⓒ	Ⓓ	48	Ⓐ	Ⓑ	Ⓒ	Ⓓ	88	Ⓐ	Ⓑ	Ⓒ	Ⓓ	128	Ⓐ	Ⓑ	Ⓒ	Ⓓ
9	Ⓐ	Ⓑ	Ⓒ	Ⓓ	49	Ⓐ	Ⓑ	Ⓒ	Ⓓ	89	Ⓐ	Ⓑ	Ⓒ	Ⓓ	129	Ⓐ	Ⓑ	Ⓒ	Ⓓ
10	Ⓐ	Ⓑ	Ⓒ	Ⓓ	50	Ⓐ	Ⓑ	Ⓒ	Ⓓ	90	Ⓐ	Ⓑ	Ⓒ	Ⓓ	130	Ⓐ	Ⓑ	Ⓒ	Ⓓ
11	Ⓐ	Ⓑ	Ⓒ	Ⓓ	51	Ⓐ	Ⓑ	Ⓒ	Ⓓ	91	Ⓐ	Ⓑ	Ⓒ	Ⓓ	131	Ⓐ	Ⓑ	Ⓒ	Ⓓ
12	Ⓐ	Ⓑ	Ⓒ	Ⓓ	52	Ⓐ	Ⓑ	Ⓒ	Ⓓ	92	Ⓐ	Ⓑ	Ⓒ	Ⓓ	132	Ⓐ	Ⓑ	Ⓒ	Ⓓ
13	Ⓐ	Ⓑ	Ⓒ	Ⓓ	53	Ⓐ	Ⓑ	Ⓒ	Ⓓ	93	Ⓐ	Ⓑ	Ⓒ	Ⓓ	133	Ⓐ	Ⓑ	Ⓒ	Ⓓ
14	Ⓐ	Ⓑ	Ⓒ	Ⓓ	54	Ⓐ	Ⓑ	Ⓒ	Ⓓ	94	Ⓐ	Ⓑ	Ⓒ	Ⓓ	134	Ⓐ	Ⓑ	Ⓒ	Ⓓ
15	Ⓐ	Ⓑ	Ⓒ	Ⓓ	55	Ⓐ	Ⓑ	Ⓒ	Ⓓ	95	Ⓐ	Ⓑ	Ⓒ	Ⓓ	135	Ⓐ	Ⓑ	Ⓒ	Ⓓ
16	Ⓐ	Ⓑ	Ⓒ	Ⓓ	56	Ⓐ	Ⓑ	Ⓒ	Ⓓ	96	Ⓐ	Ⓑ	Ⓒ	Ⓓ	136	Ⓐ	Ⓑ	Ⓒ	Ⓓ
17	Ⓐ	Ⓑ	Ⓒ	Ⓓ	57	Ⓐ	Ⓑ	Ⓒ	Ⓓ	97	Ⓐ	Ⓑ	Ⓒ	Ⓓ	137	Ⓐ	Ⓑ	Ⓒ	Ⓓ
18	Ⓐ	Ⓑ	Ⓒ	Ⓓ	58	Ⓐ	Ⓑ	Ⓒ	Ⓓ	98	Ⓐ	Ⓑ	Ⓒ	Ⓓ	138	Ⓐ	Ⓑ	Ⓒ	Ⓓ
19	Ⓐ	Ⓑ	Ⓒ	Ⓓ	59	Ⓐ	Ⓑ	Ⓒ	Ⓓ	99	Ⓐ	Ⓑ	Ⓒ	Ⓓ	139	Ⓐ	Ⓑ	Ⓒ	Ⓓ
20	Ⓐ	Ⓑ	Ⓒ	Ⓓ	60	Ⓐ	Ⓑ	Ⓒ	Ⓓ	100	Ⓐ	Ⓑ	Ⓒ	Ⓓ	140	Ⓐ	Ⓑ	Ⓒ	Ⓓ
21	Ⓐ	Ⓑ	Ⓒ	Ⓓ	61	Ⓐ	Ⓑ	Ⓒ	Ⓓ	101	Ⓐ	Ⓑ	Ⓒ	Ⓓ	141	Ⓐ	Ⓑ	Ⓒ	Ⓓ
22	Ⓐ	Ⓑ	Ⓒ	Ⓓ	62	Ⓐ	Ⓑ	Ⓒ	Ⓓ	102	Ⓐ	Ⓑ	Ⓒ	Ⓓ	142	Ⓐ	Ⓑ	Ⓒ	Ⓓ
23	Ⓐ	Ⓑ	Ⓒ	Ⓓ	63	Ⓐ	Ⓑ	Ⓒ	Ⓓ	103	Ⓐ	Ⓑ	Ⓒ	Ⓓ	143	Ⓐ	Ⓑ	Ⓒ	Ⓓ
24	Ⓐ	Ⓑ	Ⓒ	Ⓓ	64	Ⓐ	Ⓑ	Ⓒ	Ⓓ	104	Ⓐ	Ⓑ	Ⓒ	Ⓓ	144	Ⓐ	Ⓑ	Ⓒ	Ⓓ
25	Ⓐ	Ⓑ	Ⓒ	Ⓓ	65	Ⓐ	Ⓑ	Ⓒ	Ⓓ	105	Ⓐ	Ⓑ	Ⓒ	Ⓓ					
26	Ⓐ	Ⓑ	Ⓒ	Ⓓ	66	Ⓐ	Ⓑ	Ⓒ	Ⓓ	106	Ⓐ	Ⓑ	Ⓒ	Ⓓ					
27	Ⓐ	Ⓑ	Ⓒ	Ⓓ	67	Ⓐ	Ⓑ	Ⓒ	Ⓓ	107	Ⓐ	Ⓑ	Ⓒ	Ⓓ					
28	Ⓐ	Ⓑ	Ⓒ	Ⓓ	68	Ⓐ	Ⓑ	Ⓒ	Ⓓ	108	Ⓐ	Ⓑ	Ⓒ	Ⓓ					
29	Ⓐ	Ⓑ	Ⓒ	Ⓓ	69	Ⓐ	Ⓑ	Ⓒ	Ⓓ	109	Ⓐ	Ⓑ	Ⓒ	Ⓓ					
30	Ⓐ	Ⓑ	Ⓒ	Ⓓ	70	Ⓐ	Ⓑ	Ⓒ	Ⓓ	110	Ⓐ	Ⓑ	Ⓒ	Ⓓ					
31	Ⓐ	Ⓑ	Ⓒ	Ⓓ	71	Ⓐ	Ⓑ	Ⓒ	Ⓓ	111	Ⓐ	Ⓑ	Ⓒ	Ⓓ					
32	Ⓐ	Ⓑ	Ⓒ	Ⓓ	72	Ⓐ	Ⓑ	Ⓒ	Ⓓ	112	Ⓐ	Ⓑ	Ⓒ	Ⓓ					
33	Ⓐ	Ⓑ	Ⓒ	Ⓓ	73	Ⓐ	Ⓑ	Ⓒ	Ⓓ	113	Ⓐ	Ⓑ	Ⓒ	Ⓓ					
34	Ⓐ	Ⓑ	Ⓒ	Ⓓ	74	Ⓐ	Ⓑ	Ⓒ	Ⓓ	114	Ⓐ	Ⓑ	Ⓒ	Ⓓ					
35	Ⓐ	Ⓑ	Ⓒ	Ⓓ	75	Ⓐ	Ⓑ	Ⓒ	Ⓓ	115	Ⓐ	Ⓑ	Ⓒ	Ⓓ					
36	Ⓐ	Ⓑ	Ⓒ	Ⓓ	76	Ⓐ	Ⓑ	Ⓒ	Ⓓ	116	Ⓐ	Ⓑ	Ⓒ	Ⓓ					
37	Ⓐ	Ⓑ	Ⓒ	Ⓓ	77	Ⓐ	Ⓑ	Ⓒ	Ⓓ	117	Ⓐ	Ⓑ	Ⓒ	Ⓓ					
38	Ⓐ	Ⓑ	Ⓒ	Ⓓ	78	Ⓐ	Ⓑ	Ⓒ	Ⓓ	118	Ⓐ	Ⓑ	Ⓒ	Ⓓ					
39	Ⓐ	Ⓑ	Ⓒ	Ⓓ	79	Ⓐ	Ⓑ	Ⓒ	Ⓓ	119	Ⓐ	Ⓑ	Ⓒ	Ⓓ					
40	Ⓐ	Ⓑ	Ⓒ	Ⓓ	80	Ⓐ	Ⓑ	Ⓒ	Ⓓ	120	Ⓐ	Ⓑ	Ⓒ	Ⓓ					

Physical Sciences Test

Time: 70 minutes

Questions 1–52

DIRECTIONS: Most of the questions in the following Physical Sciences test are organized into groups, with a descriptive passage preceding each group of questions. Study the passage, then select the single best answer to each question in the group. Some of the questions are not based on a descriptive passage; you must also select the best answer to these questions. If you are unsure of the best answer, eliminate the choices that you know are incorrect, then select an answer from the choices that remain. Indicate your selection by blackening the corresponding oval on your answer document. A periodic table is provided below for your use with the questions.

Periodic Table of the Elements

1 H 1.0																	2 He 4.0
3 Li 6.9	4 Be 9.0											5 B 10.8	6 C 12.0	7 N 14.0	8 O 16.0	9 F 19.0	10 Ne 20.2
11 Na 23.0	12 Mg 24.3											13 Al 27.0	14 Si 28.1	15 P 31.0	16 S 32.1	17 Cl 35.5	18 Ar 39.9
19 K 39.1	20 Ca 40.1	21 Sc 45.0	22 Ti 47.9	23 V 50.9	24 Cr 52.0	25 Mn 54.9	26 Fe 55.8	27 Co 58.9	28 Ni 58.7	29 Cu 63.5	30 Zn 65.4	31 Ga 69.7	32 Ge 72.6	33 As 74.9	34 Se 79.0	35 Br 79.9	36 Kr 83.8
37 Rb 85.5	38 Sr 87.6	39 Y 88.9	40 Zr 91.2	41 Nb 92.9	42 Mo 95.9	43 Tc (98)	44 Ru 101.1	45 Rh 102.9	46 Pd 106.4	47 Ag 107.9	48 Cd 112.4	49 In 114.8	50 Sn 118.7	51 Sb 121.8	52 Te 127.6	53 I 126.9	54 Xe 131.3
55 Cs 132.9	56 Ba 137.3	57 La * 138.9	72 Hf 178.5	73 Ta 180.9	74 W 183.9	75 Re 186.2	76 Os 190.2	77 Ir 192.2	78 Pt 195.1	79 Au 197.0	80 Hg 200.6	81 Tl 204.4	82 Pb 207.2	83 Bi 209.0	84 Po (209)	85 At (210)	86 Rn (222)
87 Fr (223)	88 Ra 226.0	89 Ac † 227.0	104 Rf (261)	105 Db (262)	106 Sg (263)	107 Bh (264)	108 Hs (269)	109 Mt (268)	110 Ds (269)	111 Rg (272)	112 Uub (277)	113 Uut (284)	114 Uuq (289)	115 Uup (288)	116 Uuh (292)	117 Uus (291)	118 Uuo (293)

*	58 Ce 140.1	59 Pr 140.9	60 Nd 144.2	61 Pm (145)	62 Sm 150.4	63 Eu 152.0	64 Gd 157.3	65 Tb 158.9	66 Dy 162.5	67 Ho 164.9	68 Er 167.3	69 Tm 168.9	70 Yb 173.0	71 Lu 175.0
†	90 Th 232.0	91 Pa (231)	92 U 238.0	93 Np (237)	94 Pu (244)	95 Am (243)	96 Cm (247)	97 Bk (247)	98 Cf (251)	99 Es (252)	100 Fm (257)	101 Md (258)	102 No (259)	103 Lr (260)

GO ON TO THE NEXT PAGE.

Passage 1 (Questions 1–5)

A continuous spectrum of light, sometimes called blackbody radiation, is emitted from a region of the sun called the photosphere. Although the continuous spectrum contains light of all wavelengths, the intensity of the emitted light is much greater at some wavelengths than at others. The relationship between the most intense wavelength of blackbody radiation and the temperature of the emitting body is given by Wien's law, $\lambda = 2.9 \ \lambda \ 10^6/T$, where λ is the wavelength in nanometers and T is the temperature in Kelvins.

As the blackbody radiation from the sun passes through the cooler gases in the sun's atmosphere, some of the photons are absorbed by the atoms in these gases. A photon will be absorbed if it has just enough energy to excite an electron from a lower energy state to a higher one. The absorbed photon will have an energy equal to the energy difference between these two states. The energy of a photon is given by $E = hf = hc/\lambda$, where h $= 6.63 \times 10^{-34}$ J•s is Planck's constant and c $= 3 \times 10^8$ m/s is the speed of light in a vacuum.

The sun is composed primarily of hydrogen. Electron transitions in the hydrogen atom from energy state $n = 2$ to higher energy states are listed below along with the energy of the absorbed photon.

Final Energy State	Energy ($\times 10^{-19}$ J)
$n = 3$	3.02
$n = 4$	4.08
$n = 5$	4.57
$n = 6$	4.84
$n = \infty$	5.44

1. If the temperature of the sun's photosphere is 5,800 K, what wavelength of radiation does the sun emit with the greatest intensity?

   A. 2 nm
   B. 50 nm
   C. 500 nm
   D. 4,500 nm

2. From the data in the table, what is the approximate wavelength of a photon emitted in the electron transition from energy state $n = 4$ to energy state $n = 3$?

   A. 5 nm
   B. 30 nm
   C. 100 nm
   D. 2,000 nm

3. The energy absorbed by a hydrogen atom as its electron undergoes a transition from the $n = 1$ energy state to the $n = \infty$ state is (Note: The $n = 1$ energy state is the ground state of hydrogen.)

   A. infinite.
   B. equal to the binding energy of the electron.
   C. equal to the energy of a zero-frequency photon.
   D. smaller than the energy absorbed in the $n = 2$ to $n = \infty$ transition.

GO ON TO THE NEXT PAGE.

4. At the center of the visible spectrum is light with a wavelength of $\lambda = 550$ nm. What is the frequency of this light?

    A. 9.0×10^8 Hz
    B. 1.8×10^{12} Hz
    C. 5.4×10^{14} Hz
    D. 1.8×10^{16} Hz

5. If a star suddenly doubles in size but remains at the same temperature, how does its continuous spectrum change?

    A. The peak intensity occurs at the same wavelength.
    B. The peak intensity occurs at a longer wavelength.
    C. The peak intensity occurs at a shorter wavelength.
    D. The intensity peak narrows.

GO ON TO THE NEXT PAGE.

Passage II (Questions 6–12)

The lead-acid battery, also called a lead storage battery, is the battery of choice for starting automobiles. It contains six cells connected in series, each composed of a lead oxide cathode "sandwiched" between two lead anodes. Insulating separators are placed between the electrodes to prevent internal short circuits. Aqueous sulfuric acid is the electrolyte.

When the battery is being discharged, the following reaction takes place:

$$Pb(s) + PbO_2(s) + 2\ H_2SO_4(aq) \rightarrow$$
$$2\ PbSO_4(s) + 2\ H_2O$$

Reaction 1

The electrode reactions, both written as reductions, are shown in Table 1.

Table 1

Half-reaction	E°(V)
$PbO_2(s) + SO_4^{2-}\ (aq) + 4H^+$ $(aq) + 2e^- \rightarrow PbSO_4(s) + 2H_2O$	1.69
$PbSO_4(s) + 2e^- \rightarrow Pb\ (s) +$ $SO_4^{2-}\ (aq)$	−0.36

As a car operates, the battery is recharged by electricity produced by the car's alternator, an AC generator whose ultimate power source is the car's internal combustion engine. In spite of this, batteries eventually lose their power. The battery is said to be "dead" when Reaction 1 has proceeded completely to the right.

6. How many cells would be required to produce a 20-volt lead-acid battery of the type described in the passage?

    A. 5
    B. 10
    C. 15
    D. 20

7. Which reaction takes place at the anode as the battery is discharging?

    A. The first half-reaction, proceeding to the left
    B. The first half-reaction, proceeding to the right
    C. The second half-reaction, proceeding to the left
    D. The second half-reaction, proceeding to the right

8. Where does oxidation occur in the lead storage battery?

    A. At the lead oxide cathodes
    B. At the lead oxide anodes
    C. At the lead cathodes
    D. At the lead anodes

9. Which of the following occurs as the battery is being recharged?

    A. An increase in the concentration of H^+ ions
    B. An increase in the amount of $PbSO_4$ and lead
    C. An increase in the concentration of H_2O
    D. A decrease in the amount of PbO_2

GO ON TO THE NEXT PAGE.

10. The graph below shows the change in potential versus time of a 12 V lead storage battery during discharge.

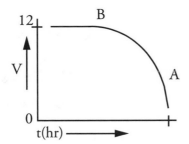

Which of the following is true?

A. The electrolyte density at point A is greater than it is at point B.
B. The electrolyte density at point A is less than it is at point B.
C. The electrolyte density at point A is the same as that at point B.
D. The electrolyte density at points A and B cannot be compared without more information.

11. Currents as small as 0.1 A can be fatal to humans. If the typical resistance of the human body is 10 k⎟, what is the minimum voltage that could be fatal?

A. 0.1 V
B. 1 V
C. 100 V
D. 1,000 V

12. Often in cold weather, the battery goes "dead." Thermodynamic data confirm that the voltage of most electrochemical cells decrease, with decreasing temperature. If the battery is warmed to room temperature, it often recovers its ability to deliver normal power. The battery appeared "dead" because

I. the resistance of the electrolyte had decreased.
II. the viscosity of the electrolyte had increased.
III. the viscosity of the electrolyte had decreased.

A. I only
B. II only
C. I and II only
D. I and III only

GO ON TO THE NEXT PAGE.

Questions 13 through 15 are NOT based on a descriptive passage.

---

13. How many neutrons does the daughter nucleus (X) have after the following radioactive decay?

$$^{60}_{27}\text{Co} \longrightarrow ^{A}_{Z}\text{X} + e^-$$

    A. 28
    B. 31
    C. 32
    D. 33

14. Heat is supplied to a gas that is constrained within a rigid container. The work done by the gas is:

    A. negative, because the internal energy of the gas increases.
    B. zero, because the pressure remains constant.
    C. zero, because the volume remains constant.
    D. positive, because the gas is an isolated system.

15. What is the ratio of the maximum possible number of f electrons to the maximum possible number of p electrons?

    A. 2:1
    B. 4:1
    C. 7:3
    D. 15:6

GO ON TO THE NEXT PAGE.

Passage III (Questions 16–20)

The resistance of a resistor is defined as the ratio of the voltage drop across it to the current passing through it. The resistance of a resistor can be measured using the circuit illustrated in Figure 1.

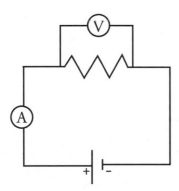

Figure 1

In the above circuit, a variable voltage source with negligible internal resistance is connected to a resistor. The voltage across the resistor is measured by a voltmeter, and the current through the resistor is measured by an ammeter.

Additional resistors may be added to the circuit. The total resistance can be calculated as follows: If R_1 and R_2 are two resistances of two resistors, then the total resistance is given by $R_{total} = R_1 + R_2$ when the resistors are connected in series and by $1/R_{total} = 1/R_1 + 1/R_2$ when the resistors are connected in parallel.

Circuits similar to the one above are used in the common household appliance known as the toaster. The rate by which energy in the form of heat is dissipated by the resistor equals I^2R, where I is the current that passes through the resistor and R is the resistance of the resistor. Energy is dissipated in a resistor because moving electrons collide with atoms in the resistor, causing the atoms to vibrate.

16. The variable voltage supply in the circuit in Figure 1 is replaced by a battery connected in series with the resistor and ammeter. The battery has a small internal resistance. How will the circuit be affected?

   A. The current measured by the ammeter at a specific voltage will be larger in the circuit with the battery.
   B. The current measured by the ammeter at a specific voltage will be smaller in the circuit with the battery.
   C. The resistance of the resistor at a specific voltage will be larger in the circuit with the battery.
   D. The resistance of the resistor at a specific voltage will be smaller in the circuit with the battery.

17. In which direction do the electrons travel, and in which direction does the current flow in the circuit in Figure 1?

   A. The electrons travel clockwise, and the current flows counterclockwise.
   B. The electrons travel clockwise, and the current flows clockwise.
   C. The electrons travel counterclockwise, and the current flows clockwise.
   D. The electrons travel counterclockwise, and the current flows counterclockwise.

GO ON TO THE NEXT PAGE.

18. For the ammeter to have a very small effect on the current flowing through the resistor, the ammeter should

   A. be connected to the resistor with insulated wire.
   B. be connected nearest to the positive terminal of the voltage source.
   C. have a very low resistance.
   D. be sensitive to currents flowing either way around the circuit.

19. As current passes through a resistor, the temperature of the resistor will increase. Which of the following is a reason the temperature increases?

   A. The average kinetic energy of the atoms in the resistor increases as a result of collisions with the electrons in the current.
   B. The average potential energy of the atoms in the resistor increases as a result of collisions with the electrons in the current.
   C. The average kinetic energy of the electrons in the current increases as a result of collisions with the atoms in the resistor.
   D. The average potential energy of the electrons in the current increases as a result of collisions with the atoms in the resistor.

20. What is the energy delivered to a piece of toast in 1 second when it is inside a toaster in which a 4×10^{-3} A current passes through a 10 k| resistor?

   A. 0.04 J
   B. 0.16 J
   C. 2.5 J
   D. 40 J

GO ON TO THE NEXT PAGE.

Passage IV (Questions 21–26)

It is critical that human blood be kept at a pH of approximately 7.4. Decreased and increased blood pH are called acidosis and alkalosis, respectively; both are serious metabolic problems that can cause death. The table below lists the major buffers found in the blood and/or kidneys.

Table 1

Buffer	pK_a of a typical conjugate acid:[1]
$HCO_3^- \rightleftharpoons CO_2 + H_2O$	6.1
Histidine side chains	6.3
$HPO_4^{2-} \rightleftharpoons H_2PO_4^-$	6.8
Organic phosphates	7.0
N-terminal amino groups	8.0
$NH_3 \rightleftharpoons NH_4^+$	9.2

[1]For buffers in many of these categories, there is a range of actual pK_a values.

The relationship between blood pH and the pK_a of any buffer can be described by the Henderson-Hasselbach equation:

$$pH = pK_a + \log([\text{conjugate base}]/[\text{conjugate acid}])$$

Equation 1

Bicarbonate, the most important buffer in the plasma, enters the blood in the form of carbon dioxide, a by-product of metabolism, and leaves in two forms: exhaled CO_2 and excreted bicarbonate. Blood pH can be adjusted rapidly by changes in the rate of CO_2 exhalation. The reaction given below, which is catalyzed by carbonic anhydrase in the erythrocytes, describes how bicarbonate and CO_2 interact in the blood.

$$CO_2 + H_2O \rightleftharpoons H^+ + HCO_3^-$$

Reaction 1

21. If the pH of blood were to increase to 7.6, what would be the likely outcome?

   A. An increase in carbonic anhydrase activity
   B. A decrease in carbonic anhydrase activity
   C. An increase in the rate of CO_2 exhalation
   D. A decrease in the rate of CO_2 exhalation

22. The equilibrium, as shown in Reaction 1, is most likely to proceed through which of the following intermediates?

   A. H_2CO_3
   B. $2H^+$ and CO_3^{2-}
   C. CO_2 and H_3O^+
   D. CO_2 and H_2

23. What would be the order of conjugate acid strength in the following buffers?

   A. Histidine side chains = organic phosphates > NH_4^+
   B. NH_4^+ > organic phosphates > histidine side chains
   C. Histidine side chains > organic phosphates > NH_4^+
   D. NH_4^+ > organic phosphates = histidine side chains

GO ON TO THE NEXT PAGE.

24. The following graph shows the titration of 0.01 *M* H_3PO_4 with 10 *M* NaOH. Within which area of the titration curve will the concentration of $H_2PO_4^-$ become equal to that of HPO_4^{2-}?

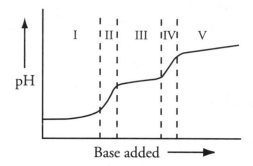

A. ll
B. lll
C. IV
D. V

25. How does the titration of a weak monoprotic acid with a strong base differ from the titration of a strong monoprotic acid with a strong base?

A. The equivalence point will occur at a higher pH.
B. The equivalence point will occur at a lower pH.
C. The equivalence point will occur at the same pH.
D. Whether the equivalence point is higher or lower depends on the particular acids used.

26. What would be the nature of the compensatory change that would take place in response to acidosis caused by organic acids?

A. Breathing rate would increase, and total blood CO_2/HCO_3^- concentration would increase.
B. Breathing rate would increase, and total blood CO_2/HCO_3^- concentration would decrease.
C. Breathing rate would decrease, and total blood CO_2/HCO_3^- concentration would increase.
D. Breathing rate would decrease, and total blood CO_2/HCO_3^- concentration would decrease.

GO ON TO THE NEXT PAGE.

27. The mouthpiece of a telephone handset has a mass of 100 g, and the earpiece has a mass of 150 g. To balance the handset on one finger, that finger must be (Note: Assume the bridge connecting the mouthpiece and the earpiece has a negligible mass.)

    A. one-and-one-half times farther from the earpiece than from the mouthpiece.
    B. two times farther from the earpiece than from the mouthpiece.
    C. one-and-one-half times farther from the mouthpiece than from the earpiece.
    D. two times farther from the mouthpiece than from the earpiece.

28. The reaction below is not spontaneous at any temperature.

    $$2ICl(g) \rightarrow I_2(g) + Cl_2(g)$$

    Which of the following is TRUE?

    A. $\Delta H > 0$, $\Delta S > 0$
    B. $\Delta H > 0$, $\Delta S < 0$
    C. $\Delta H < 0$, $\Delta S > 0$
    D. $\Delta H < 0$, $\Delta S < 0$

29. Which of the following is the reason that water boils at a much higher temperature than hydrogen sulfide?

    A. The intramolecular O–H bonds are stronger than the intramolecular S–H bonds.
    B. The enthalpy of vaporization of water is less than that of hydrogen sulfide.
    C. The relative molecular mass of water is less than that of hydrogen sulfide.
    D. The intermolecular O–H bonds are stronger than the intermolecular S–H bonds.

30. In the figure below, aqueous solutions A and B are separated by a semipermeable membrane. Which of the following will occur?

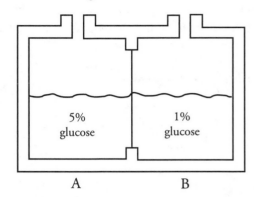

A   B

    A. Glucose molecules will move from side B to side A.
    B. Glucose molecules will move from side A to side B.
    C. Both water and glucose molecules will move from side A to side B.
    D. Water molecules will move from side B to side A.

31. What is the normality of a solution containing 49 g of H_3PO_4 (MW 98) in 2,000 mL of solution?

    A. 0.25
    B. 0.50
    C. 0.75
    D. 1.50

GO ON TO THE NEXT PAGE.

Passage V (Questions 32–36)

A helium-neon gas discharge laser, as shown in Figure 1 below, generates a coherent beam of monochromatic light at a wavelength of 632.8 nm.

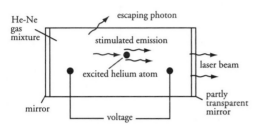

Figure 1

A discharge current of electrons is created in the tube by an applied voltage. When these electrons collide with the helium atoms, they can excite ground-state helium electrons to an energy level of 20.61 eV. The excited electrons cannot decay back to the ground state by emitting a photon because such a transition does not conserve angular momentum. Instead, if the excited helium atom collides with a neon atom, a ground-state electron in the neon atom can be excited to an energy level of 20.66 eV, and the helium electron can return to its ground state.

The above process occurs quite often in the tube, until the percentage of neon atoms with electrons in the 20.66-eV energy level is greater than the percentage of neon atoms with electrons in lower levels. This condition is called a population inversion. An excited electron in one of the neon atoms can then spontaneously decay by emitting a photon of wavelength 632.8 nm in a random direction. The photon will stimulate the same transition in another excited atom. The photon radiated by this stimulated emission process travels in the same direction as the original photon. The resulting light is then reflected back and forth inside the tube until it escapes through the partially transparent mirror. (Note: A photon's energy in eV is given by $E = 1{,}240/\lambda$, where λ is the photon's wavelength in nm. The helium and neon ground state energies are both 0 eV.)

32. What is the energy of the photon with wavelength 632.8 nm?

   A. 0.05 eV
   B. 1.96 eV
   C. 20.61 eV
   D. 20.66 eV

33. A population inversion exists when

   A. the percentage of neon atoms with electrons in the ground state is greater than the percentage of neon atoms with electrons in higher energy levels.
   B. the percentage of neon atoms with electrons in a higher energy level is greater than the percentage of neon atoms with electrons in lower energy levels.
   C. the percentage of neon atoms with electrons in a higher energy level is equal to the percentage of neon atoms with electrons in the ground state.
   D. all the neon atoms have electrons in the ground state only.

GO ON TO THE NEXT PAGE.

34. A helium atom with an electron in the 20.61 eV energy level collides with a neon atom with an electron in the ground state. The result is that the helium electron returns to the ground state and the ground state neon electron is excited to an energy level of 20.66 eV. What is the minimum kinetic energy lost by the helium atom?

    A. 0.05 eV
    B. 1.96 eV
    C. 10.30 eV
    D. 20.61 eV

35. A laser produces light with a wavelength of 200 nm at a power of 6.2×10^{15} eV/s. How many photons per second does this laser deliver?

    A. 1.0×10^{15}
    B. 2.0×10^{15}
    C. 4.0×10^{15}
    D. 10.0×10^{15}

36. Why is stimulated emission of photons necessary in order to produce a coherent beam of light instead of spontaneous emission alone?

    A. Stimulated emission produces photons of higher energy than those produced by spontaneous emission.
    B. Stimulated emission produces photons that travel in the same direction as the photon that induces their emission.
    C. Stimulated emission produces photons with longer wavelengths than those produced by spontaneous emission.
    D. Either spontaneous or stimulated emission alone would be sufficient to produce laser light.

GO ON TO THE NEXT PAGE.

37. A deep-sea research module has a volume of 150 m³. If ocean water has an average density of 1,025 kg/m³, what will be the buoyant force on the module when it is completely submerged in the water? (Note: The acceleration due to gravity is 9.8 m/s².)

    A. 9.8 N
    B. 60 N
    C. 1×10^3 N
    D. 1.5×10^6 N

38. If a spring is 64 cm long when it is unstretched and is 8 percent longer when a 0.5 kg mass hangs from it, how long will it be with a 0.4 kg mass suspended from it?

    A. 66 cm
    B. 68 cm
    C. 70 cm
    D. 74 cm

39. Which of the following will halve the magnitude of the electrostatic force of attraction between two charged particles?

    A. Doubling the distance between the particles
    B. Halving the charge on each particle
    C. Halving the charge on one of the particles only
    D. Placing a positively charged particle midway between the particles

40. When performing bomb calorimetry, which of the following conditions best applies to the combustion of a sample?

    A. Constant P
    B. Constant T
    C. Constant V
    D. Constant n

41. In which atomic orbital(s) does(do) the alkaline earth elements contain valence electrons?

    A. s
    B. d
    C. s and d
    D. s, d, and p

GO ON TO THE NEXT PAGE.

Passage VI (Questions 42–46)

When softball players take batting practice, they often use a machine called an "automatic pitcher," which is essentially a cannon that uses air pressure to launch a projectile. In a prototype automatic pitcher, a softball is loaded into the barrel of the cannon and rests against a flat disk. This disk is locked into place, and a high air pressure is built up behind it. When the disk is released, the softball is pushed along the barrel of the cannon and ejected at a speed of v_0.

Figure 1 shows the batter and automatic pitcher. The angle of the barrel to the horizontal is ⊠. The unit vectors **i** and **j** point in the horizontal and vertical directions, respectively.

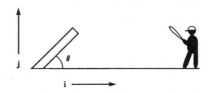

Figure 1

The height above the ground y of the softball as a function of time t is shown in Figure 2, where $t = 0$ at Point A, $t = t_B$ at Point B, and $t = t_C$ at Point C. The softball is ejected from the barrel of the cannon at Point A, it reaches its maximum height at Point B, and the batter hits the softball at Point C. (Note: Assume that the effects of air resistance are negligible, unless otherwise stated.)

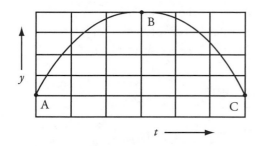

Figure 2

42. What physical quantity is NOT the same at Point C as it is at Point A?

    A. The velocity of the softball
    B. The speed of the softball
    C. The gravitational potential energy of the softball
    D. The horizontal component of the velocity of the softball

43. What is the acceleration of the softball t seconds after it exits the barrel?

    A. $-g\,\mathbf{j}$
    B. $-v_0/t\,\mathbf{i}$
    C. $-v_0/t\,\mathbf{j}$
    D. $-v_0/t\,\mathbf{i} - g\,\mathbf{j}$

44. How will v_0 change if the impulse on the softball remains the same but its mass is doubled?

    A. It will decrease by a factor of 4.
    B. It will decrease by a factor of 2.
    C. It will not change.
    D. It will increase by a factor of 2.

GO ON TO THE NEXT PAGE.

45. What is the ratio of the horizontal distance travelled by the softball at Point B to the horizontal distance travelled at Point C?

   A. 5:1

   B. 4:1

   C. 3:3

   D. 1:2

46. How does the work done by the automatic pitcher change as the angle of the barrel to the horizontal increases?

   A. The work done increases, because the softball's maximum height increases.

   B. The work done decreases, because the softball lands closer to the cannon.

   C. The work done does not change, because the air pressure behind the disk is unchanged.

   D. The work done does not change, because gravity is a conservative force.

GO ON TO THE NEXT PAGE.

Passage VII (Questions 47–52)

A researcher investigated the equilibrium between CO_2, C, and CO as a function of temperature. The equation is given below.

$$CO_2(g) + C(s) \rightleftharpoons 2\ CO(g)$$

Carbon dioxide, at 298 K and 1 atm, and an excess of powdered carbon were introduced into a furnace, which was then sealed so that pressure would increase as the temperature rose. The furnace was heated to and held constant at a predetermined temperature. The pressure within the furnace chamber was recorded after it had remained unchanged for one hour. The table below shows the pressures recorded for a series of temperatures together with the pressures expected if no reaction had taken place.

Table 1

T(K)	P_r (P recorded after reaction, in atm)	P_e (P expected without reaction, in atm)
900	3.4	3.0
950	3.8	3.2
1,000	4.3	3.4
1,050	5.0	3.5
1,200	7.2	4.0

47. When the system stabilized at 1,200 K, a sample of helium was injected into the furnace. What should happen to the amount of carbon dioxide in the system?

    A. It should increase.

    B. It should decrease.

    C. It should be completely converted to carbon monoxide.

    D. It will remain the same.

48. What can be said about the value of $\Delta S°$ of the reaction?

    A. It is positive.

    B. It is negative.

    C. It is zero.

    D. It cannot be determined from the information given.

49. How many pi bonds are in the carbon dioxide molecule?

    A. 0

    B. 1

    C. 2

    D. 3

GO ON TO THE NEXT PAGE.

50. Which of the following is NOT necessarily true about the equilibrium reaction among CO_2, C, and CO?

    A. The standard entropy change is positive.
    B. A decrease in pressure at constant temperature would shift the equilibrium to the right.
    C. Addition of CO will shift the equilibrium to the left.
    D. The standard Gibbs free energy change is negative.

51. Which of the following shows the correct Lewis structure of carbon monoxide?

    A.

    $:C \!=\! \ddot{O}$

    C.

    $:C \!\equiv\! O:$

    B.

    $\ddot{C} \!=\! \ddot{O}$

    D.

    $:C \!\equiv\! \ddot{O}$

52. How are the values of P_e calculated?

    A. $(T/273)(1 \text{ atm})$
    B. $(T/298)(1 \text{ atm})$
    C. $[(T - 273)/273](1 \text{ atm})$
    D. $[(T - 298)/298](1 \text{ atm})$

GO ON TO THE NEXT PAGE.

Verbal Reasoning Test

Time: 60 minutes
Questions 53–92

DIRECTIONS: There are six passages in this Verbal Reasoning test. Each passage is followed by several questions. After reading a passage, select the one best answer to each question. If you are not certain of an answer, eliminate the alternatives that you know to be incorrect and then select an answer from the remaining alternatives. Indicate your selection by blackening the corresponding oval on your answer document.

Passage 1 (Questions 53–58)

Although nihilism is commonly defined as a form of extremist political thought, the term has a broader meaning. Nihilism is in fact a complex intellectual stance with venerable roots in the history of ideas, which forms the theoretical basis for many positive assertions of modern thought. Its essence is the systematic negation of all perceptual orders and assumptions. A complete view must account for the influence of two historical crosscurrents: philosophical skepticism about the ultimacy of any truth, and the mystical quest for that same pure truth. These are united by their categorical rejection of the "known."

The outstanding representative of the former current, David Hume (1711–1776), maintains that external reality is unknowable, since sense perceptions give no information whatsoever about what really exists. Hume points out that sense impressions are actually part of the contents of the mind. Their presumed correspondence to external "things" cannot be verified, since it can be checked only by other sense impressions. Hume further asserts that all abstract conceptions turn out, on examination, to be generalizations from sense impressions. He concludes that even such an apparently objective phenomenon as a cause-and-effect relationship between events may be no more than a subjective fabrication of the observer. Stanley Rosen notes: "Hume terminates in skepticism because he finds nothing within the subject but individual impressions and ideas."

For mystics of every faith, the "experience of nothingness" is the goal of spiritual practice. Buddhist meditation techniques involve the systematic negation of all spiritual and intellectual constructs to make way for the apprehension of pure truth. St. John of the Cross similarly rejected every physical and mental symbolization of God as illusory. St. John's spiritual legacy is, as Michael Novak puts it, "the constant return to inner solitude, an unbroken awareness of the emptiness at the heart of consciousness. It is a harsh refusal to allow idols to be placed in the sanctuary. It requires also a scorching gaze upon all the bureaucracies, institutions, manipulators, and hucksters who employ technology and its supposed realities to bewitch and bedazzle the psyche."

Novak's interpretation points to the way these philosophical and mystical traditions prepared the ground for the political nihilism of the nineteenth and twentieth centuries. The rejection of existing social institutions and their claims to authority is in the most basic sense made possible by Humean skepticism. The political nihilism of the Russian intelligentsia combined this radical skepticism with a near-mystical faith in the power of a new beginning. Hence, their desire to destroy became a revolutionary affirmation; in the words of Stanley Rosen, "Nihilism is an attempt to overcome or repudiate the past on behalf of an unknown and unknowable, yet hoped-for, future." This fusion of skepticism and mystical re-creation can be traced in contemporary thought, for example, as an element in the counterculture of the 1960s.

GO ON TO THE NEXT PAGE.

53. The author's working definition of *nihilism*, as it functions in the passage, is

    A. systematic doubt of that which one takes for granted.

    B. a mystical quest for nothingness.

    C. a form of extremist political thought.

    D. rejection of all presently established institutions.

54. In the passage, quotations from writers about nihilism are used in order to

    I. summarize specific points made in the course of the passage.

    II. contrast points of view on the subject under discussion.

    III. make transitions between points in the discussion.

    A. I only

    B. I and II only

    C. I and III only

    D. II and III only

55. Novak's interpretation of St. John's spiritual legacy (paragraph 3) is important to the author's argument primarily because it

    A. characterizes the essence of St. John's mystical doctrine.

    B. gives insight into the historical antecedents of political nihilism.

    C. draws a parallel between Christian mysticism and the Humean tradition of philosophical skepticism.

    D. suggests that St. John's teachings are influential mainly because of their sociopolitical implications.

56. The author uses all of the following techniques in developing the topic EXCEPT

    A. discussion of individuals as representative of intellectual trends.

    B. a contrast between a common definition and his own.

    C. identification of the common elements in distinct intellectual traditions.

    D. examination of the practical consequences of a social doctrine.

GO ON TO THE NEXT PAGE.

57. In the last paragraph, the author quotes Stanley Rosen in order to make the point that modern nihilism is

   A. impractical because of its faith in an unknowable future.
   B. more than just a movement to do away with existing institutions.
   C. a living doctrine rather than merely a part of the history of political theory.
   D. based more on the tradition of philosophical skepticism than on that of mystical affirmation.

58. Which of the following provides the best continuation for the final paragraph of the passage?

   A. Thus, the negative effects of nihilism are still being felt.
   B. Classical nihilism has thus been superseded by a new and unrelated type.
   C. The revolutionaries of that time did, after all, reject society and hope for something better.
   D. The study of nihilism, then, belongs to the past rather than to the present.

GO ON TO THE NEXT PAGE.

Passage II (Questions 59–64)

Agonistic behavior, or aggression, is exhibited by most of the more than 3 million species of animals on this planet. Animal behaviorists still disagree on a comprehensive definition of the term, but *aggressive behavior* can be loosely described as any action that harms an adversary or compels it to retreat. Aggression may serve many purposes, such as gathering food, establishing territory, and enforcing social hierarchy. In a general Darwinian sense, however, the purpose of aggressive behavior is to increase the individual animal's—and thus, the species'—chance of survival.

Aggressive behavior may be directed at animals of other species, or it may be conspecific—that is, directed at members of an animal's own species. One of the most common examples of conspecific aggression occurs in the establishment and maintenance of social hierarchies. In a hierarchy, social dominance is usually established according to physical superiority; the classic example is that of a pecking order among domestic fowl. The dominance hierarchy may be viewed as a means of social control that reduces the incidence of attack within a group. Once established, the hierarchy is rarely threatened by disputes because the inferior animal immediately submits when confronted by a superior.

Two basic types of aggressive behavior are common to most species: attack and defensive threat. Each type involves a particular pattern of physiological and behavioral responses, which tends not to vary regardless of the stimulus that provokes it. For example, the pattern of attack behavior in cats involves a series of movements, such as stalking, biting, seizing with the forepaws and scratching with the hind legs, that changes very little regardless of the stimulus—that is, regardless of who or what the cat is attacking.

The cat's defensive threat response offers another set of closely linked physiological and behavioral patterns. The cardiovascular system begins to pump blood at a faster rate in preparation for sudden physical activity. The eyes narrow and the ears flatten against the side of the cat's head for protection, and other vulnerable areas of the body such as the stomach and throat, are similarly contracted. Growling or hissing noises and erect fur also signal defensive threat. As with the attack response, this pattern of responses is generated with little variation regardless of the nature of the stimulus.

Are these aggressive patterns of attack and defensive threat innate, genetically programmed, or are they learned? The answer seems to be a combination of both. A mouse is helpless at birth, but by its twelfth day of life can assume a defensive threat position by backing up on its hind legs. By the time it is one month old, the mouse begins to exhibit the attack response. Nonetheless, copious evidence suggests that animals learn and practice aggressive behavior; one need look no further than the sight of a kitten playing with a ball of string. All the elements of attack—stalking, pouncing, biting, and shaking—are part of the game, which prepares the kitten for more serious situations later in life.

59. The passage asserts that animal social hierarchies are generally stable because

    A. the behavior responses of the group are known by all its members.
    B. the defensive threat posture quickly stops most conflicts.
    C. inferior animals usually defer to their physical superiors.
    D. the need for mutual protection from other species inhibits conspecific aggression.

GO ON TO THE NEXT PAGE.

60. According to the author, what is the most significant physiological change undergone by a cat assuming the defensive threat position?

    A. An increase in cardiovascular activity
    B. A sudden narrowing of the eyes
    C. A contraction of the abdominal muscles
    D. The author does not say which change is most significant.

61. Based on the information in the passage about agonistic behavior, it is reasonable to conclude that

    I.   the purpose of agonistic behavior is to help ensure the survival of the species.
    II. agonistic behavior is both innate and learned.
    III. conspecific aggression is more frequent than interspecies aggression.

    A. I only
    B. II only
    C. I and II only
    D. I, II, and III

62. The author suggests that the question of whether agonistic behavior is genetically programmed or learned

    A. still generates considerable controversy among animal behaviorists.
    B. was first investigated through experiments on mice.
    C. is outdated since most scientists now believe the genetic element to be most important.
    D. has been the subject of extensive clinical study.

63. Which of the following topics related to agonistic behavior is NOT explicitly addressed in the passage?

    A. The physiological changes that accompany attack behavior in cats
    B. The evolutionary purpose of aggression
    C. Conspecific aggression that occurs in dominance hierarchies
    D. The relationship between play and aggression

64. Which of the following would be most in accord with the information presented in the passage?

    A. The aggressive behavior of sharks is closely linked to their need to remain in constant motion.
    B. The inability of newborn mice to exhibit the attack response proves that aggressive behavior must be learned.
    C. Most animal species that do not exhibit aggressive behavior are prevented from doing so by environmental factors.
    D. Members of a certain species of hawk use the same method to prey on both squirrels and gophers.

GO ON TO THE NEXT PAGE.

Passage III (Questions 65–70)

The Gypsies, or Romani people, are found throughout Europe, as well as in the Americas, the Middle East, and Asia. The Romani have emerged as a culturally linked constellation of nomadic groups, little understood by outsiders, which include, but are not limited to, the Kalderash, Machavaya, Lovari, Churari, Roanichal, Gitanoes, Kalo, Sinti, Rudari, Manush, Boyash, Ungaritza, Luri, Bashalde, Romongro, and Xoraxai. What led to the original Romani diaspora remains shrouded in mystery. Historical linguists, however, have begun to trace their migratory paths, as well as to estimate when their migrations occurred.

Most scholars agree on their basic migratory route, which began in northwestern India between 800 and 950 ce and progressed through the upper Indus Valley, across the Himalayas, and down the Silk Road to the southern shores of the Caspian Sea. From there, they followed the west coast to the foothills of the Caucasus, through Armenia, and into the Byzantine Empire. Romani then entered the Balkans and drifted throughout Europe. There is considerably less consensus, however, about whether there was one migration or several and what exactly was the time frame of the migration.

Linguists who support a single emigration hypothesis cite linguistic similarities between Romani and a group of Sanskrit-based languages that includes Rajasthani, Hindi, Gujarati, Bengali, and Multani. According to these linguists, Romani developed in parallel with these languages until the 11th century ce and then diverged from the others, which continued to develop in synchronicity. Furthermore, they point to the fact that all European Romani dialects include the same "loan words" from Dardic, Persian, Armenian, Byzantine Greek, Old Slavic, and Romanian.

Other scholars, however, use linguistic evidence to show that the Romani, who today fall into three major subgroups—the Domari or "Dom," Lomavren or "Lom," and Romani or "Rom"—did not separate from one original group but were rather three distinct groups who left India at three different times. These researchers look to the linguistic dissimilarities among the three branches, such as the fact that although all three branches show lexical adoption from Persian, there are no specific items shared by all three branches. Further, vestiges of a third grammatical gender in Lom and Rom indicate to these linguists that these groups left India later than the Dom.

The very flexibility of the Romani language ensures that historical linguists will continue to debate the migratory paths of the various Romani tribes. In one Sinto dialect, for instance, the word *svigardaj* (mother-in-law) has been constituted from *daj* (mother, of Sanskrit origin) and an adaptation of the German word *Schweiger* (*Schwieger-mutter* means mother-in-law). Among Muslim Romani in the south of Yugoslavia, the word *ledome* (frozen) can be traced to the Slav word *led* (ice) followed by the suffix *me*, which is of Greek origin. While these linguistic borrowings clearly enrich the language of the Romani and provide endless fodder for speculation among academics, it also makes the difficulties of understanding between the different groups more acute, as the dialects continue to diverge.

Even the origin of the name *Gypsy* is subject to linguistic debate. Some scholars claim that the word *Gypsy* refers to the dark-skinned people from the Middle East who were brought to Europe before the arrival of the Romani to serve as entertainers and were loosely known as "Egyptians." When the Romani arrived, they, too, were identified as Egyptian, which was later shortened to Gypsy. Others, however, trace the origin of the name to the Byzantine Empire, where Romani were falsely linked with the heretical sect of Athiganoi, thus leading to the Italian *zingari*, the French *tsiganes*, the German *Zigeuner*, the Czech *cikan*, and, among others, the English word *Gypsy*.

GO ON TO THE NEXT PAGE.

65. The author introduces the debate over the origin of the word *Gypsy* to show that

A. the Romani share cultural traditions with Egyptians and Greeks.

B. the Romani language is difficult to pronounce accurately in modern European languages.

C. the Romani have been falsely identified as a unified group when, in fact, their members comprise three culturally and linguistically independent groups.

D. the Romani history is incomplete and highly debated, even among scholars.

66. According to the passage, the Romani have migrated to which of the following countries?

I. France

II. Armenia

III. China

A. I only

B. II only

C. I and II

D. I, II, and III

GO ON TO THE NEXT PAGE.

67. Which of the following pieces of information, if offered as new evidence, would support the multiple emigration hypothesis described in the fourth paragraph?

    A. A Hindi text from the ninth century CE refers to both the Dom and the Lom.
    B. Many Persian words have three or four distinct meanings.
    C. A 13th-century Armenian folk tale mentions Gypsies.
    D. Descendants of the Romani still live in India.

68. The author of this passage would most likely look for information relevant to the arguments made in the passage in

    A. a religious text of the *zingari*.
    B. a poem written in both Bengali and Romani.
    C. an 11th-century Romani painting.
    D. a comparison of Dom and Rom cuisines.

69. Which of the following would cast doubt on the single emigration theory?

    A. The Romani had an oral history of the migration from India that was finally committed to writing only in the 19th century.
    B. The similarities between Romani and Hindi stem from a relation between each of them and a third language that arose in the 15th century.
    C. Linguistic analysis is shown to be more useful for tracing migratory paths than for fixing the dates of migrations.
    D. Linguists supporting this theory are not involved in the linguistic debate over the origin of the word *Gypsy*.

70. Which of the following best characterizes the author's claim that the Romani are "little understood by outsiders" (paragraph 1)?

    A. It is contradicted by the historiography of the Romani migration.
    B. It is strongly supported by objective data presented throughout the passage.
    C. It is perhaps true but is not explicitly supported by any objective data in the passage.
    D. It is refuted by the author's many references to linguistic evidence.

GO ON TO THE NEXT PAGE.

Passage IV (Questions 71–77)

The rich analyses of Fernand Braudel and his fellow *Annales* historians have made significant contributions to historical theory and research. In a departure from traditional historical approaches, the *Annales* historians assume (as do Marxists) that history cannot be limited to a simple recounting of conscious human action but must be understood in the context of forces and material conditions that underlie human behavior. Braudel was the first *Annales* historian to gain widespread support for the idea that history should synthesize data from various social sciences, especially economics, in order to provide a broader view of human societies over time (although Febvre and Bloch, founders of the *Annales* school, had originated this approach).

Braudel conceived of history as the dynamic interaction of three temporalities. The first of these, the *evenementielle*, involved short-lived dramatic "events," such as battles, revolutions, and the actions of great men, which had preoccupied traditional historians like Carlyle. *Conjonctures* was Braudel's term for larger cyclical processes that might last up to half a century. The *longue durée*, a historical wave of great length, was for Braudel the most fascinating of the three temporalities. Here he focused on those aspects of everyday life that might remain relatively unchanged for centuries. What people ate, what they wore, their means and routes of travel—for Braudel these things create "structures" that define the limits of potential social change for hundreds of years at a time.

Braudel's concept of the *longue durée* extended the perspective of historical space as well as time. Until the *Annales* school, historians had taken the juridical political unit the nation-state, duchy, or whatever as their starting point. Yet, when such enormous time spans are considered, geographical features may well have more significance for human populations than national borders. In his doctoral thesis, a seminal work on the Mediterranean during the reign of Philip II, Braudel treated the geohistory of the entire region as a "structure" that had exerted myriad influences on human lifeways since the first settlements on the shores of the Mediterranean Sea. And so the reader is given such arcane information as the list of products that came to Spanish shores from North Africa, the seasonal routes followed by Mediterranean sheep and their shepherds, and the cities where the best ship timber could be bought.

Braudel has been faulted for the imprecision of his approach. With his Rabelaisian delight in concrete detail, Braudel vastly extended the realm of relevant phenomena; but this very achievement made it difficult to delimit the boundaries of observation, a task necessary to beginning any social investigation. Further, Braudel and other *Annales* historians minimize the differences among the social sciences. Nevertheless, the many similarly designed studies aimed at both professional and popular audiences indicate that Braudel asked significant questions that traditional historians had overlooked.

71. The author refers to the work of Febvre and Bloch in order to

A. illustrate the limitations of the *Annales* tradition of historical interpretation.

B. suggest the relevance of economics to historical investigation.

C. debate the need for combining various sociological approaches.

D. show that previous *Annales* historians anticipated Braudel's focus on economics.

GO ON TO THE NEXT PAGE.

72. According to the passage, all of the following are aspects of Braudel's approach to history EXCEPT that he

    A. attempted to draw on various social sciences.
    B. studied social and economic activities that occurred across national boundaries.
    C. pointed out the link between increased economic activity and the rise of nationalism.
    D. examined seemingly unexciting aspects of everyday life.

73. In the third paragraph, the author is primarily concerned with discussing

    A. Braudel's fascination with obscure facts.
    B. Braudel's depiction of the role of geography in human history.
    C. the geography of the Mediterranean region.
    D. the irrelevance of national borders.

74. The passage suggests that, compared to traditional historians, *Annales* historians are

    A. more interested in other social sciences than in history.
    B. critical of the achievements of famous historical figures.
    C. skeptical of the validity of most economic research.
    D. more interested in the underlying context of human behavior.

75. Which of the following statements would be most likely to follow the last sentence of the passage?

    A. Few such studies, however, have been written by trained economists.
    B. It is time, perhaps, for a revival of the Carlylean emphasis on personalities.
    C. Many historians believe that Braudel's conception of three distinct "temporalities" is an oversimplification.
    D. Such diverse works as Gascon's study of Lyon and Barbara Tuchman's *A Distant Mirror* testify to his relevance.

76. The author is critical of Braudel's perspective for which of the following reasons?

    A. It seeks structures that underlie all forms of social activity.
    B. It assumes a greater similarity among the social sciences than actually exists.
    C. It fails to consider the relationship between short-term events and long-term social activity.
    D. It rigidly defines boundaries for social analysis.

GO ON TO THE NEXT PAGE.

77. Which of the following statements is most in keeping with the principles of Braudel's work as described in the passage?

    A. All written history is the history of social elites.
    B. The most important task of historians is to define the limits of potential social change.
    C. Those who ignore history are doomed to repeat it.
    D. People's historical actions are influenced by many factors of which they may be unaware.

GO ON TO THE NEXT PAGE.

Passage V (Questions 78–83)

The Russia that emerged from the terrible civil war after the 1917 Revolution was far from the Bolsheviks' original ideal of a nonexploitative society governed by workers and peasants. By 1921, the regime was weakened by widespread famine, persistent peasant revolts, a collapse of industrial production stemming from the civil war, and the consequent dispersal of the industrial working class—the Bolsheviks' original base of support. To buy time for recovery, the government in 1921 introduced the New Economic Policy which allowed private trade in farm products (previously banned) and relied on a fixed grain tax instead of forced requisitions to provide food for the cities. The value of the ruble was stabilized. Trade unions were again allowed to seek higher wages and benefits and even to strike. However, the Bolsheviks maintained a strict monopoly of power by refusing to legalize other parties.

After the death of the Revolution's undisputed leader, Lenin, in January 1924, disputes over the long-range direction of policy led to an open struggle among the main Bolshevik leaders. Since open debate was still possible within the Bolshevik Party in this period, several groups with differing programs emerged in the course of this struggle.

The program supported by Nikolai Bukharin—a major ideological leader of the Bolsheviks with no power base of his own—called for developing agriculture through good relations with wealthy peasants, or *kulaks*. Bukharin favored gradual industrial development, or "advancing towards Socialism at a snail's pace." In foreign affairs, Bukharin's policy was to ally with non-Socialist regimes and movements that were favorable to Russia.

A faction led by Leon Trotsky, head of the Red Army and the most respected revolutionary leader after Lenin, called for rapid industrialization and greater central planning of the economy, financed by a heavy tax on the kulaks. Trotsky rejected the idea that a prosperous, humane Socialist society could be built in Russia alone (Stalin's slogan of "Socialism in One Country") and, therefore, called for continued efforts to promote working-class revolutions abroad. As time went on, he became bitterly critical of the new privileged elite emerging within both the Bolshevik Party and the Russian state.

Joseph Stalin, General Secretary of the party, was initially considered a "center," conciliating figure, not clearly part of a faction. Stalin's eventual supremacy was ensured by three successive struggles within the party, and only during the last did his own program become clear.

First, in 1924–25, Stalin isolated Trotsky, allying for this purpose with Grigori Zinoviev and Lev Kamenev, Bolshevik leaders better known than Stalin himself whom Trotsky mistakenly considered his main rivals. Stalin maneuvered Trotsky out of leadership of the Red Army, his main potential power base. Next, Stalin turned on Zinoviev and Kamenev, using his powers as head of the Party organization to remove them from Party leadership in Leningrad and Moscow, their respective power bases. Trotsky, Zinoviev, and Kamenev then belatedly formed the "Joint Opposition" (1926–27). With Bukharin's help, Stalin easily outmaneuvered the Opposition: Bukharin polemicized against Trotsky, while Stalin prevented the newspapers from printing Trotsky's replies, organized gangs of toughs to beat up his followers, and transferred his supporters to administrative posts in remote regions. At the end of 1927, Stalin expelled Trotsky from the Bolshevik Party and exiled him. (Later, in 1940, he had him murdered.) Zinoviev and Kamenev, meanwhile, recanted their views in order to remain within the Party.

GO ON TO THE NEXT PAGE.

The final act now began. A move by kulaks to gain higher prices by holding grain off the market touched off a campaign against them by Stalin. Bukharin protested, but with the tradition of Party democracy now all but dead, Stalin had little trouble silencing Bukharin. Meanwhile, he began a campaign to force all peasants—not just kulaks—onto state-controlled "collective farms" and a crash industrialization program during which he deprived the trade unions of all rights and cut real wages by 50 percent. Out of the factional struggle in which he emerged by 1933 as sole dictator of Russia, Stalin's political program of building up heavy industry on the backs of both worker and peasant emerged with full clarity.

78. All of the following were among the factors contributing to the weakness of the Bolshevik regime in 1921 EXCEPT

 A. the aftereffects of the civil war.
 B. low production.
 C. opposition by peasants.
 D. lack of democracy within the Party.

79. The main feature of the New Economic Policy of 1921 was

 A. a strict economic centralization.
 B. stimulation of the economy through deliberate inflation.
 C. a limitation of trade union activity.
 D. a relaxation of economic controls.

80. An important feature of Bukharin's program was

 A. a tax on the peasants.
 B. avoiding confrontations with the trade unions.
 C. forming alliances with friendly foreign regimes.
 D. maintaining open debate within the Party.

81. According to the passage, a similarity between Stalin and Trotsky was their attitude and policy toward

 A. the elite of the Bolshevik Party.
 B. the importance of industrialization.
 C. democracy within the party.
 D. trade unions.

82. In his struggle with rival factions of the Party, Stalin was apparently MOST helped by

 A. his control of the party organization.
 B. his control of the army.
 C. Trotsky's misjudgment of threats to his position.
 D. the appearance of standing above factional politics.

83. The passage supports the idea that struggles within the Bolshevik Party were primarily

 A. reflections of struggles among important groups in the general population.
 B. the result of differences over economic policy.
 C. the result of differences over foreign policy.
 D. caused by Russian social elites outside the Party.

Passage VI (Questions 84–87)

In examining "myths of women" in literature, Simone de Beauvoir found the images put forward by Stendhal romantic, yet feministic. Stendhal's ideal woman was the one best able to reveal him to himself. For Stendhal, such a task required an equal. Women's emancipation was required, then, not simply in the name of liberty but—more importantly—for the sake of individual happiness and fulfillment.

De Beauvoir wrote: "Stendhal wants his mistress intelligent, cultivated, free in spirit and behavior: an equal." Love, in Stendhal's scheme, will be more true if woman, being man's equal, is able to understand him more completely.

De Beauvoir found it rather refreshing—a kind of relief—that in Stendhal, at least, we can find a man who lived among women of flesh and blood. He rejected the mystification of women: his women were "not fury, nymph, morning star, nor siren, but human." Humanity sufficed for Stendhal, and no dream or myth could have been more entrancing.

Stendhal believed that the human, living souls of women, having rejected "the heavy sleep in which humanity is mired," may rise through passion to heroism, if they can find an objective worthy of them— an objective worthy of their spiritual and creative powers, their energies, and the ferocity and purity of total dedication. Certainly Stendhal believed such an objective exists for woman, and it is man. It is in this belief that Stendhal became ultimately unsatisfying to de Beauvoir. While Stendhal did grant women emotions, aspirations, and some sense of self, the only way he believed they can fully realize and fulfill their own selves is through man. It is in loving a man that the ennui of these truly living souls is driven away. Any boredom—any lack of focus, in essence, the lack of men—represents also a lack of any reason for living or dying, absolute stagnation. Meanwhile, passion—the love of a man—has an aim, and that is enough justification for woman's life.

Yet de Beauvoir was still compelled by Stendhal. She found him unique—or, at least, distinct—in going to the point of projecting himself into a female character. He did not "hover over" as Lamiel did but assumed her destiny. On account of that, de Beauvoir noted, "Lamiel's outline remains somewhat speculative," but also singularly significant.

Lamiel is typical of Stendhal's women. Her creator has raised every imaginable obstacle before her: she is a poor peasant, raised by coarse, ignorant people imbued with all sorts of common prejudices. But, as de Beauvoir noted, "she clears from her path all moral barriers once she understands the full meaning of the little words: 'that's silly'. It is her freedom of mind that allows her to see through the meaninglessness and superficiality of so much social ritual, so that she may act in the world in her own fashion, responding fully to the impulses of her own curiosity and ambition, and shaping a destiny worthy of herself in a mediocre world."

In this, Lamiel conveys Stendhal's ultimate message to his readers: there is no comfortable place for great souls in society as it exists. It is in this sense that his men and women are the same: equals. Together, two who may have the chance to know each other in love, man and woman, defy time and universe—and come into absolute harmony with it. Such a couple is sufficient unto itself and realizes the absolute.

GO ON TO THE NEXT PAGE.

84. According to the passage, Stendhal believed that in order to experience self-realization, an individual requires the presence of

    A. a muse.
    B. God.
    C. an equal.
    D. family.

85. The author suggests de Beauvoir considered Stendhal's portrait of Lamiel "somewhat speculative" (paragraph 5) because Stendhal

    A. based his story upon myths.
    B. sensationalized his plot.
    C. took on the identity of a woman.
    D. exaggerated the aspirations of his female characters.

86. The passage mentions that de Beauvoir saw the mystification of women in all of the following forms EXCEPT

    A. nymph.
    B. morning star.
    C. fury.
    D. mistress.

87. It can be inferred from the passage that Stendhal's notion of love between a man and woman both includes and requires

    A. faithfulness in the relationship.
    B. the mystification of woman.
    C. understanding of each other.
    D. the blessing of the union before God.

GO ON TO THE NEXT PAGE.

Passage VII (Questions 88-92)

The new field of molecular anthropology has provided important new data on primate evolution, but many paleontologists have been slow to accept them. They argue that fossils are the only direct evidence and that molecules are not relevant to the study of extinct species. With regard to human origins, fossil bones and teeth may appear to conflict with molecular data, but, as we have seen with Ramapithecus, the fossil evidence is often fragmentary and subject to more than one interpretation.

The two approaches are quite different: Paleontologists dig up bones from the earth, study their shapes, and compare them to other living and extinct species in order to establish their place in an evolutionary phylogeny.

Molecular anthropologists study the proteins of living species and deduce how long ago two species diverged from a common ancestor . . . Proteins are made up of various combinations of the basic twenty amino acids, arranged in definite sequences. A given protein may include hundreds to thousands of amino acids. The proteins of closely related species, such as horse and donkey or dog and fox, are nearly identical; whereas species that diverged more than 100 [million years ago], such as shrew and opossum, have many sequence differences.

These differences can be measured precisely, and their number is approximately proportional to the divergence time. Such "molecular clocks" are particularly valuable for evolutionary study because results can be, and have been, replicated in numerous laboratories, whereas the analysis of fossil bones and teeth is somewhat subjective, and agreement between researchers may be difficult to achieve. Paleontological phylogenies have indicated a long, independent evolution for the five living hominid groups. They have suggested that Pliopithecus was an early gibbon; that different species of Dryopithecus were ancestral to gorilla, chimpanzee, and orangutan; and that Ramapithecus was ancestral to the human line.

In contrast, the molecular phylogenies show a relatively recent divergence for all the apes, with the Asian apes splitting off earlier than the rest. This rules out the possibility that Pliopithecus is an ancestral gibbon or that Dryopithecus or Proconsul are ancestral apes. The three-way divergence between human, chimpanzee, and gorilla about 5 [million years ago] does not preclude Australopithecus as an early representative of the human family. So, aside from the equivocal fossil evidence itself, the molecular findings make it even less likely that Ramapithecus could have been a human ancestor.

To consider Ramapithecus as hominid, one would have to assume that primate proteins have evolved at half the rate of shark, fish, frog, snake, kangaroo, mouse, and elephant proteins. Some have argued that proteins evolve more slowly in animals with more time between generations—a presumption refuted by the evidence that mouse and elephant proteins have evolved at the same rate, as have loris and human proteins. This external check on the statistical constancy of the molecular clock is further supported by internal evidence: numerous proteins with different rates of change (cytochrome c, albumin, transferrin, hemoglobin, and histones) indicate similar divergence times. That is like timing the same event with an hour hand, minute hand, and second hand and finding out that the times come out the same. The statistical constancy of the molecular clock is not an assumption but an observation based on an enormous amount of data.

From the biochemical evidence, then, there was but one ancestor prior to the ape–human split, not three different ones, for humans and the African apes. The molecular information had made it clear that we cannot look at human origins as an isolated phenomenon, but must consider the event as part of the radiation that included the African apes. If Ramapithecus has a place in human ancestry, it will have a place in chimpanzee and gorilla ancestry as well.

GO ON TO THE NEXT PAGE.

88. The author would agree with which of the following statements regarding the origins of the five living hominid groups?

   I. Pliopithecus was an early gibbon.
   II. Dryopithecus and Proconsul are ancestral apes.
   III. Australopithecus is a human ancestor.

   A. I only
   B. I and II only
   C. III only
   D. I, II, and III

89. Based on the information presented in the passage, what would the author believe is most significant to anthropologists regarding the findings of molecular phylogenies?

   A. It is less likely that Ramapithecus could have been a human ancestor.
   B. Fossil evidence is fragmentary and subject to more than one interpretation.
   C. Ape and human origins prior to the ape-human split are much more closely related than was previously thought.
   D. The invention of the molecular clock was made possible.

90. Which of the following statements would be most relevant to the first paragraph of the passage?

   A. Almost 200 years ago, French paleontologist Cuvier boasted that he could reconstruct an animal from its teeth alone. But paleontologists have learned the hard way that teeth do not tell the whole story.
   B. Ramapithecus, first found in India, was named in the 1930s after the Hindu prince "Rama," hence "Rama's ape."
   C. The famous nineteenth-century anatomist Thomas Henry Huxley, in his 1863 book, *Evidence As to Man's Place in Nature,* argued on anatomical grounds that humans were most similar to the African apes, a conclusion confirmed 100 years later by biochemistry.
   D. A comparison of developmental stages among vertebrates led Ernst Haeckel (1834–1919) to propose his famous principle "ontogeny recapitulates phylogeny."

91. Which of the following would most help to reconcile the disagreement between molecular anthropologists and paleontologists regarding hominid ancestry?

   A. Evidence that ape and human proteins have evolved at the same rate
   B. The finding by paleontologists that the Asian apes did not split off earlier than the rest
   C. Evidence that Australopithecus was an early human
   D. The finding of a complete intact fossil specimen of Ramapithecus with characteristics that are as much apelike as human

GO ON TO THE NEXT PAGE.

92. The author claims, but offers no supporting evidence, that:

A. the analysis of fossil bones and teeth is subjective.
B. Ramapithecus is ancestral to the gorilla.
C. the molecular clock has statistical constancy.
D. we cannot look at human origins as an isolated phenomenon.

STOP.

IF YOU FINISH BEFORE TIME HAS EXPIRED, CHECK YOUR WORK.
YOU MAY GO BACK TO ANY QUESTION IN THIS PART ONLY.

Biological Sciences Test

Time: 70 minutes

Questions 93–144

DIRECTIONS: The majority of the questions in the following Biological Sciences test are arranged in groups addressing a preceding descriptive passage. Select the single best answer to each question in the group after thorough analysis of the passage. Some discrete questions are not based on a descriptive passage. Similarly, select the best answer to these questions. If you are not certain of an answer, eliminate the answer choices known to be incorrect and select an answer from the remaining alternatives. Indicate your answer selection hy blackening the corresponding oval on your answer document. A periodic table is provided below for your assistance with the passages and questions.

Periodic Table of the Elements

1 H 1.0																	2 He 4.0
3 Li 6.9	4 Be 9.0											5 B 10.8	6 C 12.0	7 N 14.0	8 O 16.0	9 F 19.0	10 Ne 20.2
11 Na 23.0	12 Mg 24.3											13 Al 27.0	14 Si 28.1	15 P 31.0	16 S 32.1	17 Cl 35.5	18 Ar 39.9
19 K 39.1	20 Ca 40.1	21 Sc 45.0	22 Ti 47.9	23 V 50.9	24 Cr 52.0	25 Mn 54.9	26 Fe 55.8	27 Co 58.9	28 Ni 58.7	29 Cu 63.5	30 Zn 65.4	31 Ga 69.7	32 Ge 72.6	33 As 74.9	34 Se 79.0	35 Br 79.9	36 Kr 83.8
37 Rb 85.5	38 Sr 87.6	39 Y 88.9	40 Zr 91.2	41 Nb 92.9	42 Mo 95.9	43 Tc (98)	44 Ru 101.1	45 Rh 102.9	46 Pd 106.4	47 Ag 107.9	48 Cd 112.4	49 In 114.8	50 Sn 118.7	51 Sb 121.8	52 Te 127.6	53 I 126.9	54 Xe 131.3
55 Cs 132.9	56 Ba 137.3	57 La * 138.9	72 Hf 178.5	73 Ta 180.9	74 W 183.9	75 Re 186.2	76 Os 190.2	77 Ir 192.2	78 Pt 195.1	79 Au 197.0	80 Hg 200.6	81 Tl 204.4	82 Pb 207.2	83 Bi 209.0	84 Po (209)	85 At (210)	86 Rn (222)
87 Fr (223)	88 Ra 226.0	89 Ac † 227.0	104 Rf (261)	105 Db (262)	106 Sg (263)	107 Bh (264)	108 Hs (269)	109 Mt (268)	110 Ds (269)	111 Rg (272)	112 Uub (277)	113 Uut (284)	114 Uuq (289)	115 Uup (288)	116 Uuh (292)	117 Uus (291)	118 Uuo (293)

	58 Ce 140.1	59 Pr 140.9	60 Nd 144.2	61 Pm (145)	62 Sm 150.4	63 Eu 152.0	64 Gd 157.3	65 Tb 158.9	66 Dy 162.5	67 Ho 164.9	68 Er 167.3	69 Tm 168.9	70 Yb 173.0	71 Lu 175.0
*														
†	90 Th 232.0	91 Pa (231)	92 U 238.0	93 Np (237)	94 Pu (244)	95 Am (243)	96 Cm (247)	97 Bk (247)	98 Cf (251)	99 Es (252)	100 Fm (257)	101 Md (258)	102 No (259)	103 Lr (260)

GO ON TO THE NEXT PAGE.

Passage 1 (Questions 93–98)

Glycolysis is the sequence of reactions in the cytosol that converts glucose into two molecules of pyruvate with the concomitant generation of 2 ATP and 2 NADH. Under anaerobic conditions, NAD^+ is regenerated from NADH by the reduction of pyruvate to either lactate or ethanol. Alternatively, under aerobic conditions, NAD^+ is regenerated by the transfer of electrons from NADH to O_2 through the electron-transport chain. Glycolysis serves two main functions: It generates ATP, and it provides carbon skeletons for biosynthesis.

Phosphofructokinase, which is the enzyme that catalyzes the committed step in glycolysis, is the most important control site. A high concentration of ATP inhibits phosphofructokinase. This inhibitory effect is enhanced by citrate and reversed by AMP. Thus, the rate of glycolysis depends on the cell's need for ATP, as signaled by the ATP/AMP ratio, and on the need for building blocks, as signaled by the concentration of citrate. These relationships are shown in Figure 1.

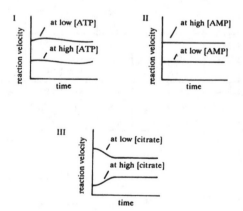

Figure 1

In liver cells, the most important regulator of phosphofructokinase activity is *fructose 2,6-bisphosphate (F-2,6-BP)*. F-2,6-BP is formed by the phosphorylation of fructose 6-phosphate in a reaction catalyzed by *phosphofructokinase 2 (PFK2)*. When blood glucose is low, a glucagon-triggered cascade leads to the phosphorylation of PFK2 and inhibition of phosphofructokinase. The control of the synthesis and degradation of F-2,6-BP is shown in Figure 2.

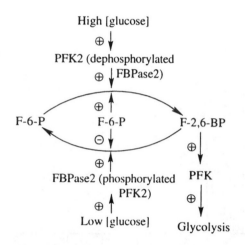

⊕ = stimulation
⊖ = inhibition

Figure 2

93. In an experiment with glycolytic enzymes, 10 mol of glucose produced 2 mol of ATP. This result fails to conform to the theoretical yield from 10 mol of glucose, which should produce

    A.   1 mol of ATP.
    B.   5 mol of ATP.
    C.   10 mol of ATP.
    D.   20 mol of ATP.

GO ON TO THE NEXT PAGE.

94. One of the reactions of aerobic respiration is the addition of water to fumarate, which is shown below. This reaction is catalyzed by the enzyme fumarase and occurs stereospecifically with water approaching on only one side of the molecule.

fumarase

X

The product of the reaction, X, is

A. a racemic mixture.
B. an optically active molecule.
C. a molecule with two chiral centers.
D. an achiral molecule.

95. It can be inferred from the passage that glucagon

A. stimulates the phosphorylation of fructose 6-phosphate.
B. stimulates F-2,6-BP synthesis.
C. inhibits phosphorylation of PFK2.
D. inhibits glycolysis.

96. Which of the following conditions would most enhance the rate of glycolysis?

A. Low concentration of F-2,6-BP
B. High ATP/AMP ratio
C. High concentration of AMP
D. High concentration of citrate

97. A high fructose-6-phosphate concentration will lead to all of the following EXCEPT

A. increased F-2,6-BP synthesis.
B. decreased F-2,6-BP degradation.
C. stimulation of phosphofructokinase.
D. decreased ATP/AMP ratio.

98. Two bacterial colonies, A and B, are grown anaerobically on separate petri plates containing a glucose-rich medium and are found to be of equal size. The two plates are then incubated for 72 hours in an O_2-rich atmosphere. After incubation, Colony A exhibited growth, and an assay of the medium revealed that most of the glucose in the plate had been consumed; Colony B had nearly disappeared. These results suggest that Colonies A and B most likely contain

A. facultative aerobes and obligate aerobes, respectively.
B. facultative aerobes and obligate anaerobes, respectively.
C. obligate aerobes and obligate anaerobes, respectively.
D. obligate anaerobes and facultative aerobes, respectively.

GO ON TO THE NEXT PAGE.

Passage II (Questions 99–104)

There are four phases of the *human immunodeficiency virus (HIV)* life cycle. In *binding and entry,* the virus binds to the CD4 receptor on CD4$^+$ T-cells via the viral glycoprotein, *gp120.* The binding results in the fusion of the viral and cellular membranes, followed by the entrance of the viral core into the cell. After entry, *synthesis and integration* occurs, during which viral RNA is transcribed into double-stranded DNA by reverse transcriptase. Viral DNA enters the nucleus and integrates into the host genome. Following integration, *expression* of viral genes occurs. Finally, during *assembly and release,* viral structural proteins are synthesized and assemble into particles containing the viral enzymes and two copies of the viral RNA. The particles bud from the cell.

One of the most puzzling cytopathic effects of HIV is the depletion of T-cells, despite the fact that relatively few cells are actually infected. Four models that attempt to account for this effect are summarized below.

Hypothesis 1

HIV particles that fail to integrate into the CD4$^+$ T-cell genome produce a toxic factor that functionally impairs T-cells and eventually leads to cell death.

Hypothesis 2

HIV integration promotes the synthesis of terminal maturation factors in CD4$^+$ T-cells, increasing their susceptibility to the body's normal cell-destruction process.

Hypothesis 3

Viral glycoproteins (gp120 and gp41) expressed on the surface of HIV-infected T-cells fuse with CD4 receptors on healthy cells, forming a nonfunctional cell mass (syncytia formation).

Hypothesis 4

gp120 molecules are released into circulation by infected T-cells and bind to the CD4 receptors on healthy T-cells, making the latter subject to an autoimmune attack by anti-gp120 antibodies.

99. A researcher wanting to study the process by which viral mRNA is transcribed in an HIV-infected CD4+ T-cell would add all of the following reagents to the cell culture EXCEPT

    A. radiolabeled thymine.
    B. radiolabeled guanine.
    C. radiolabeled uracil.
    D. radiolabeled adenine.

100. If Hypothesis 1 were true, which of the following pairs of processes would HIV have to undergo before a toxic factor could be produced?

    A. Binding and entry; synthesis and integration
    B. Reverse transcription and host cell death
    C. Binding and entry
    D. Reverse transcription; synthesis and integration

101. Which of the following supports Hypothesis 3?

    A. Some CD4$^+$ T-cell lines do not form syncytia but are susceptible to the cytopathic effects of HIV.
    B. Syncytia formation is transient in some CD4$^+$ T-cell lines.
    C. gp120 and gp41 bind almost irreversibly to CD4 receptor molecules in vitro.
    D. Syncytia formation does not lead to cell death in some CD4$^+$ T-cell lines.

GO ON TO THE NEXT PAGE.

102. Hypothesis 4 is based on the assumption that

    A. healthy CD4+ T-cells are not normally subject to autoimmune attacks.
    B. healthy CD4+ T-cells will produce anti-gp120 cells in response to exposure to the HIV virus.
    C. healthy CD4+ T-cells normally synthesize gp120.
    D. proteins travel through the body by way of the immune system.

103. If Hypothesis 3 were true, which of the following cellular organelles would be responsible for directing the newly synthesized gp120 and gp41 molecules toward the plasma membrane, on which they would eventually be expressed?

    A. Centrioles
    B. Golgi complex
    C. Mitochondria
    D. Lysosomes

104. HIV infection is detected by the presence of anti-HIV antibodies in the blood. This indicates that during infection

    A. helper T-cells are still able to activate cytotoxic T-cell proliferation.
    B. B-lymphocytes are still able to produce antibodies in response to the foreign antigens of HIV.
    C. anti-HIV antibodies are effective against the virus.
    D. HIV has not infected host macrophages.

GO ON TO THE NEXT PAGE.

Question 105 through 107 are NOT associated with a passage .

105. What is the name of the product formed when $CH_3CH=CH_3$ is reacted with hot, basic $KMnO_4$?

   A.   Acetic acid
   B.   2,3–butanediol
   C.   Ethanal
   D.   Ethylene glycol

106. Which of the following is formed as an intermediate when 1-butyne reacts with HBr, but not formed as an intermediate when 1-butene reacts with HBr?

   A.   A secondary carbocation
   B.   A vinylic anion
   C.   A vinylic cation
   D.   A tertiary carbocation

107. Mammalian fetal circulation is similar to amphibian adult circulation in that:

   A.   gas exchange occurs only in the lungs.
   B.   gas exchange occurs only in the blastopore.
   C.   the heart has only three chambers prior to birth.
   D.   oxygenated and deoxygenated blood coexists within the same chambers of the heart.

GO ON TO THE NEXT PAGE.

Passage III (Questions 108–113)

An epidemiologist was called in to investigate an outbreak of illness following a sewage leak into a city's water supply. Blood tests of the affected individuals revealed the presence of an unknown infectious agent, which the epidemiologist determined to be either viral or bacterial. Further examination determined that the infectious agent was bacterial, and when the results were more closely analyzed, it appeared that more than one strain of bacteria was infecting the patients. Four different strains of bacteria, labeled Microbe Q, Microbe R, Microbe S, and Microbe T, were eventually isolated.

Four different types of nutrient plates were prepared, each containing only four amino acids, and the microbes were inoculated onto the plates to determine the essential amino acids of each strain. Those amino acids that an organism cannot synthesize are said to be *essential* to that organism.

Plate 1:   cysteine, phenylalanine, serine, threonine

Plate 2:   cysteine, phenylalanine, proline, tryptophan

Plate 3:   cysteine, proline, threonine, tryptophan

Plate 4:   phenylalanine, serine, threonine, tryptophan

The results are shown in Table 1.

Table 1

Microbe

	Q	R	S	T
Plate 1	+	+	–	+
Plate 2	–	+	+	+
Plate 3	+	–	–	–
Plate 4	–	–	–	+

+ = growth; – = no growth

After the microbes were isolated, it was determined that Microbe R and Microbe S were not pathogenic. Potential antibiotics against Microbe Q and Microbe T were then selected, and the microbes were inoculated onto their respective growth media. Antibiotic discs X, Y, and Z were then placed on each nutrient plate. After 24 hours of incubation (enough time to allow growth), the plates were re-examined. The shaded areas of Figure 1 represent regions of good bacterial growth.

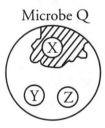 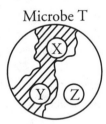

Figure 1

GO ON TO THE NEXT PAGE.

108. Which of the following techniques would have been MOST effective in helping the epidemiologist determine that the infectious agent was bacterial?

    A. Hybridize the infectious agent with radiolabeled probes specific for the genes encoding viral structural proteins; only viral genes would hybridize.
    B. Analyze a patient's serum in a spectrophotometer to measure its absorption wavelength; the photosynthetic pigments found in all bacteria would distinguish them from viruses, which lack such pigments.
    C. Stain the infectious agent for the presence of RNA; only bacteria would stain positive.
    D. Stain the infectious agent for the presence of protein; only bacteria would stain positive.

109. Which of the following structures would NOT have been detected when the epidemiologist determined Microbe R's structural composition?

    A. Nuclear membrane
    B. DNA
    C. Cell wall
    D. Ribosomes

110. According to Table 1, which of the following amino acids is essential to Microbe Q?

    A. Serine
    B. Threonine
    C. Phenylalanine
    D. Proline

111. According to Table 1, which of the four nutrient media could the epidemiologist have used when determining the effectiveness of the antibiotic discs against the pathogenic microbes?

    A. The medium from Plate 1
    B. The medium from Plate 2
    C. The medium from Plate 3
    D. The medium from Plate 4

112. Based on the information in Figure 1, which of the following antibiotics would be most effective in treating patients infected with both Microbe Q and Microbe T?

    A. Antibiotic X
    B. Antibiotic Y
    C. Antibiotic Z
    D. Antibiotic Y and Antibiotic Z are equally effective.

GO ON TO THE NEXT PAGE.

113. Which of the following would be the easiest method to isolate Microbe Q from Microbe T when they coexist in the same patient?

    A. Centrifuge a serum sample from a patient infected with both bacteria; the two strains would layer at different levels and could thus be isolated.

    B. Take a blood sample from a patient infected with both bacteria. Put some blood on a nutrient plate containing only phenylalanine and some on another plate containing only cysteine. Incubate and isolate what grows.

    C. Take a blood sample from a patient infected with both bacteria. Put some on a nutrient plate with all the amino acids except cysteine and some on another plate with all the amino acids except phenylalanine. Incubate and isolate what grows.

    D. There is no way to isolate the two bacteria, since all bacteria are similar in their structure and nutritional requirements.

Questions 114 through 118 are NOT based on a descriptive passage.

114. Which of the following would form the most stable carbocation?

A. $(CH_3)_2CHBr$ dissolved in toluene
B. $(CH_3CH_2)_3COH$ dissolved in acetone
C. $(CH_3)_3COH$ dissolved in H_2SO_4
D. CH_3CH_2I dissolved in diethyl ether

115. The hormone calcitonin acts as a regulator of serum Ca^{2+} levels by promoting the incorporation of Ca^{2+} into bone. Which of the following hormones is antagonistic to calcitonin?

A. Parathyroid hormone
B. Prolactin
C. ACTH
D. Thyroxine

116. In a healthy individual, which of the following blood vessels has the highest partial pressure of carbon dioxide?

A. Pulmonary arteries
B. Pulmonary veins
C. Aorta
D. Coronary arteries

117. Which of the following structures is NOT derived from embryonic ectoderm?

A. Eye lens
B. Pituitary gland
C. Digestive tract
D. Adrenal medulla

118. 2-pentene has two melting points because it can exist as either of two

A. anomers
B. enantiomers
C. conformational isomers
D. geometric isomers

GO ON TO THE NEXT PAGE.

Passage IV (Questions 119–123)

Alkanes, in the presence of light, react with halogens to produce alkyl halides. The reactions result in the substitution of halogen atoms for hydrogen atoms on the carbon skeleton. The reactions involve free radical intermediates, as illustrated in this general mechanism:

Initiation: X_2 $\xrightarrow{\text{light}}$ $2X \bullet$ (1)

Propagation: $RH + X \bullet$ $\rightarrow$ $R \bullet + HX$ (2)

     $X_2 + R \bullet$ $\rightarrow$ $RX + X \bullet$ (3)

(R = alkyl chain, X = F, Cl, Br, I)

The reactivity of an alkane depends on the types of hydrogens that are available to be substituted. Differences in the bond strengths, and in the energies of the transition states, make tertiary hydrogens most reactive, followed by secondary and then primary hydrogens. For instance, in substitution by bromine, tertiary hydrogens are five times more reactive than primary ones.

The order of reactivity of the halogens is as follows:

$$F > Cl > Br > I$$

119. The chlorination of butane is accompanied by which of the following?

    I.   The formation of chiral products
    II. No observed change in optical rotation
    III. The formation of achiral products

    A. I only
    B. III only
    C. II and III only
    D. I, II, and III

120. Reaction of alkanes containing equal numbers of primary and tertiary hydrogens with fluorine produces approximately equal amounts of each possible product. By contrast, reaction with bromine produces five times as much tertiary product as primary. Which of the following statements is most strongly supported by these facts and the passage?

    A. The reactivity of the halogens is inversely related to their selectivity between hydrogens in free-radical substitutions.
    B. Bromine is a more efficient halogenating reagent for all classes of alkanes than fluorine.
    C. Fluorine is less reactive with respect to substitution of tertiary hydrogens in alkanes than bromine.
    D. Fluorine forms stronger bonds to primary carbons than bromine does.

121. Light of low intensity is sufficient to cause the alkanes and halogens to react because

    A. the reactions have low activation energies.
    B. only a small, catalytic amount of X radicals must be produced in Step 1.
    C. the bonds in the halogen molecules are weak.
    D. alkanes are very reactive molecules.

GO ON TO THE NEXT PAGE.

122. Which of the following represents a chain termination step?

A. $Br + Br_2$ $\rightarrow$ $Br_2 + Br$
B. $Br + R$ $\rightarrow$ RBr
C. $RH + Br_2$ $\rightarrow$ $RBr + HBr$
D. $Br_2 + R \bullet$ $\rightarrow$ $RBr + Br$

123. What is the IUPAC name of the product formed when the most reactive hydrogen of 2-methylpropane is substituted by a bromine atom?

A. 2-bromomethylpropane
B. 2-bromobutane
C. 1-bromo-2-methylpropane
D. 2-bromo-2-methylpropane

GO ON TO THE NEXT PAGE.

Passage V (Questions 124–129)

Current theories of carcinogenesis are based on the concept of cellular and viral *oncogenes*. It is believed that the genome of any eukaryotic cell contains DNA segments, called *proto-oncogenes,* which normally code for cell growth-related proteins such as transcription factors, growth factors, growth-factor receptors, and tyrosine kinases (enzymes thought to regulate cell division). These cellular proto-oncogenes can be transformed into tumorigenic oncogenes (*c-onc*) by a number of mechanisms.

A common mechanism by which a cellular proto-oncogene is transformed into a *c-onc* is point mutation, which leads to formation of a defective protein. For example, one well-studied cellular proto-oncogene codes for the *ras* protein. *Ras* proteins have GTPase activity, and their activity is regulated by the presence of GTP or GDP. In the wild-type protein, growth-factor receptors with tyrosine kinase activity stimulate *ras* to exchange GDP with GTP through an indirect process involving intermediate proteins. *Ras* then activates a cytosolic kinase (also an oncogene) *c-raf. c-raf* then activates *MAP kinase-kinase,* which in turn activates *MAP-kinase. MAP-kinase* appears capable of phosphorylating transcription factors in the nucleus. After the appropriate genes have been transcribed, *ras* GTPase activity hydrolyzes GTP, converting *ras* to its inactive form. Mutant *ras* proteins are unable to hydrolyze GTP and, and therefore, remain in the active GTP-bound form.

Alternatively, a proto-oncogene may become an oncogene through a mutation that causes it to produce an excess of a normal protein. Such a mutation may place the gene under the control of a stronger promoter via either chromosomal translocation or by the integration of a provirus with a strong promoter in the immediate proximity of the proto-oncogene. An excess of a normal protein may also be caused by gene amplification of the proto-oncogene.

Another mechanism of carcinogenesis that depends on oncogenes is viral carcinogenesis, which is caused by transforming viruses. Transforming viruses, which occur widely in the avian and animal kingdoms, are retroviruses whose genomes contain oncogenes (called viral oncogenes, or *v-onc*) derived from their former eukaryotic hosts. Such viruses can later cause other host cells to become tumorigenic.

124. Which of the following activities would you expect to increase in a tumorigenic cell?

   I.   mRNA synthesis
   II. Ribosomal assembly
   III. Cell division

   A. I only
   B. I and II only
   C. II and III only
   D. I, II, and III

125. A *c-onc* activated by point mutation differs from the proto-oncogene from which it was derived by

   A. a single base-pair.
   B. two base-pairs.
   C. a triplet insertion.
   D. a triplet deletion.

GO ON TO THE NEXT PAGE.

126. Based on the information in the passage, cellular proto-oncogenes can become tumorigenic oncogenes by all of the following mechanisms EXCEPT

    A. a mutation that results in the synthesis of a faulty protein.
    B. a chromosomal translocation that produces an excess of a protein.
    C. binding of complementary nucleic acid sequences to proto-oncogene transcripts.
    D. a mutation that causes gene amplification of the proto-oncogene.

127. Comparison of a *v-onc* sequence with a corresponding *c-onc* sequence reveals that the organization of the viral gene corresponds to the mRNA of the *c-onc* gene, rather than to its own genomic organization. Which of the following best accounts for this observation?

    A. The *v-onc* gene contains only *c-onc* introns.
    B. The *v-onc* gene has a greater level of expression than the corresponding *c-onc* gene.
    C. The *v-onc* gene was captured from a host cell in the form of RNA during a retroviral infection.
    D. Since retroviral DNA is incorporated into the cellular genome, the alternating exons and introns in the *v-onc* gene are spliced by cellular enzymes.

128. Which of the following processes function in an analogous way to *ras* activity?

    A. Formation of antibody-antigen complexes during an immune response
    B. Sodium–potassium pump in neurons
    C. Krebs cycle in mitochondria
    D. Second messenger system involving cAMP

129. The incorporation of a strong promoter near a proto-oncogene may lead to cancer because the stronger promoter most likely

    A. increases the rate of translation.
    B. increases the rate of transcription.
    C. increases the rate of translocation.
    D. increases the rate of point mutations.

GO ON TO THE NEXT PAGE.

Passage VI (Questions 130–135)

Radioimmunoassay (RIA) is a technique used for measuring hormone concentrations in blood serum based on highly specific antigen-antibody interactions. To carry out an RIA for a particular human hormone, an antibody to that hormone is prepared by immunizing mice or rabbits with an extract from the human endocrine gland that produces the hormone. A measured quantity of this antibody is then mixed with a known concentration of isotopically labeled hormone and the blood sample to be assayed, which contains an unknown concentration of unlabeled hormone. RIA is based on the principle that as long as there is too little antibody to bind both the labeled hormone and unlabeled hormone completely, then the unlabeled and the labeled hormone will compete for antibody-binding sites. Thus, as the concentration of unlabeled hormone in the sample increases, the percentage of antibody-bound radiolabeled hormone decreases.

Hormone concentrations can be calculated by comparing the radioactivity counts obtained from the original RIA to a standard curve, such as the one shown in Figure 1. To generate a standard curve for a particular hormone, RIAs are performed on a series of solutions containing different known concentrations of unlabeled hormone. After the radioactivity of each solution is measured, these concentrations are then plotted against the percentage of antibody-bound radiolabeled hormone.

For most hormones, the form that circulates in the blood (the active form) is different from that extracted from the tissues and used to prepare the antibodies and standard curve used for RIAs (the precursor form), though typically, the two forms are very similar in structure and chemistry.

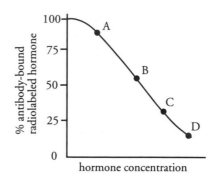

Figure 1

130. According to the passage, an antibody to a particular human hormone is prepared by immunizing laboratory animals with an extract of the human hormone. Which of the following best explains why this technique works?

A. The lab animal's immune system recognizes the human hormone as "foreign," or antigenic, and produces antibodies in response to its presence.

B. Human gland cells must first be injected into a host organism, such as a mouse or rabbit, before they can produce the antibodies.

C. Human hormones will elicit antibody production in mice and rabbits but not in other animals, such as rats and chimpanzees.

D. Immunization with human hormone, prior to actual exposure to the hormone, protects the lab animal from infection upon second exposure to the hormone.

GO ON TO THE NEXT PAGE.

131. An RIA for antidiuretic hormone (ADH) performed on a healthy person yielded a concentration of 3 pg/mL. If an RIA were performed on a patient suffering from severe blood loss, which of the following ADH concentrations would the RIA most likely yield?

    A. 0.5 pg/mL
    B. 2 pg/ml.
    C. 3 pg/mL
    D. 5 pg/mL

132. If Figure 1 were the standard curve for FSH, which point on the graph would most likely represent FSH concentration in a woman before pregnancy and in her 16th week of pregnancy, respectively?

    A. Point A and Point D
    B. Point B and Point D
    C. Point C and Point D
    D. Point B and Point A

133. RIA is based on the principle that radiolabeled and unlabeled hormone will compete for binding sites on the antibody. Which of the following conditions would NOT compromise the validity of an RIA?

    A. The antibody binds the radiolabeled hormone with a greater affinity than the unlabeled hormone.
    B. The antibody binds the radiolabeled hormone and the unlabeled hormone with equal affinity.
    C. There is enough antibody in the solution to completely bind with the radiolabeled and the unlabeled hormone.
    D. The radiolabeled hormone binds to a site on the antibody other than the antigen-binding site, inducing a conformational change that inhibits the binding of unlabeled hormone.

134. If Figure 1 were the standard curve for insulin, which points on the graph would most likely represent the serum insulin concentration calculated from the RIA performed before and 1 hour after glucose infusion, respectively?

    A. Point B and Point A
    B. Point B and Point D
    C. Point C and Point C
    D. Point C and Point A

135. Suppose that a researcher who wanted to measure the concentration of a particular *active* hormone unwittingly used its *precursor* form to develop the antibodies and generate the standard curve used for the RIA. If the researcher then performed an RIA on a sample of unlabeled active hormone contaminated with unlabeled precursor hormone, how would this affect the RIA?

    A. The standard curve generated for the precursor form would be inaccurate and, therefore, could not be used to calculate unknown concentrations of that form.
    B. The percentage of antibody-bound radiolabeled hormone would be greater than normal, because there would be twice as much unlabeled hormone for the radiolabeled hormone to compete with.
    C. The calculated concentration of the active hormone would be greater than its actual concentration, because the antibody would bind to both the active hormone and its precursor form.
    D. The calculated concentration of the active hormone would be less than its actual concentration, because the antibody would bind to both the active hormone and its precursor form.

GO ON TO THE NEXT PAGE.

Questions 136 through 140 are NOT based on a descriptive passage.

136. Marine and freshwater fish have different problems in maintaining their internal salt and water balances. Osmosis causes freshwater fish to gain water and marine fish to lose water. Based on this information, which of the following must be true?

    A. Marine fish live in an environment hypertonic to their body fluids.
    B. Marine fish live an environment hypotonic to their body fluids.
    C. Freshwater fish live in an environment hypertonic to their body fluids.
    D. Freshwater fish live in an environment isotonic to their body fluids.

137. Myoglobin, which is an oxygen-carrying protein found in muscle tissue, consists of a single polypeptide chain with an attached heme group. In contrast, hemoglobin consists of four heme-carrying polypeptide subunits. Which of the following best accounts for the difference in shape between the hemoglobin and myoglobin oxygen-dissociation curves?

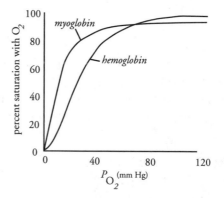

    A. Bohr effect
    B. Cooperative binding of oxygen to myoglobin
    C. Difference in P_{O_2} between blood and muscle
    D. Cooperative binding of oxygen to hemoglobin

GO ON TO THE NEXT PAGE.

138. Which of the following is NOT a *meta*-directing group in electrophilic aromatic substitution?

A. $-\overset{\overset{\displaystyle O}{\|}}{C}-OH$

B. $-NH_2$

C. $-\overset{\overset{\displaystyle O}{\|}}{C}-R$

D. $-SO_3H$

139. An amino acid is subjected to electrophoresis at pH 8.5 and is observed to migrate to the anode. The isoelectric point of this amino acid

A. is less than 8.5.
B. is more than 8.5.
C. is equal to 8.5.
D. cannot be determined without more information.

140. It is hypothesized that the binding of testosterone to corticosteroid receptors in the hypothalamus of a developing male fetus accounts for the sexual differentiation of the human brain. This binding causes the hypothalamus to switch from cyclic production of gonadotropin-releasing factors (which is characteristic of females) to acyclic production. This switch, therefore, is likely to affect the release patterns of

A. LH.
B. FSH.
C. both LH and FSH.
D. neither LH nor FSH.

GO ON TO THE NEXT PAGE.

Passage VII (Questions 141–144)

Ketones are known to readily react with halogens in the presence of acid or base to form alpha-halogenated products. The overall reaction is shown below:

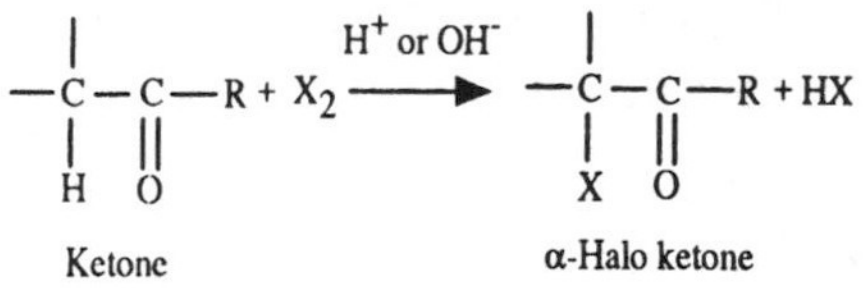

Reaction 1

In basic solution (Figure 1), the hydroxide ion removes a proton from the alpha carbon, yielding a carbanion intermediate (Step 1). Finally, the alpha-halogenated ketone is formed by the addition of a positively polarized bromide to the carbanion (Step 2):

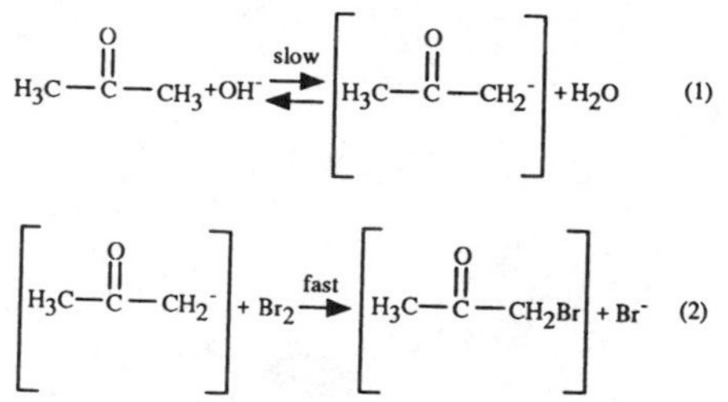

Figure 1

Alpha halogenation under acidic conditions (Figure 2) initially involves protonation of the carbonyl oxygen, resulting in the formation of an enol (Step 2). This molecule then undergoes electrophilic addition to yield another intermediate that can then be deprotonated to form the α-halo ketone (Step 4).

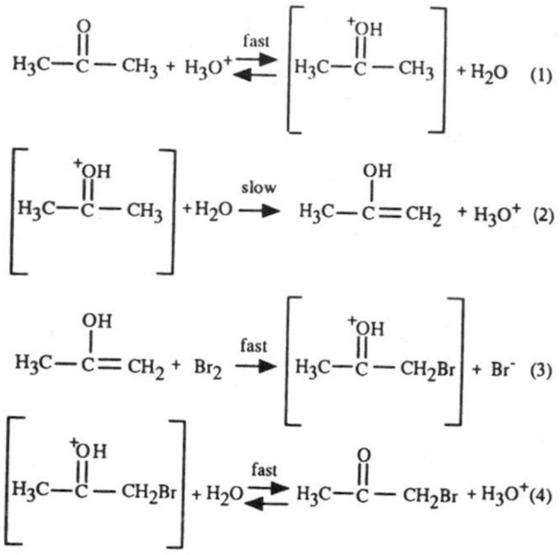

Figure 2

141. What is the function of the hydrogen and hydroxide ions in the acidic and basic solutions, respectively?

A. They both act as catalysts.
B. They are both reactants.
C. The hydrogen ion is a reactant, while the hydroxide ion acts as a catalyst.
D. The hydrogen ion acts as a catalyst, while the hydroxide ion is a reactant.

142. In Figure 2, the first two steps are characteristic of isomerization between which of the following?

I.   Tautomers
II. Enantiomers
III. Geometric isomers

A. I only
B. III only
C. I and II only
D. I, II, and III

GO ON TO THE NEXT PAGE.

143. Alpha halogenation of acetone in basic solution usually results in multiple halogenations on the alpha carbon (known as the Haloform reaction). This reaction occurs because

   A. introduction of the first halogen makes the remaining α-hydrogens more acidic and, therefore, easily removed by the base.
   B. the base is very strong and will easily abstract protons.
   C. α-halo ketones are highly unstable and susceptible to further reaction.
   D. the first halogen stabilizes any carbocations that are formed.

144. From the mechanism drawn in Figure 1, the overall rate of reaction for alpha halogenation is dependent on the concentration of which of the following?

   I. CH_3COCH_3
   II. Br_2
   III. OH^-

   A. I only
   B. II only
   C. I and III only
   D. I, II, and III

STOP.

IF YOU FINISH BEFORE TIME HAS EXPIRED, CHECK YOUR WORK.
YOU MAY GO BACK TO ANY QUESTION IN THIS PART ONLY.

Practice Test 2 Answer Key

Full-Length Practice MCAT

PHYSICAL SCIENCES

1. C	9. A	17. C	25. A	33. B	41. A	49. C
2. D	10. B	18. C	26. B	34. A	42. A	50. D
3. B	11. D	19. A	27. C	35. A	43. A	51. C
4. C	12. B	20. B	28. B	36. B	44. B	52. B
5. A	13. C	21. D	29. D	37. D	45. D	
6. B	14. C	22. A	30. D	38. B	46. C	
7. C	15. C	23. C	31. C	39. C	47. D	
8. D	16. B	24. B	32. B	40. C	48. A	

VERBAL REASONING

53. A	59. C	65. D	71. D	77. D	83. B	89. C
54. C	60. D	66. C	72. C	78. D	84. C	90. A
55. B	61. C	67. A	73. B	79. D	85. C	91. D
56. D	62. D	68. B	74. D	80. C	86. D	92. A
57. B	63. A	69. B	75. D	81. B	87. C	
58. C	64. D	70. B	76. B	82. A	88. C	

BIOLOGICAL SCIENCES

93. D	101. C	109. A	117. C	125. A	133. B	141. D
94. B	102. A	110 B	118. D	126. C	134. B	142. A
95. D	103. B	111. A	119. D	127. C	135. C	143. A
96. C	104. B	112. C	120. A	128. D	136. A	144. C
97. D	105. A	113. C	121. B	129. B	137. D	
98. B	106. C	114. C	122. B	130. A	138. B	
99. A	107. D	115. A	123. D	131. D	139. A	
100. C	108. A	116. A	124. D	132. D	140. C	

Score Conversion Chart

Full-Length Practice MCAT

Physical Science		Verbal Reasoning		Biological Science	
Raw Score*	Estimated Scaled Score*	Raw Score*	Estimated Scaled Score*	Raw Score*	Estimated Scaled Score*
0 to 10	1	0 to 16	1	0 to 13	1
11 to 12	2	17 to 18	2	14 to 16	2
13 to 15	3	19 to 20	3	17 to 19	3
16 to 17	4	21 to 22	4	20 to 22	4
18 to 19	5	23 to 24	5	23 to 25	5
20 to 21	6	25 to 27	6	26 to 28	6
22 to 24	7	28 to 29	7	29 to 31	7
25 to 26	8	30 to 32	8	32 to 34	8
27 to 28	9	33 to 34	9	35 to 37	9
29 to 31	10	35	10	38 to 39	10
32 to 34	11	36	11	40 to 42	11
35 to 36	12	37	12	43 to 45	12
37 to 39	13	38	13	46 to 48	13
40 to 42	14	39	14	49 to 51	14
43 to 52	15	40	15	52	15

*No test or score conversion chart can exactly predict actual Test Day performance.

Answers and Explanations

Physical Sciences

Passage 1 (Questions 1–5)

1. C

To answer this question, you need to use Wien's law, which is given in the passage. It states that $\lambda = 2.9 \times 10^6/T$, where λ is the most intense wavelength emitted in nm and T is the temperature in kelvins. Since the temperature of the sun's photosphere is 5,800 K, the most intense wavelength emitted is given by $\lambda = 2.9 \times 10^6/5,800 = 500$ nm, which is **choice (C)**.

2. D

When an electron makes a transition from a higher energy state to a lower energy state, a photon is emitted with energy equal to the difference between the energies of the two states. The table in the passage provides energies for photon transitions from energy state $n = 2$ to various higher energy states in hydrogen. The absolute energy difference between states $n = 4$ and $n = 3$ is equal to the difference between their energies relative to the $n = 2$ state. Therefore, the energy of the photon emitted in the transition from $n = 4$ to $n = 3$ is $4.08 \times 10^{-19} - 3.02 \times 10^{-19} = 1.06 \times 10^{-19} \times 10^{-19}$J.

The energy of a photon E is given by $E = hc/\lambda$, where h is Planck's constant, c is the speed of light in a vacuum, and λ is the photon's wavelength. Rearranging to solve for λ gives $\lambda = hc/E$. Using $E = 10^{-19}$ J from above, we find

$$\lambda = (6.6 \times 10^{-34})(3 \times 108)/(10^{-19}) \text{ m}$$

Rounding to the nearest integer gives $\lambda = 20 \times 10^{-34 + 8 + 19}$ m $= 2 \times 10^{-6}$ m. Since 1 nm $= 10^{-9}$ m, $\lambda = 2,000$ nm, which is **choice (D)**.

3. B

The binding energy of an electron is by definition the energy required to detach an electron from an atom in its ground state. Hydrogen's ground state is the $n = 1$ state. When the atom is ionized, the electron is separated from the atom and makes a transition to the highest energy state, the $n = \infty$ state. This is not a distinct energy state, but rather it defines the minimum energy that must be transferred to the electron to free it from the atom. Hence, the energy difference between the $n = \infty$ and the $n = 1$ state is the binding energy of the electron in the hydrogen atom, and **choice (B)** is correct.

Choices (A), (C), and (D) can all be ruled out based on the data presented in the passage, which indicate that the energy increases as n increases. This implies that the energy of the $n = 2$ state is greater than that of the $n = 1$ state by some finite, positive amount E_{12}. Furthermore, according to the table, the energy of the $n = \infty$ state is 5.44×10^{-19} J greater than the energy of the $n = 2$ state. Since the energy difference between $n = \infty$ and $n = 1$ is the sum of these two finite, positive quantities ($E_{12} + 5.44 \times 10^{-19}$ J), it must also be finite and positive. Therefore, **choice (A)** is wrong. **Choice (C)** is wrong because a zero frequency photon would correspond to zero energy, as shown by the formula $E = hf$, but as discussed above, the energy absorbed must be positive. **Choice (D)** is wrong because the sum $E_{12} + 5.44 \times 10^{-19}$ J is clearly greater than 5.44×10^{-19} J, the energy absorbed in the $n = 2$ to $n = \infty$ transition.

4. C

This question asks for the frequency f of light given its wavelength λ. If you didn't remember the relationship between the two, you could have figured it out from the formula $hf = hc/\lambda$ given in the passage. Dividing both sides by h, we obtain $f = c/\lambda$, where c is the speed of light in a vacuum. Plugging in $\lambda = 550$ nm, we obtain

$$f = \frac{3 \times 10^8 \, \text{m/s}}{550 \, \text{nm}} = 5 \times 10^{14} \, \text{Hz}$$

which most closely corresponds to **choice (C)**.

5. A

This question asks you to apply Wien's law to the case of a star changing its size and temperature. Wien's law, $\lambda = 2.9 \times 10^6/T$, indicates that the wavelength of the peak intensity depends only on temperature. Therefore, if the star's temperature doesn't change when it doubles in size, the wavelength of the peak intensity of the star's radiation will not change. **Choice (A)** is therefore the correct answer, and **choices (B)** and **(C)** are wrong. Since the shape of the spectrum, like the location of the peak, is also a function of temperature, **choice (D)** is wrong as well.

Passage 11 (Questions 6–12)

6. B

When the half-reactions are written as reductions—as they are here—the cell voltage is determined by the equation

$$E_{cell} = E_{cathode} - E_{anode}$$

(Remember that E_{cell} must be greater than zero for the reaction to be spontaneous.) The cell voltage is therefore 2.05 V:

$$1.69 \text{ V} - (-0.36 \text{ V}) = 2.05 \text{ V}$$

Since the potentials of cells connected in series are additive, a 20 V battery needs ten 2.05 V cells, choice (B). Choice (A) is a 10 V battery, choice (C) is a 30 V battery, and choice (D) is a 40 V battery.

7. C

Oxidation—the loss of electrons—occurs at the anode. When both half-reactions are written as reductions, the following equation is used to determine the cell potential:

$$E_{cell} = E_{cathode} - E_{anode}$$

(Again, remember that E_{cell} must be greater than zero for the reaction to be spontaneous.) The cell potential is positive when the reduction potential of the second reaction in Table 1 is subtracted from the first reaction, making the first reaction the cathode and the second reaction the anode. Since oxidation occurs at the anode, the reaction must proceed to the left, making choice (C) the correct answer.

Choice (A) and choice (B) are wrong because the first reaction is the cathode reaction, not the anode reaction. Choice (D) is wrong because the second reaction proceeds to the left, not to the right.

8. D

Oxidation occurs when a species' oxidation number increases; reduction occurs when a species' oxidation number decreases. Also discussed earlier, oxidation occurs at the anode, and reduction occurs at the cathode. From the answer choices, it can be seen that lead oxide and lead are the only species that have to be investigated. In Reaction 1, Pb^{4+}, in lead oxide, is going to Pb^{2+}, in lead sulfate. Since lead's oxidation number has decreased, it has been reduced. Choice (A), choice (B), and choice (C) can, therefore, all be eliminated, leaving choice (D) as the correct answer. Choice (D) is correct because lead is being reduced at the anode—where oxidation occurs—from Pb to Pb^{2+}.

9. A

The battery is being recharged, so Reaction 1 is proceeding to the left. Since aqueous sulfuric acid, H_2SO_4, is one of the products of recharging, the concentration of H^+ will increase, making choice (A) the correct answer.

Choice (B) is wrong because $PbSO_4(s)$ is serving as a reactant during recharging and is, therefore, consumed during the reaction. Choice (C) is wrong because water is also a reactant during recharging. Choice (D) is wrong because the amount of lead oxide increases, not decreases, as the battery is being recharged.

10. B

As can be seen in Reaction 1, when the lead-acid battery is being discharged, sulfuric acid, a reactant, is being consumed. Since the passage states that sulfuric acid is the electrolyte, the density will decrease as the discharge progresses, so the density at point A is less than that at point B.

Choice (A) is wrong because at point A, there is less electrolyte present, not more. Choice (C) is wrong because the density decreases as the discharge progresses. Choice (D) is wrong because there °is a direct relationship between the density of the electrolyte and the state of discharge.

11. D

Remembering that a $k\Omega$ is 10^3 Ω and using the relationship that $V = IR$, a current of 0.1 A times a resistance of 10,000 Ω gives a voltage of 1,000 V. You might have chosen **choice (B)** if you did not convert kilo-ohms to ohms. **Choices (A)** and **(C)** represent other conversion errors.

12. B

The reason that the battery "goes dead" with decreasing temperature is that the viscosity of the electrolyte increases. At higher viscosities, the ions are moving much slower, which leads to an increase in resistance and a decrease in the power output. Roman numeral I states that the resistance of the electrolyte has decreased. This is not true, the resistance of the electrolyte increases with decreasing temperature. Since **choice (A)**, **choice (C)**, and **choice (D)** all contain Roman numeral I, they can be eliminated, leaving **choice (B)** as the correct answer.

Discrete Questions

13. C

To determine how many neutrons the daughter nucleus has, we'll need to conserve charge and mass number for this decay. Consulting the periodic table, a cobalt nucleus has 27 protons. The electron on the other side of the decay has a proton number of -1. Consequently, the proton number for the daughter nucleus X must be 28: $27 = Z - 1$, $Z = 28$. The mass of the cobalt nucleus is 60, and the mass of an electron is zero; so the mass number for the daughter nucleus must be $A = 60$. Since 28 of the 60 nucleons are protons, the remaining 32 must be neutrons and **choice (B)** is correct.

14. C

A gas can only do work by expanding and pushing. If the gas is compressed, then work is done on it, which is the same as saying that the gas does negative work. Since the gas in this question is contained within a constant volume, it cannot expand, and therefore it does zero work. So **(C)** is correct.

15. C

Each electron shell can be divided into up to four subshells, designated s, p, d, and f. The s subshell contains 1 orbital, the p subshell contains 3, the d subshell contains 5, and the f subshell contains 7. Since each orbital can hold two electrons, the numbers of electrons that can be held by these four subshells are 2, 6, 10, and 14, respectively. So the ratio of f electrons to p electrons in the f subshell is 14 to 6, which is equal to 7 to 3, **choice (C)**.

Passage III (Questions 16–20)

16. B

The question stem states that the voltage source, which according to the passage has negligible internal resistance, is replaced by a battery with a small but significant internal resistance. A battery with significant internal resistance can be modeled as a voltage source connected in series with a resistor. Hence, the new circuit is the same as the one in Figure 1, except for the addition of a second resistor (call its resistance R_{int}) in series with the original resistor (call its resistance R_0). To determine how this additional resistance affects the circuit, use Ohm's law $V = IR$, where V is the voltage, I is the current, and R is the resistance. Solving for I gives $I = V/R$. Thus, in the original circuit, the voltage source supplies a voltage V, and the ammeter measures a current $I_{original} = V/R_0$. In the new circuit, the total resistance is given by the addition rule for resistors in series, $R_{total} = R_0 + R_{int}$. Therefore, the current measured by the ammeter in the new circuit will be $I_{new} = V/(R_0 + R_{int})$, which is clearly smaller than $I_{original}$ since its denominator is larger. So choice (B) is correct, and choice (A) is wrong.

Choices (C) and (D) are wrong because the resistance of a resistor is a property that does not change with the addition of other resistors to the circuit. The resistance of a resistor remains constant when the voltage across it or the current through it changes.

17. C

Like charges repel each other, and opposite charges attract each other. Since electrons have negative charge, they will move away from a negative terminal and move toward a positive terminal. This corresponds to the counterclockwise direction. So choices (A) and (B) can be ruled out.

By convention, current flows in the direction that positive charge would flow. This means that in the circuit in Figure 1, the current flows in the clockwise direction, from the positive terminal to the negative terminal, and choice (C) is the correct answer.

If you couldn't figure out the direction of current flow or the direction that the electrons travel, but you knew they were opposite directions, you could have eliminated choices (B) and (D).

18. C

Ammeters, like all components of electric circuits, have some internal resistance. Therefore, adding an ammeter to the circuit is like adding another resistor in series. If the ammeter has a large resistance, then the current flowing through the resistor will be significantly reduced when it is added to the circuit. If it has a small resistance, the current will be only slightly affected. So choice (C) is correct.

Choice (A) is wrong since insulated wires are wires surrounded by a nonconducting material, which prevents unintended contact with the current. Insulating the wires won't directly affect the current through the resistor and won't affect the way that the ammeter works. Choice (B) is wrong as well: The current in the wire to the right of the resistor is the same as the current to the left of the resistor, so an ammeter will function identically at either location. In both cases, the ammeter is in series with the resistor. You can eliminate choice (D) because although an ammeter that can detect current in either direction might be useful, whether it can or not is unrelated to its effect on the current flowing through the resistor.

19. A

When the electrons collide with the atoms of the resistor, the vibration of the atoms increases, and the atoms' kinetic energy, which is the energy of motion, increases as well. By definition, the temperature of a gas, liquid, or solid is a measure of the average kinetic energy of the atoms that make up the substance. Thus, the increase in the kinetic energy of the atoms is directly related to the increase in temperature, and **choice (A)** is correct.

Since temperature is related to the average kinetic energy and not the potential energy, **choices (B)** and **(D)** are wrong. As for **choice (C)**, the passage states that the atoms vibrate as a result of the collisions. A moving electron hits an atom, which is basically stationary, and starts it in motion. This means that the electron transfers some of its kinetic energy to the atom. So the electron's kinetic energy actually decreases as a result of the collisions, and **choice (C)** is wrong.

20. B

The energy delivered to a piece of toast must be equal to the energy dissipated by the toaster's resistor. The rate of energy dissipation, or the energy released per unit time, is known as the power. Mathematically, this can be expressed as $P = E/t$, where P is the power and E is the energy released in time t. The passage gives the relation $P = I^2 R$, where P is the power, I is the current, and R is the resistance of the resistor. Equating the two expressions for power and solving for E gives $E = I^2 R t$. Now we substitute the values given in the question stem into the last equation for the energy and obtain

$$E = (4 \times 10^{-3} \text{ A})^2 (10 \times 10^3 \Omega) (1 \text{ s}) = 0.16 \text{ J}$$

which is **choice (B)**. As is often the case with questions involving calculations, the wrong answer choices are the results of math errors. For example, you would have obtained **choice (D)** if you forgot to square the current.

Passage IV (Questions 21–26)

21. D

If the pH of blood increases to 7.6, it becomes more alkaline, and the pH of blood must be kept at approximately pH 7.4. Since the second sentence of the last paragraph states that blood pH can be adjusted rapidly by changes in the rate of CO_2 exhalation, **choice (A)** and **choice (B)** can be eliminated. To bring the pH of blood back to its normal value of 7.4, it must become more acidic; it becomes more acidic by increasing the concentration of H^+. Reaction 1 has H^+ as a product, and according to Le Châtelier's principle, you should know that a reaction will proceed in a direction that will consume an added reactant or product. In other words, the concentration of a product can be increased by increasing the concentration of a reactant. If the concentration of carbon dioxide is allowed to increase, it will react to produce more H^+, resulting in a lowering of the pH. The concentration of carbon dioxide will increase if it is not exhaled, making **choice (D)** the correct response.

22. A

Carbonic acid, H_2CO_3, is the intermediate formed when carbon dioxide and water combine, making **choice (A)** the correct response. You should be able to recognize that when the products of Reaction 1 combine, carbonic acid will result.

Choice (B) is incorrect because it is just not a logical intermediate: Water and carbon dioxide would not react to form H^+ and CO_3^{2-}. **Choices (C)** and **(D)** can be eliminated because they both contain carbon dioxide, which is one of the two reactants.

23. C

You should know that the smaller the pK_a, the stronger the acid. Looking at Table 1, it can be seen that the histidine side chains buffer has a stronger conjugate acid than both the organic phosphates buffer and the ammonium buffer. **Choice (C)** is therefore the correct response.

Choice (A) is wrong because the pK_a of the histidine side chains buffer is not equal to the organic phosphates buffer. **Choice (B)** is wrong because it is the reverse of what it should be. **Choice (D)** is wrong because, again, the pK_a of the histidine side chains buffer is not equal to the organic phosphates buffer.

24. B

In Region I, the following reaction takes place:

$$H_3PO_4(aq) + OH^-(aq) \rightarrow H_2PO_4^-(aq) + H_2O$$

As OH^- is added, $H_2PO_4^-$ is formed, and a buffer is realized. So in this region, there is a point where the concentration of H_3PO_4 will equal that of $H_2PO_4^-$. In Region II, there is a point where exactly enough base has been added to react with all of the H_3PO_4; this point is called an equivalence point. In Region III, the following reaction takes place:

$$H_2PO_4^-(aq) + OH^-(aq) \rightarrow HPO_4^{2-}(aq) + H_2O$$

Again, this system constitutes a buffer, and there is a point in this region where—after enough base has been added—the concentration of $H_2PO_4^-$ will equal that of HPO_4^{2-}. **Choice (B)** is therefore the correct response. In Region IV, there is another equivalence point when exactly enough base has been added to react with all of the $H_2PO_4^{-}$. In Region V the following reaction takes place:

$$HPO_4^{2-}(aq) + OH^-(aq) \rightarrow PO_4^{3-}(aq) + H_2O$$

This system is, of course, a buffer as well.

25. A

When a weak acid is reacted with a strong base, the equivalence point will be in the basic region. Consider the titration of equimolar solutions of acetic acid and NaOH. Before the equivalence point, the following reaction takes place:

$$HC_2H_3O_2(aq) + OH^-(aq) \rightarrow H_2O + C_2H_3O_2^-(aq)$$

At the equivalence point, only $C_2H_3O_2^-$ exists. When $C_2H_3O_2^-$ undergoes hydrolysis (i.e., reacts with water), hydroxide ions are formed according to the following equilibrium:

$$C_2H_3O_2^-(aq) + H_2O \rightleftharpoons HC_2H_3O_2(aq) + OH^-(aq)$$

The numerical value of the equilibrium constant along with the initial concentration of acetate is all that is needed to determine the hydroxide ion concentration. When equimolar solutions of a strong acid and a strong base are titrated, the equivalence point will be neutral. It is neutral because neither of the ions present at the equivalence point can undergo hydrolysis. **Choice (A)** is therefore the correct response. **Choice (B)** would be correct if a weak base was titrated with a strong acid.

26. B

As the passage states, the immediate buffering effect of bicarbonate is controlled by changes in the breathing rate. When acidosis occurs, the concentration of H^+ is too high. As discussed earlier, Le Châtelier's principle applies: To decrease the concentration of H^+, the concentration of carbon dioxide must decrease. If the breathing rate increases, more carbon dioxide is exhaled, and its concentration in the blood decreases. Since the effect of this rapid breathing is to remove carbon dioxide from the body, the ultimate effect is to decrease the total CO_2/HCO_3^- concentration in the blood. Therefore **choice (B)** is correct.

Choice (A) is wrong because the ratio of CO_2 to HCO_3^- would decrease, not increase. **Choices (C)** and **(D)** are wrong because the breathing rate would increase, not decrease.

Discrete Questions

27. C

Since rotation about a point is at issue, an understanding of torques is necessary to solve the problem. The torque τ, or rotational force on a rigid body resting on a pivot point, is given by $\tau = rF$, when a force F acts at a distance r from the pivot in a direction perpendicular to the axis of rotation. Balance is achieved when the net torque is zero (i.e., the clockwise torque equals the counterclockwise torque).

Draw a little sketch of the telephone handset, balanced horizontally on a pivot point. The weight of the mouthpiece is (100 grams)g, where g is the acceleration due to gravity. Call the distance between the point where this force acts and the pivot r_m. Similarly, the weight of the earpiece is (150 grams)g and acts a distance r_e from the pivot. To achieve balance, the opposing torques must be equal to each other, so (100 grams) gr_m = (150 grams)gr_e. Solving for r_m and canceling out g gives $r_m = (3/2)r_e$. So the mouthpiece must be (3/2) times farther from the pivot than the earpiece, and **choice (C)** is correct.

28. B

The relationship between ΔG, ΔH, ΔS, and temperature is

$$\Delta G = \Delta H - T\Delta S$$

For a reaction to be spontaneous, ΔG must be less than zero. If a reaction is not spontaneous at any temperature, ΔH must be positive, and ΔS must be negative. No matter what the temperature, ΔG will always be positive, and the reaction will be nonspontaneous. **Choice (B)** is, therefore, the correct response.

Choice (A) is for a reaction that would be spontaneous if the temperature is sufficiently high. **Choice (C)** is for a reaction that is spontaneous at *all* temperatures. **Choice (D)** is for a reaction that would be spontaneous if the temperature is sufficiently low.

29. D

To achieve boiling, intermolecular forces holding the liquid together have to be overcome so that the molecules of the substance can enter the vapor phase. Boiling points of substances, therefore, often reflect the strength of the intermolecular forces operating among the molecules. **Choice (D)** is correct because the intermolecular hydrogen–oxygen bonds in water are stronger than the intermolecular hydrogen–sulfur bonds in hydrogen sulfide. When hydrogen is bonded to a strongly electronegative element, such as nitrogen, oxygen, or fluorine, very strong intermolecular forces exist. These forces are called hydrogen bonds.

Choice (A) is wrong because, although it is true that intramolecular oxygen–hydrogen bonds are stronger than intramolecular sulfur–hydrogen bonds, this is not the reason that water boils at a higher temperature than hydrogen sulfide. **Choice (B)** is wrong because if the enthalpy of vaporization of water is less than that of hydrogen sulfide, less energy is required to evaporate a given quantity of water at a constant temperature than for hydrogen sulfide. This is not what happens: The heat of vaporization of water is greater than that of hydrogen sulfide, so water boils at a higher temperature. **Choice (C)** is wrong because it is the ability of water to hydrogen-bond that makes it boil at a higher temperature.

30. D

A semipermeable membrane allows the movement of solvent molecules but not solute molecules. This means that water molecules can move through the semipermeable membrane and that glucose molecules cannot. **Choice (A), choice (B)**, and **choice (C)** can all be eliminated, leaving **choice (D)** as the correct response. You should be aware that osmosis is the net movement of solvent molecules through a semipermeable membrane from a pure solvent or a dilute solution to a more concentrated solution. In this case, solution A, which is 5 percent glucose, is more concentrated than solution B, which is only 1 percent glucose. So there will be a movement from the more dilute solution, solution B, to one of higher concentration, which is solution A.

31. C

Normality is defined as the number of equivalents of solute per liter of solution. An equivalent of an acid is the amount of acid required to give 1 mole of H^+. Phosphoric acid, which contains 3 moles of protons per mole of acid, therefore contains 3 equivalents per mole. A one-molar solution of phosphoric acid is said to be 3 normal. The solution in question contains 49 grams of phosphoric acid, and the molar mass of phosphoric acid is 98. Since 49 is half of 98, the amount of phosphoric acid in this sample is half of the 3 equivalents in each mole of the acid. So there are 1.5 equivalents of phosphoric acid in this solution. We know the total volume of the solution is 2,000 milliliters, or 2 liters. So this solution contains 1.5 equivalents of acid per 2 liters. This comes to 0.75 equivalents per liter, which is a 0.75 N solution.

Passage V (Questions 32–36)

32. B

This question is a straightforward application of the equation given in the passage, $E = 1{,}240/\lambda$. In this equation, E is the energy in electron-volts of a photon having a wavelength λ in nanometers. Note that this formula is a variant of the more familiar equation $E = hc/\lambda$. Plugging in $\lambda = 632.8$ nm, we obtain $E = 1{,}240/632.8 = 2.0$ eV, which is closest to **choice (B)**. It is a good idea to save time by estimating because the answer choices are relatively far apart.

33. B

To answer this question, you have to refer to the passage to find the description of the condition called a population inversion. The passage states that a population inversion exists when the percentage of neon atoms with electrons in the 20.66 eV energy level is greater than the percentage of neon atoms with electrons in lower levels. The distinctive characteristic of this distribution is that the percentage of atoms with electrons in a higher energy level is greater than the percentage of atoms with electrons in lower levels. Only **choice (B)** is consistent with this information.

34. A

To solve this problem, apply the law of conservation of energy to atomic systems. In the absence of dissipative forces, the total energy of a system, which is the sum of the kinetic and potential energies, is conserved. In the case of atoms, the potential energy is the energy stored when the electron moves to a higher energy state by absorbing a photon.

In the collision between the helium and neon atoms, the helium atom loses 20.61 eV of potential energy because its electron returns to the ground state, and the neon atom gains 20.66 eV of potential energy. Since energy is conserved, the helium atom must have lost some kinetic energy as well. The neon atom cannot gain more energy than the helium atom loses. Therefore, the minimum amount of kinetic energy that the helium atom must lose is equal to the difference between the two potential energies. This is equal to $20.66 - 20.61 = 0.05$ eV, which is **choice (A)**. If the helium atom loses only this amount of kinetic energy, then the neon atom's kinetic energy will not change during the collision. If the helium atom loses more than 0.05 eV, then the neon atom's kinetic energy will increase.

35. A

The power of the laser is 6.2×10^{15} eV/s, which means that the laser produces 6.2×10^{15} eV of energy each second. This energy takes the form of photon energy. To solve for the number of photons produced per second, figure out how many photons correspond to an energy of 6.2×10^{15} eV. The formula given in the passage states that the energy (in eV) of one photon is given by $E = 1{,}240/\lambda$, where λ is the photon's wavelength in nm. Hence, the energy of n photons must given by $n(1{,}240/\lambda)$. Setting this expression equal to 6.2×10^{15} eV and solving for n, we obtain $n = \lambda(6.2 \times 10^{15}/1{,}240)$. The question stem states that for this laser, $\lambda = 200$ nm. Substituting in, we calculate $n = 200(6.2 \times 10^{15}/1{,}240) = 1.0 \times 10^{15}$, which is **choice (A)**.

36. B

To answer this question, you have to figure out the difference between stimulated and spontaneous emission. The passage states that a photon is emitted in a random direction when an atom spontaneously decays. This process is called spontaneous emission. It also states that a photon can stimulate an electron transition in an atom. The photon that is emitted in this process, called stimulated emission, travels in the same direction as the stimulating photon. Therefore, spontaneous emission produces photons that travel in random directions, whereas stimulated emission produces photons that travel in the same direction as the stimulating photon. A coherent beam of light consists of photons travelling in the same direction.

Choices (A) and (C) are wrong because, as stated in the third paragraph, the photon produced by spontaneous emission causes stimulated emission by inducing the *same* electron transition in another excited atom. Since the electron transition is the same, the photon energy released by the transition is the same, and the photon wavelengths must be the same because energy and wavelength are related by the formula $E = 1,240/\lambda$.

Choice (D) is incorrect because stimulated emission is necessary to obtain a large number of photons traveling in the same direction.

Discrete Questions

37. D

Archimedes's principle states that the buoyant force exerted by a fluid on a submerged object is equal to the weight of the fluid displaced. In this case, the submerged object is the research module, and the fluid is ocean water. Mathematically, the buoyant force is given by $F = m_w g$, where m_w is the mass of the water and g is the acceleration due to gravity. Since we are not given the mass of the water displaced, we express it as $m_w = \rho_w V_w$, where ρ_w is the density of the water and V_w is the volume of the water displaced. But the volume of the water displaced is identical to the volume of the submerged module, V_0. Hence, $m_w = \rho_w V_w = \rho_w V_0$, and $F = m_w g = \rho_w V_0 g$. Since the answer choices are far apart, we round off the values given in the question and calculate:

$$F = \rho_w V_0 g \approx (1,000 \text{ kg/m}^3)(150 \text{ m}^3)(10 \text{ m/s}^2) = 1.5 \times 10^6 \text{ N}$$

This is **choice (D)**. Note that no conversions are necessary since all the values are given in SI units.

38. B

To solve this problem, apply Hooke's law, $F = kx$, where F is the force applied to the spring, x is the distance the spring stretches, and k is the spring constant. The forces applied in this case are weights. Since weight is proportional to mass, the distance the spring stretches is also proportional to the mass of the object attached to the spring.

The spring starts out with a length of 64 cm. When the 0.5 kg mass is attached, it stretches 8 percent longer, or $64(0.08) = 5.12$ cm. Since the distance stretched and the mass attached are proportional, the ratio of the distance stretched to the mass attached is (5.12 cm)/(0.5 kg) $\approx 5/(0.5) = 10$ cm/kg. In other words, each kilogram attached to the spring stretches it 10 cm. Thus, when the 0.4 kg mass is attached, the spring is stretched a distance $(0.4 \text{ kg})(10 \text{ cm/kg}) = 4$ cm. Therefore, the total length of the spring is its original length plus the distance it stretches, or $64 + 4 = 68$ cm. This is **choice (B)**.

39. C

The electrostatic force between two charged particles is given by $F = kq_1q_2/r^2$, where k is a constant, q_1 and q_2 are the charges on the particles, and r is the distance between the two charges. Since the force is proportional to each of the charges, halving the charge on one of the particles will also halve the force, and **choice (C)** is correct.

Halving the charge on both particles will reduce the force by one-fourth, so **choice (B)** is wrong. Since the force is inversely proportional to the square of the distance, doubling the distance will reduce the force by one-fourth, and **choice (A)** is wrong. Watch out for **choice (D)**. It is wrong because the presence of a third charge will not change the force of attraction between the first and second charges. The third charge, however, will change the net force on the first and second charges because it interacts with each separately.

40. C

The combustion is performed in a heavy canister. When the gaseous products are made, they create additional pressure inside the container, so the pressure is not constant. A crucial measurement of bomb calorimetry is the temperature rise, so the temperature is not constant during the process. The number of moles of substances usually changes during any chemical reaction; therefore, the amount of material is not defined to be constant. The only parameter that is essentially constant is the volume inside the bomb, so **choice (C)** is the best answer.

41. A

The alkaline earth elements are those in the second column from the left of the periodic table. The first two columns of the periodic table are the s-block elements, so their valence electrons are in the s subshell. The alkaline earth elements have two valence electrons and therefore, a complete s subshell in their outer electron shell. They lose these two electrons to gain a valence number of +2. Anyway, all of these valence electron properties aside, the correct answer to the question is the s orbital, **choice (A)**.

Passage VI (Questions 42–46)

42. A

The velocity of the softball is a vector, which means that it has both a magnitude and direction. At Point A, the velocity vector points up and to the right, because the softball is traveling in this direction. At Point C, however, the velocity vector points down and to the right. Since the velocity's direction has changed, it is not the same at Points A and C, and **choice (A)** is correct.

You should know that the gravitational potential energy of the softball is given by $U = mgy$, where m is the mass, g is the acceleration due to gravity, and y is the height above the earth. Since Points A and C are at the same height y, the gravitational potential is the same, and **choice (C)** is incorrect.

The passage says to ignore air resistance, so the total mechanical energy, which is the kinetic plus potential energy, is conserved in this system. Since the gravitational potential is the same at Points A and C, the kinetic energy $(1/2)\, mv^2$ must be the same as well. Because the mass m does not change, the speed v must be the same at both points also, and **choice (B)** is wrong.

Since air resistance is negligible, the only force present is that of gravity, which acts in the vertical direction. Consequently, there is no horizontal force on the softball, which means there can be no horizontal acceleration. Therefore, the horizontal component of the velocity must remain the same throughout the softball's flight, and **choice (D)** is wrong.

43. A

Newton's second law, $F = ma$, states that a force produces an acceleration in the same direction as the force. In the absence of a force, there is no acceleration. In this situation, the only force present is the force of gravity, which is the same at all times during the softball's flight. Near the earth's surface, the gravitational force is directed downward, and its magnitude is given by $F = mg$, where m is the softball's mass and g is the acceleration due to gravity. Putting the gravitational force into Newton's second law, we obtain $ma = mg$. Canceling the masses, we obtain $a = g$. In other words, the acceleration of the softball is the same as the acceleration due to gravity.

Figure 1 shows that the unit vector **j** points upward, which means that –**j** points downward. Because **j** is a unit vector, its magnitude is 1. Since the softball accelerates downward with a magnitude of g, the acceleration is symbolically given by $g(-\mathbf{j}) = -g\mathbf{j}$. Thus, **choice (A)** is correct.

Choice (C) is incorrect because it has the wrong magnitude. **Choices (B)** and **(D)** are wrong because they both include an acceleration in the horizontal direction –**i**.

44. B

You should know that the change in momentum of a body is equal to the impulse applied to that body. The magnitude of the momentum of a body is given by mv, where m is its mass and v is its speed. In this situation, an impulse is applied to the softball to launch it from the cannon. Before the impulse, the speed of the softball is zero, so we can write $J = \Delta(mv) = mv_0 - m(0) = mv_0$, where J is the impulse. Solving for v_0, we obtain $v_0 = J/m$. Since m is inversely proportional to v_0, doubling the mass will halve v_0, so **choice (B)** is correct.

45. D

Figure 2 shows that the curve is symmetric around $t = t_b$. Since the axes of graphs are always linear unless otherwise stated, the time elapsed at Point C is twice the time elapsed at Point B. There are no horizontal forces because air resistance is negligible. Therefore, the horizontal speed is the constant v_0 throughout the softball's flight. The horizontal distance traveled is then given by $x = v_0 t$, where t is the time elapsed. Since the time elapsed at Point C is twice the time elapsed at Point B, the horizontal distance traveled at Point C is twice the horizontal distance traveled at Point B, and **choice (D)** is correct.

46. C

The softball starts off at rest and acquires a speed v_0 as it is launched from the cannon. The work-energy theorem states that the work done equals the change in the kinetic energy. Since the softball acquires a kinetic energy equal to $(1/2)mv_0^2$, the automatic pitcher must have done work on it. The pitcher uses air pressure, which builds up behind a disk, to do the work when the disk is released. The angle of the barrel to the horizontal will not affect this mechanism, and the softball will still be ejected with the same kinetic energy. Hence, the work done by the pitcher does not change.

Although it is true that the softball's maximum height increases and that the distance it lands from the cannon decreases, the work done by the pitcher does not change, so **choices (A)** and **(B)** are wrong. Although it is also true that gravity is a conservative force, it is irrelevant because the question asks about the work done by the pitcher, not the work done by gravity. Hence, **choice (D)** is incorrect as well.

Passage VII (Questions 47-52)

47. D

You should know that helium, a noble gas, is very unreactive and would almost certainly not react with any of the species in the furnace. Because the helium does not react with any of the species that participate in the equilibrium, the equilibrium is unaffected by the addition of helium. Even though it increases the total pressure inside the system, the partial pressures of the reacting gases are unchanged (Dalton's law), and, therefore, they keep on behaving as if the helium weren't present. The correct selection is **choice (D)**.

48. A

The entropy of a reaction is a measure of the disorder of the system. The sign of the value of the entropy indicates whether the products of a reaction are more or less disordered than the reactants. A reaction that experiences an increase in disorder in going from reactants to products would have a positive ΔS for the reaction. Similarly, a reaction that decreases its disorder would have a negative ΔS for the reaction. In this reaction, 1 mole of carbon dioxide, a gas, reacts with 1 mole of solid carbon to give 2 moles of carbon monoxide gas. Since there are more moles of gas in the products than in the reactants, there is an increase in entropy, meaning that the sign of the change is positive.

49. C

The carbon dioxide molecule has a central carbon bonded to two oxygen atoms: Carbon shares two electrons with each oxygen, and each oxygen shares two electrons with carbon. As a result of this sharing pattern, two double bonds are formed. You should know that a double bond consists of one sigma bond and one pi bond. Since there are two double bonds, there are two pi bonds, making **choice (C)** correct.

50. D

You should know the relationship $\Delta G = \Delta H - T\Delta S$. ΔS for this reaction is positive, because there are more moles of gaseous products than reactants, but there is no information about the sign of ΔH. Since ΔH cannot be determined, neither can ΔG.

Choice (A) is wrong (that is, the statement is certainly true) because, as was just stated, the entropy change is positive. **Choice (B)** is wrong because, according to Le Châtelier's principle, a decrease in pressure will favor the side of the reaction with more moles of gas. In this case, it is the products side, and the equilibrium is said to have shifted to the right. **Choice (C)** is wrong because, again according to Le Châtelier's principle, addition of a product will shift the equilibrium to the left; that is, the reactants side.

51. C

The first thing that should be done is to determine which choices have the proper number of valence electrons. Carbon monoxide must have a total of 10 electrons: 6 from the oxygen and 4 from the carbon. **Choice (B)** and **choice (D)** can be eliminated because they both have 12 electrons. In **choice (A)**, the carbon has one pair of unbonded electrons, plus 4 more electrons in the double bond. This gives the carbon a total of only 6 electrons in its valence shell, so the carbon doesn't have a complete octet, and **choice (A)** must be wrong.

Choice (C) shows the correct Lewis structure for carbon monoxide: Each atom has a complete octet, and there are a total of 10 electrons.

52. B

P_e, as the table explains, is the expected pressure at each temperature if no reaction had taken place. When the carbon dioxide is introduced into the furnace chamber, it is at a pressure of 1 atmosphere and a temperature of 298 K. Above 298 K, P_e is greater than 1 atmosphere because, at constant volume, the pressure increases as the temperature increases. Since P_e is the pressure if no reaction had taken place, any change in the number of moles of gas present does not have to be considered. Since the pressure of a gas is directly proportional to its temperature in Kelvins, the ratio of the *expected* pressure to the original pressure of 1 atmosphere must be equal to the ratio of the temperature of the trial to the original temperature of 298 K. The equation is as follows:

$$P_e / (1 \text{ atm}) = T/298$$

Solving for P_e yields answer **choice (B)**.

Verbal Reasoning

Passage 1 (Questions 53–58)

53. A

This question asks you for the author's working definition of *nihilism*.

The definition that reflects the author's own thinking is provided in the second and third sentences of paragraph 1. The author says there that nihilism is a complex intellectual stance whose essence is systematic negation of perceptual orders and assumptions.

Remember that the author's definition is not the same as the usual definition of nihilism, a form of extremist political thought, so **(C)** is not correct. **Choice (B)** defines the essence of mysticism, not nihilism. **Choice (D)** is too narrow, being an aspect of political nihilism derived purely from skepticism.

54. C

Statement I is true. There are three quotations used in the passage, two by Stanley Rosen in the second and fourth paragraphs and one by Novak in paragraph 3. Rosen's first quote, at the end of paragraph 2, summarizes Hume's argument, and Rosen's second quote sums up what the author wants to say about the political nihilism of the Russian intelligentsia. Statement I will, therefore, be part of the correct answer; this eliminates **choice (D)**.

Statement II is false because the author never presents any contrasting points of view in the passage. This rules out **choice (B)**.

Statement III, on the other hand, is true. In the opening sentence of paragraph 4, the author refers to the quote from Novak in the previous paragraph to make the transition from the discussion of mysticism to the larger point about how skepticism and mysticism paved the way for nihilism. Since Statements I and III are true, **choice (C)** is correct.

55. B

In the beginning of the last paragraph, the author says that Novak's quote "points to the way [the] philosophical and mystical traditions prepared the ground for the political nihilism of the 19th and 20th centuries." Correct **choice (B)** paraphrases this statement.

Although Novak does characterize St. John's doctrine, this is not why his interpretation is important to the author's argument, so (A) is wrong. Novak does not draw a parallel between Humean skepticism and Christian mysticism, which rules out **choice (C)**, nor does he say that St. John's teachings were influential, so (D) is wrong as well.

56. D

You have to pick the choice that is a technique *not* used by the author to develop his thesis. The best approach to this type of question is simply to go through the choices one by one.

The author discusses David Hume as a representative of skepticism and St. John of the Cross as a representative of mysticism, so **choice (A)** is not the answer. (B) is out, too; the author contrasts the common definition of *nihilism* with his own definition in the first three sentences of the passage. Also in the first paragraph, the author states that skepticism and mysticism are "united by their categorical rejection of the known"; this identification of the common element in the two traditions is **choice (C)**. Eliminating these three choices leaves us with **choice (D)** as the correct answer. The author never examines the practical consequences of any social doctrine, let alone those of nihilism.

57. B

The author uses Rosen's quote to support his own thesis that the Russian political nihilists combined radical skepticism and the rejection of existing institutions with a faith in the power of a new beginning: "their desire to destroy becomes a revolutionary affirmation." The quote confirms that nihilism is more than just the desire to reject or destroy society.

Neither the author nor Rosen suggests that the nihilists were impractical, so (A) is wrong. (C) can't be correct because the author never speaks of nihilism as a doctrine that is currently "alive." **Choice (D)** suggests that the fusion of the skeptical and mystical traditions in nihilism is weighed more heavily toward skepticism than toward mysticism, but the author never says anything to this effect, so it can be eliminated as well.

58. C

You are looking for a choice that follows logically from the flow of the author's argument, so you can bet that the right answer will somehow refer to the counterculture movement of the 1960s that is mentioned in the passage's final sentence.

Choice (A) suggests that the negative effects of nihilism are still being felt, but the author never hints that any form of nihilism had a negative effect on anything. The nihilistic element of the counterculture movement is not new and different from classical nihilism, so (B) is wrong. **Choice (C)** would conclude the passage by commenting further on the nihilism of the 1960s revolutionaries—this is more like what you're looking for. A quick look at **choice (D)** confirms that **choice (C)** is the best answer. Since the author has obviously been studying nihilism, he isn't going to say that the study of nihilism belongs to the past but not the present.

Passage 11 (Questions 59-64)

59. C

The reason for the stability of these hierarchies is revealed in the final sentence of paragraph 2; hierarchies are rarely threatened by disputes because the inferior animal immediately submits when confronted by a superior. Correct **choice (C)** paraphrases this assertion.

Choice (A) doesn't make any sense; even if the behavior responses of the group (whatever those behavior responses are supposed to be) are known by all of the members, this won't automatically make the hierarchy stable. The author never says that the defensive threat posture stops most conflicts (**choice (B)**) or that conspecific aggression is inhibited by the need for protection from other species (**choice (D)**).

60. D

The defensive threat response is discussed primarily in paragraph 4. An increase in cardiovascular activity (**choice (A)**), narrowing of the eyes (**choice (B)**), and stomach muscle contraction (**choice (C)**) are all mentioned in the paragraph as being part of the defensive threat response. However, the author never says that one of these is more significant than the others, so **choice (D)** is correct.

61. C

The entire passage is about agonistic, or aggressive, behavior, so you need to rely on your memory or passage map of the topics of different paragraphs if you want to go back and verify the statements in this Roman numeral question.

Statement I is taken practically verbatim from the final sentence of paragraph 1. Since the statement is true, you can eliminate **choice (B)**. Statement II paraphrases the entire final paragraph, so it is true as well, and **choice (A)** has to be ruled out. Statement III, on the other hand, is not supported by anything in the passage; all you know from the second paragraph is that both conspecific and interspecies aggression exist. **Choice (C)** is the correct answer.

62. D

This question centers on the nature-versus-nurture argument discussed in the final paragraph. Keep the author's conclusion—that aggressive patterns are both innate and learned—in mind when you're looking for the right choice.

The author's conclusion allows you to rule out **choice (C)** immediately, since it is clear that scientists have not resolved the question in favor of genetics. The only thing the passage says is controversial is the definition of *aggression*, so **choice (A)** is wrong. **Choice (B)** is out because the author never says that the experiments on mice were the first investigations done to answer the nature-nurture question. This leaves **choice (D)** as the only possible correct answer, and it seems reasonable to infer from the author's remark, "copious evidence suggests that animals learn and practice aggressive behavior," that a lot of study has been devoted to this subject.

63. A

Scan the choices and eliminate the ones that look familiar. **Choice (B)**, the evolutionary purpose of aggression, is explicitly addressed in the final sentence of paragraph 1. Conspecific aggression occurring in dominance hierarchies, **choice (C)**, is discussed in paragraph 2. The relationship between play and aggression, **choice (D)**, is mentioned in the final two sentences of the passage. **Choice (A)** seems to be the winner by the process of elimination. Indeed, the physiological changes that accompany aggressive behavior were discussed in detail only with respect to defensive threat response and not with respect to attack behavior in cats.

64. D

You already know a considerable amount from the passage about aggressive behavior in animals; you just have to decide which new assertion fits in with what you already know.

The author doesn't say anything about a link between aggressive behavior and breathing (the reason a shark has to stay in motion), so **choice (A)** is out. The inability of newborn mice to exhibit the attack response is *not* proof that aggressive behavior must be learned, as **choice (B)** claims. On the contrary, mice attack after only a month, too short a time to have learned this behavior, which is why the author cites this as evidence that aggressive behavior is partially genetic. **Choice (C)** is wrong because the author never discusses animal species that don't exhibit aggressive behavior.

That leaves **choice (D)**, which says that certain hawks use the same means of attack on both squirrels and gophers. This fits right in with the facts of the passage, since the second sentence of paragraph 3 states that the physiological and behavioral patterns that make up aggressive behavior change very little regardless of the stimuli that provoke them (the stimuli here being the squirrels and the gophers).

Passage III (Questions 65–70)

65. D

This question asks you why a piece of information was included in the passage. Why was the word *Gypsy* discussed at some length? Examples are generally included to further illustrate a main point, which in this case is that the history of the Romani people is little understood by outsiders.

Choice (A) takes details outside their context, details used to explain the origin of the word *Gypsy* rather than the other way around. Choice (B) involves information that was never mentioned in the passage. Choice (C) distorts information from paragraph 4, one of the hypotheses about Romani migratory patterns, and takes it as truth. Even if the detail were uncontested, however, it still would not relate to why the word *Gypsy* was highlighted in the last paragraph. Choice (D) gives us exactly the explanation we are seeking.

66. C

This question requires you to locate the relevant details within the passage. Paragraph 2 discusses what is known about the Romani migration, and there Armenia is explicitly mentioned, eliminating choice (A). The phrase "throughout Europe" clearly implies that the Romani also migrated to France, so choice (B) is also out. China is never mentioned in the passage at all, so choice (C) is the correct answer.

67. A

The word *support* means that the answer should strengthen the argument. The fourth paragraph deals with the fundamental dissimilarities among the three branches of Romani.

Choice (A) is a good choice because the ninth century is when the Romani began to leave India, according to paragraph 2. If the two branches were distinct that early, it supports the idea that the Romani were already distinct groups that far back and less likely to be migrating as a single group. **Choice (B)** is irrelevant; differences in meaning within Persian have no bearing on Romani. The 13th-century date mentioned in **choice (C)** is too late to be relevant to the migrations, which are dated in the ninth, tenth, and 11th centuries in paragraphs 2 and 3. Nothing in the passage suggests that all Romani left India in the migrations, so **choice (D)** adds nothing.

68. B

The passage deals entirely with linguistic evidence. **Choice (B)** refers to the Romani language and Bengali, one of the languages listed as "Sanskrit-based." So this would be a likely source of further data on the relationships between these language groups.

The *zingari*, **choice (A)**, are mentioned once, in paragraph 6, in the context of the possible origin of the word *Gypsy*—not in reference to the competing migration theories. Nor does the passage suggest that religious beliefs or differences are relevant. The passage never discusses evidence from painting or cuisine, so **choices (C) and (D)** are out.

69. B

To answer this question, you should research paragraph 3, which reviews the evidence supporting the single migration theory. There, the similarities between Romani and Sanskrit languages such as Hindi are cited as evidence that these languages developed in synchronicity until the late 11th century and then diverged during the single migration. The correct answer, **choice (B)**, throws this evidence into doubt, thus weakening the single migration theory. The other choices would have no effect on the argument as presented in the third paragraph.

70. B

The entire passage refers to the many ways outsiders disagree with each other over the history and origins of the Romani, so **choice (B)** is correct.

Choices (A) and (D) are contrary to all the evidence given; clearly the author wouldn't make such a statement only to contradict it with the ensuing argument. **Choice (C)** is wrong because the many linguistic debates discussed—everything from the competing migration theories to the debate over the origin of the word *Gypsy*—clearly support the statement.

Passage IV (Questions 71–77)

71. D

The reason that the author refers to Febvre and Bloch is explained in the parentheses at the end of paragraph 1. The author states that Febvre and Bloch had anticipated Braudel by originating the historical approach that emphasized economics.

Choice (A) is out because the limitations of the *Annales* approach are not discussed until the end of the passage. The relevance of economics to history has already been suggested by the time the author mentions Febvre and Bloch, so choice (B) is wrong. choice (C) is incorrect because the need for combining various sociological approaches is not debated in the first paragraph or anywhere else.

72. C

Nationalism is never mentioned in the passage. All the other choices are aspects of Braudel's approach to history. Choice (A) is mentioned in paragraph 1. Paragraph 3 explains that Braudel ignored national boundaries in favor of geographical features in his work on the Mediterranean (choice (B)). In the same paragraph, you find out that unchanging aspects of everyday life (choice (D)) were what the French historian studied most closely.

73. B

The right answer has to cover the entire paragraph; beware of choices that are just details from the paragraph in question (in this case the third paragraph), like choice (C). The author only mentions the geography of the Mediterranean in the context of discussing his real subject: Braudel's depiction of the role of geography in human history (choice (B)) when a long view of history is taken. You can eliminate choice (A) because Braudel's use of obscure facts does not mean that he was "fascinated" with them. (D) is out because the author never says that national borders are irrelevant; they were just less significant to Braudel than geographical boundaries.

74. D

The author states in paragraph 1 that unlike conventional historians, the *Annales* historians emphasized understanding history in the context of the forces and material conditions underlying human behavior. Choice (D) paraphrases this.

Annales historians are interested in synthesizing data from social sciences, but they are not more interested in other social sciences than in history, so choice (A) is wrong. Braudel incorporated the study of great figures into his framework of the three temporalities, so there is no reason to think *Annales* historians would be critical of the achievements of historical figures (choice (B)). Choice (C) is incorrect because the author states in paragraph 1 that the *Annales* historians advocate using economic data in historical research.

75. D

The author ends the paragraph by affirming the value and influence of Braudel's approach; the author cites the number of similarly designed studies as evidence. The next sentence will most likely refer to these studies in some way and be similarly upbeat about Braudel's work. Choice (D) fits the bill.

Choice (A), on the other hand, is wrong because it contradicts the positive tone the last sentence of the passage established. Choice (B) is incorrect because it does not continue the thought from the last sentence and is inconsistent with the main ideas of the passage as a whole. Choice (C) is wrong because it, too, is negative in tone when a positive sentence is appropriate.

76. B

The author voices the possible criticisms of Braudel in the last paragraph. One of them is that he minimized the differences among the social sciences.

The author is never critical of Braudel's "structures," so **choice (A)** is out. The relationship between short-term events and long-term social activity is not mentioned by the author at all, so **(C)** is wrong; and **choice (D)** can be eliminated because Braudel is criticized for having no boundaries for social analysis, not for having rigid boundaries.

77. D

The author suggests in the first paragraph that one fundamental principle of Braudel's work is that history must be understood in the context of forces and material conditions that underlie human behavior. So the assertion that historical actions are influenced by forces that individuals may be unaware of is perfectly consistent with Braudel's principles.

Choice (A), on the other hand, is wrong because neither written history nor social elites are mentioned in the passage. **Choice (B)** is incorrect because defining the limits of potential social change in the *longue durée* was but one aspect of Braudel's work and certainly not the historian's most important task. Finally, **Choice (C)** is a cliché and neither particularly relevant to nor descriptive of Braudel's analysis.

Passage V (Questions 78-83)

78. D

This is an all/except question, so you have to pick out the choice that did not contribute to the weakness of the Bolshevik regime. The author discusses the problems facing the Bolshevik regime in 1921 in the first paragraph. These problems included a collapse of industrial production stemming from the civil war (choices (A) and (B)) and persistent peasant revolts (choice (C)). A lack of democracy (choice (D)), however, did not hurt the Bolsheviks; rather, they were able to monopolize power by refusing to legalize other political parties.

79. D

The author describes the details of the New Economic Policy at the end of paragraph 1. The author lists the permission of private trade—which was previously banned—as one feature of the policy. Forced requisitions were eliminated, and trade unions were allowed to be active again. In other words, the New Economic Policy relaxed economic controls—choice (D).

Economic centralization (choice (A)) and deliberate inflation (choice (B)) can be ruled out because they are not mentioned in the first paragraph. Choice (C) directly contradicts the fact that trade unions were once again allowed to fight for higher wages and better benefits and to strike.

80. C

The features of Bukharin's program are listed in paragraph 3. At the end of the paragraph, the author states that one of Bukharin's policies was to form alliances with nonsocialist foreign regimes that were favorable to Russia.

Choice (A) is one of Trotsky's policies, not Bukharin's. Avoiding confrontations with the trade unions (choice (B)) was presumably the idea behind the New Economic Policy's lifting of restrictions; this wasn't Bukharin's policy either. Choice (D) was not a feature of anyone's program.

81. B

Details of Trotsky's and Stalin's policies and attitudes can be found in paragraphs four and seven. Trotsky called for rapid industrialization, and Stalin sought to build up heavy industry, so it's clear that industrialization was important to both of them.

Choice (A) is incorrect: the author states that Trotsky was critical of the elite, but Stalin's attitude toward them is left unstated. Similarly, you don't know how either of them felt about democracy within the party (choice (C)) or how Trotsky felt about trade unions (choice (D)).

82. A

You can throw out choices (B) and (D) right away—Trotsky had control of the Red Army, not Stalin, and there is no reason to think that Stalin's initially neutral appearance helped him at all once he began to maneuver. Trotsky's misjudgment of threats (choice (C)) enabled Stalin to force him out of Red Army leadership, but control of the party helped Stalin much more. He was able to use his powers to remove Zinoviev and Kamenev from Party leadership and to expel Trotsky from the Party and have him murdered.

83. B

You know from the second paragraph that disputes over the long-range direction of policy led to the struggles within the Bolshevik party. This rules out choices (A) and (D), and all you have to figure out is whether the policy at issue was foreign or economic policy. Since foreign policy is mentioned only once in the passage, the differences were clearly over economic policy (choice (B)).

Passage VI (Questions 84–87)

84. C

In the first paragraph, the author says that in Stendhal's view, the ideal woman is one who reveals a man to himself and in order to do so, she must be his equal. Self-realization can be attained, then, through an equal (**choice (C)**). Muses (**choice (A)**), God (**choice (B)**), and family (**choice (D)**) are not mentioned in the passage.

85. C

Go back to the sentence in question and read the surrounding sentences. Stendhal projected himself into Lamiel, his female character, de Beauvoir noted; he "assumed Lamiel's destiny." This is why Lamiel is "somewhat speculative"; Stendhal took on the identity of a woman (**choice (C)**), which means he had to rely on speculation.

Choice (A) is wrong because we know from the third paragraph of the passage that Stendhal rejected myth. Nothing in the passage indicates that Stendhal sensationalized his plots (**choice (B)**) or exaggerated the aspirations of his female characters (**choice (D)**).

86. D

According to the third paragraph, de Beauvoir rejected the mystification of women in "fury, nymph, morning star . . . siren." The choice not included here is (**D**), "mistress."

87. C

The answer appears both in the second paragraph— "love will be more true if woman, being man's equal, is able to understand him more completely"—and in the last paragraph—"two who may have the chance to know each other in love defy time." The key is clearly understanding of each other (**choice (C)**). There is no mention in the passage of faithfulness or of blessing of the union, which means **choices (A)** and **(D)** are wrong. Stendhal rejected the mystification of women, so **(B)** is wrong as well.

Passage VII (Questions 88-92)

88. C

Statements I and II are both false; paragraph 6 states that molecular phylogeny rules out both the possibility that Pliopithecus is an ancestral gibbon (statement I) and the possibility that Dryopithicus or Proconsul are early apes (statement II). This alone allows **choices (A), (B), and (D)** to be eliminated, because they contain some combination of statements I and II. But statement III is true anyway, because the 3rd sentence of paragraph 5 states that Australopithecus could be an early representative of the human family. **Choice (C) is correct.**

89. C

This is really a main idea question because of the words "most significant." The passage is a straightforward explanation of the author's view that Ramapithecus has an equal place in human history as well as in ape history, which matches **choice (C)**. This main point is reiterated in the last paragraph.

Choices **(A)** and **(B)** are both true, but those details are not the most significant in the passage, and **choice (D)** is wrong because the "molecular clock" is a metaphor, not an actual object.

90. A

What is a main point of the paragraph? Paleontologists' evidence is not as accurate as molecular anthropologists'. **Choice (A)** is the best choice because it augments the point in the first paragraph that paleontologists' evidence is not as accurate as the evidence of molecular anthropologists.

The other choices are incorrect because **choices (B)** and **(D)** are far outside the scope of the passage, and **choice (C)** is somewhat within the scope of the passage, but not relevant to the purpose of the first paragraph.

91. D

Ramapithecus represents one of the greatest differences in the findings of paleontologists and molecular anthropologists. If Ramapithecus were proven to be as much ape-like as human-like, the molecular findings that it is a common ancestor to apes and humans would be true. **Choice (D) is correct.**

Choice (A) is incorrect because the rate of evolution is not at issue between the two fields. **Choice (B)** is incorrect because it directly contradicts molecular theory, which states that the Asian apes *did* split off earlier. And **choice (C)** is incorrect because both fields already agree that Australopithecus was an early human.

92. A

Paragraph 1 states that fossil evidence is subject to more than one interpretation, but no evidence is offered in support. **(A) is correct.**

Choice (B) is incorrect because the author never makes the claim that Ramapithecus is ancestral to the gorilla. The statements in **choices (C)** and **(D)** are both made by the author, but they are also both explicitly supported in paragraph 7, so those choices are incorrect as well.

Biological Sciences

Passage 1 (Questions 93–98)

93. D

The complete catabolism of a mole of glucose yields a net of 36 moles of ATP. The glycolytic portion of this pathway, however, yields only a net of 2 moles of ATP. Therefore, if 10 moles of glucose were to undergo glycolysis, then the total ATP produced would be 10 times the amount formed from the glycolysis of 1 mole, so 10×2 moles of ATP = 20 moles of ATP. Therefore, **choice (D)** is correct, and **choice (A)**, **choice (B)**, and **choice (C)** are wrong.

94. B

If the reaction were not stereospecific, water could add to the double bond of fumarate to form two enantiomers:

Fumarate   L-Malate   D-Malate

However, the question stem states that the reaction is stereospecific. Therefore, fumarate, which is a *trans* isomer, will react differently to its *cis* counterpart, forming a stereochemically different product. As a result, only one enantiomer will be formed, which is an optically active molecule.

A racemic mixture consists of an equal quantity of enantiomers. This would only be produced if the reaction was not stereospecific. Therefore, **choice (A)** is wrong. **choice (C)** is wrong because only one chiral center is produced in the reaction. An achiral molecule is one that doesn't contain any chiral centers, or if it does, it possesses an internal plane of symmetry. Since the product has a chiral center and no internal plane of symmetry, **choice (D)** is wrong.

95. D

According to the passage and Figure 2, a low blood glucose concentration stimulates a glucagon-triggered cascade, which leads to the phosphorylation of PFK2 to form the enzyme FBPase 2. This degrades F-2,6-BP into fructose 6-phosphate, inhibiting phosphofructokinase activity in the process. Since phosphofructokinase catalyzes the committed step in glycolysis, its inhibition will in turn inhibit glycolysis. Choice (D) is thus correct, since glucagon inhibits glycolysis.

Choice (A) and choice (B) are wrong, since glucagon does not stimulate the production of F-2,6-BP; it promotes its degradation. Choice (C) is wrong, since according to Figure 2, the phosphorylation of PFK2 occurs when blood glucose levels are low. Glucagon, therefore, promotes the phosphorylation of PFK2.

96. C

According to Figure 1, a high AMP concentration results in a greater glycolytic reaction velocity than a low AMP concentration. Therefore, choice (C) enhances the rate of glycolysis and is correct.

Choice (A) is wrong because a low concentration of fructose 2,6-bisphosphate inhibits phosphofructokinase activity, which leads to an inhibition of glycolysis. A high ATP-to-AMP ratio corresponds to a high ATP concentration or a low AMP concentration. Graphs I and II tell you that a high ATP concentration and a low AMP concentration reduce the rate of glycolysis so choice (B) can be eliminated. Choice (D) is wrong since, as seen in Graph III, a high citrate concentration reduces the rate of glycolysis.

97. D

A high fructose-6-phosphate concentration will lead to increased phosphofructokinase activity and enhanced glycolysis, so there will be more ATP. Greater ATP concentration will raise the ATP/AMP ratio, so choice (D) is correct; the ATP/AMP ratio will not decrease with high concentrations of fructose 6-phosphate.

Choice (A) and choice (B) can be eliminated, since according to Figure 2, fructose 6-phosphate stimulates the synthesis of F-2,6-BP and inhibits its degradation. Choice (C) can also be discarded, since high concentrations of F-2,6-BP stimulate phosphofructokinase.

98. B

Colony A survived under both anaerobic and aerobic conditions, and it demonstrated considerable growth and glucose consumption under aerobic conditions. This implies that the Colony A bacteria are facultative aerobes. That Colony B practically disappeared when incubated under aerobic conditions implies that Colony B bacteria must be obligate anaerobes. Thus, Colonies A and B are, respectively, facultative aerobes and obligate anaerobes, so choice (B) is correct and choice (A), choice (C), and choice (D) are all incorrect.

You should have eliminated choice (A) and choice (C) right away, since the fact that the bacteria from both colonies existed for some time under anaerobic conditions implies that neither of them could be obligate aerobes, since obligate aerobes require molecular oxygen for existence.

Passage II (Questions 99–104)

99. A

The transcription of viral mRNA in an HIV-infected CD4+ T-cell requires the same reagents as does the transcription of eukaryotic mRNA in a healthy CD4+ T-cell: RNA polymerase, ribose, phosphate, adenine, cytosine, guanine, and uracil. Unlike DNA, RNA doesn't contain thymine. So if the researcher wanted to study mRNA synthesis (transcription), then she would add radiolabeled adenine, guanine, cytosine, and uracil but not radiolabeled thymine, since it wouldn't be incorporated into the mRNA transcripts.

100. C

Hypothesis 1 is based on the premise that HIV fails to integrate. These unintegrated viruses produce a factor that results in CD4+ T-cell death. So if Hypothesis 1 is true, integration doesn't occur. However, for HIV to be capable of producing a toxic factor that causes the death of its host CD4+ T-cell, it must be inside the host cell, implying that binding and entry do occur. So, choice (C) is correct.

You can immediately eliminate choice (A) and choice (D), since they both include integration. Reverse transcription is the process by which DNA is synthesized from an RNA template with the enzyme reverse transcriptase. There's not enough information in the description of Hypothesis 1 to determine whether or not reverse transcription must occur before the toxic factor can be produced. Furthermore, it would be virtually impossible for HIV to produce a toxic factor after it had already induced the death of its host cell. Thus, choice (B) is wrong.

101. C

According to Hypothesis 3, HIV-infected cells express the viral proteins gp120 and gp41 on their surfaces. These proteins bind to the CD4 receptors on healthy T-cells, yielding a mass of immune-impaired cells known as syncytia. The net result is an effective depletion of T-cell activity. If gp120 and gp41 bound almost irreversibly to CD4 receptors, then syncytia formation would account for the depletion of T-cells associated with HIV infection. Therefore, choice (C) supports Hypothesis 3 and is correct.

Choice (A) is wrong, because it contradicts Hypothesis 3 by saying that some CD4+ T-cell lines do not form syncytia yet are still susceptible to depletion due to HIV infection. Hypothesis 3 states that syncytia formation is the cause of the T-cell depletion. Choice (B) does not support Hypothesis 3, either. If syncytia formation were transient, then these T-cells would be only temporarily nonfunctional, and the supply of T-cells would not be depleted. Choice (D) neither supports nor contradicts Hypothesis 3. Although syncytia formation does lead to cell death, the cell death is not necessary for syncytia formation to render the T-cells nonfunctional.

102. A

According to Hypothesis 4, gp120 molecules are released by HIV-infected CD4+ T-cells and bind to healthy CD4+ T-cells. According to the passage, gp120 binds to the CD4 receptor molecules expressed on the surface of other T-cells. Since CD4 receptor molecules are a normal part of CD4+ T-cell structure, they are recognized by the immune system as "self." However, CD4 receptor molecules bound to gp120 molecules are recognized as "foreign," since the gp120 molecules are not normally present in the body. In response to the presence of gp120, the immune system produces anti-gp120 antibodies, thereby attacking its own CD4+ T-cells. This is known as an autoimmune response. Therefore, Hypothesis 4 only makes sense if healthy CD4+ cells are not normally subject to autoimmune attacks, and **choice (A) is correct.**

Choice (B) is wrong because the B-cells are the antibody-producing components of the immune system. **Choice (C)** is wrong because healthy CD4+ T-cells do not synthesize gp120 molecules. **Choice (D)** is wrong because it would be impossible for gp120 to travel through the body by way of the immune system, since the immune system is not a "system" in the traditional sense of the word. The immune system refers to a group of nonspecific and specific defense mechanisms mediated by specialized cells, such as B-cells, T-cells, and macrophages, which travel through the body via the circulatory system.

103. B

The Golgi complex (Golgi apparatus) is the organelle responsible for the packaging and distribution of newly synthesized proteins, including viral proteins, such as gp120 and gp41.

Choice (A) is wrong because centrioles are cylindrical structures whose role, if any, in animal cell mitosis is unclear to date. **Choice (C)** is wrong because mitochondria are the sites of cellular respiration in eukaryotic cells. **Choice (D)** is wrong because lysosomes are responsible for the digestion of various cellular and extracellular metabolites, as well as the degradation of unwanted toxins.

104. B

According to the question stem, the test for the presence of HIV is the detection of anti-HIV antibodies circulating in the blood. HIV depletes the body's supply of T-cells, which are crucial for the proliferation and activity of the B-cells that produce the anti-HIV antibodies detected in the blood. This means that at some point during HIV infection, enough healthy T-cells are in circulation to allow for the production of anti-HIV antibodies by B-cells. **Choice (B) is correct.**

Though **Choice (A)** is most likely a true statement, it is wrong because cytotoxic T-cells are not the cells responsible for the presence of anti-HIV antibodies in the blood of an HIV-infected person. **Choice (C)** is wrong because, even if it were true, it still wouldn't account for the presence of circulating anti-HIV antibodies. **Choice (D)** is wrong, since the presence of anti-HIV antibodies would not imply that macrophages have not been infected. Macrophages are phagocytic mononuclear white cells that serve accessory roles in cellular immunity; they are not directly involved in antibody production. By the way, macrophages have been shown to harbor HIV in vivo, yet they are relatively resistant to HIV cytopathic effects, most likely due to their low level of CD4 expression. Some studies have suggested that these cells may be the basis of the neurological abnormalities seen in some AIDS patients.

Discrete Questions

105. A

In hot basic potassium permanganate, nonterminal alkenes will be oxidatively cleaved to form two molecules of carboxylic acid. $CH_3CH=CHCH_3$ is symmetrical, so cleavage and subsequent oxidation will result in the formation of two molecules of acetic acid. The molecular formula of acetic acid is $C_2H_4O_2$, and since two molecules are formed, the overall result is $2C_2H_4O_2$. Choice (B) and choice (D) are incorrect because these molecules are diols and are formed when alkenes are treated with cold dilute potassium permanganate. Choice (C) is wrong because the molecular formula doesn't match. Also, aldehydes will not form under these conditions.

106. C

The addition of HBr to 1-butyne follows Markovnikov's rule: H^+ adds to the least-substituted, double-bonded carbon first to form a carbocation intermediate—$CH_3CH_2CH^+CH_3$. Br^- then adds to this molecule to form 2-bromobutane: HBr adds to CH_3CH_2ClCH in much the same way as 1-butyne. H^+ adds to the least-substituted carbon, but this time, the intermediate $CH_3CH_2C^+=CH_2$ is formed. This is called a vinylic cation—an intermediate in which the positive charge is adjacent to a double bond. Therefore, choice (C) is the correct answer. After the vinylic cation is formed, Br^- adds to form $CH_3CH_2CBr=CH_2$: The double bond can then add another molecule of HBr to form a *gem*-dihalide—$CH_3CH_2CBr_2CH_3$. Choice (A) and choice (D) are incorrect because carbocations are formed when HBr adds to alkenes, not alkynes. Choice (B) is wrong since the positive charge on the vinylic intermediate means that it is a cation, not an anion.

107. D

This is a critical thinking question that only requires knowledge of the mammalian fetal circulatory system, as amphibian biology is not tested on the MCAT. Mammalian fetal circulation involves various shunts, such as the ductus arteriosus and foramen ovale to divert blood away from the lungs, and the ductus venosus to divert blood away from the liver. Mammalian fetal gas exchange occurs in the placenta rather than the lungs, which are non-functional prior to birth. The combined effect of these factors is that both oxygenated and deoxygenated blood flow concurrently in a majority of fetal blood vessels, along with the atria and ventricles of the heart. At birth, the lungs become functional and the shunts close soon thereafter, allowing the oxygenated and deoxygenated blood to flow separately. Thus choice (D) is correct.

Choice (A) is wrong because fetal gas exchange occurs in the placenta. The lungs do not function prior to birth. Choice (B) is wrong because gas exchange occurs in the placenta. The blastopore is the opening of the archenteron (primitive gut), and eventually becomes the anus in mammals and other deuterostomes. Choice (C) is wrong because the mammalian heart always has four chambers.

Passage III (Questions 108–113)

108. A

All viruses have a protein coat consisting of protein subunits. Since all viruses are so closely related, there will be homology among the viral genes coding for the protein coats of different viruses. This means that probes specific for proteins present in the protein coats of almost all viruses can be created. By hybridizing the unknown infectious agent with probes specific for the few major variants of viral protein coats, the nature of the infectious agent can be determined. If the probes hybridize with the genes of the infectious agent, the agent must be a virus. If the probes do not hybridize with the genes, this means that the infectious agent does not contain the viral genes coding for the protein coat and the agent must be bacterial.

Choice (B) is wrong because, while viruses do not have any photosynthetic pigments, only some bacteria have them. Only the cyanobacteria, or blue-green algae, are photosynthetic, and cyanobacteria are not infectious agents in humans. Choice (C) is wrong because although most viruses are DNA viruses, RNA viruses also exist. And since all bacteria have RNA, if the infectious agent were an RNA virus, both would stain positive for the presence of RNA. Choice (D) is wrong because all bacteria and all viruses have proteins, so both would stain positive for the presence of proteins.

109. A

Since all four of the microbes are bacteria, you're looking for the structure not found in bacteria. Bacteria are prokaryotes—unicellular organisms characterized by the lack of a true nucleus as well as the absence of all other membranous organelles. Bacteria have a single circular chromosome located in a region of the cell known as the nucleoid. So choice (A) is correct, and choice (B) can be eliminated.

Choice (C) is wrong, since bacteria have cell walls. Likewise, bacteria contain all the necessary machinery for protein synthesis and reproduction, such as RNA, enzymes, ribosomes, and proteins, which is why choice (D) is wrong.

For your information, prokaryotic ribosomes are structurally different from eukaryotic ribosomes, and this difference is often exploited in the development of effective antibiotics.

110. B

By culturing the four strains of bacteria on different nutrient plates, the epidemiologist was able to determine the nutritional requirements of each strain. A strain can only grow on those plates that contain all of the amino acids essential to that strain; if any of these amino acids are lacking, growth will not occur. Microbe Q grew on Plate 1 and Plate 3, both of which contain threonine and cysteine. Microbe Q did not grow on Plate 2 or Plate 4. Plate 4 is identical to Plate 1, except that tryptophan has been substituted for cysteine. Plate 2 is identical to Plate 3, except that phenylalanine has been substituted for threonine. Since growth occurred when threonine and cysteine were both present and was prohibited when either of them was absent, it can be deduced that both threonine and cysteine are essential amino acids for Microbe Q. Therefore, choice (B) is correct.

Choice (A) and choice (C) can be eliminated because neither of these amino acids is present in Plate 3, which supported Microbe Q growth. Choice (D) is wrong: Proline can not be an essential amino acid for Microbe Q because it is missing from Plate 1, which also supported growth.

111. A

The phrase "pathogenic microbes" refers to Microbe Q and Microbe T only, since Microbes R and S were found to be nonpathogenic. To test whether the strains were affected by the antibiotics, the experimenter needed to use a medium that the strains could definitely grow on in the absence of antibiotics. With this in mind, you should have translated the question to read: Which of the four nutrient plates is capable of sustaining colonies of both Microbe Q and Microbe T?

According to Table 1, Microbe Q grew on Plate 1 and Plate 3, while Microbe T grew on Plates 1, 2, and 4. Plate 1 is, therefore, the only plate that the epidemiologist could have used in the experiment illustrated in Figure 1. Thus, choice (A) is correct, and choice (B), choice (C), and choice (D) are wrong.

112. C

An effective antibiotic is one that inhibits, if not completely prevents, bacterial growth. According to the passage, shaded areas in Figure 1 represent regions of good bacterial growth, and as can be seen, Microbe Q growth is inhibited by both Antibiotic Y and Antibiotic Z, while Microbe T is inhibited only by Antibiotic Z. Since Antibiotic Z inhibits both strains of bacteria, it makes sense that this drug would be the most effective in treating patients simultaneously infected with Microbe Q and Microbe T. Thus, choice (C) is correct, and choice (A), choice (B), and choice (D) are wrong.

113. C

The best way to approach this question is by the process of elimination. Choice (A) can be eliminated, since centrifugation separates substances on the basis of density and would, therefore, be of little use here. All the bacteria are so close in density that they would sediment into the same layer.

Choice (B) sounds like a good idea—especially if you determined from Table 1 that cysteine and threonine are essential for Microbe Q and that phenylalanine is essential for Microbe T. You might expect only Microbe Q to grow on the nutrient plate containing cysteine and only Microbe T to grow on the nutrient plate containing phenylalanine. However, Microbe Q requires both cysteine and threonine for growth, and while Microbe T would grow on the phenylalanine plate, Microbe Q would not grow on either one. So choice (B) is wrong.

Choice (C) is similar to choice (B), except that one of the plates has all of the amino acids except cysteine, and the other has all of the amino acids except phenylalanine. This means that Microbe Q would grow on the plate lacking phenylalanine but not on the plate lacking cysteine. Likewise, Microbe T would grow on the plate lacking cysteine but not on the plate lacking phenylalanine. In this way, Microbe Q could be isolated from Microbe T, so choice (C) is correct.

Choice (D) is obviously wrong, since clearly, a mechanism for isolating the two microbes does exist.

By the way, the easiest way to isolate these microbes would be to use the original Plate 3 and Plate 4. As can be seen in Table 1, Plate 3 sustained only Microbe Q, and Plate 4 sustained only Microbe T.

Discrete Questions

114. C

Choice (C) is the correct answer for two reasons. Firstly, $(CH_3)_3COH$ will form a tertiary carbocation; $(CH_3)_3C^+$. Here, there are three alkyl groups which, by electron donation through sigma bonds, can stabilize the positive charge. Secondly, the polar protic solvent H_2SO_4 is used. This drives the formation of the carbocation, since it can stabilize the transition state that forms.

Choice (A) is wrong because no nucleophilic substitution reactions can occur in a nonpolar solvent. Choice (B) is wrong because even though $(CH_3CH_2)_3COH$ would form a tertiary carbocation, acetone is a polar aprotic solvent which would not be able to stabilize the transition state as effectively as a polar protic solvent. Choice (D) is wrong because these conditions would be ideal for an S_N2 reaction, not S_N1.

115. A

Calcitonin lowers blood Ca^{2+} by promoting the incorporation of calcium ion into bone. A way to remember this is as follows: Calcitonin tones down the Ca^{2+}. Parathyroid hormone (PTH), on the other hand, increases blood Ca^{2+} concentration by promoting its removal from bone and its release into the bloodstream. PTH also decreases the excretion of Ca^{2+} from the kidneys and converts vitamin D3 into its active form, which stimulates the absorption of Ca^{2+} in the intestines.

Choice (B) is wrong because prolactin, a hormone synthesized by the anterior pituitary gland, stimulates the secretion of milk from female mammary glands. Choice (C) is incorrect because the function of ACTH, also synthesized and secreted by the anterior pituitary, is to stimulate the production of hormones from the adrenal cortex. Choice (D) is wrong because thyroxine (T_4) is a thyroid hormone involved in regulating metabolism.

116. A

The partial pressure of CO_2 in the blood is highest in those vessels carrying deoxygenated blood. Deoxygenated blood is returned to the right atrium of the heart via the inferior vena cava and the superior vena cava. From the right atrium, the deoxygenated blood drains into the right ventricle, where it is pumped into the pulmonary arteries. The pulmonary arteries deliver the blood to the capillary beds surrounding the alveoli, which is where gas exchange occurs: CO_2 is traded for O_2. The now-oxygenated blood is returned to the heart via the pulmonary veins, which empty into the left atrium. The left atrium drains into the left ventricle, which pumps the oxygenated blood into circulation via the aorta. In addition, the heart is delivered its own supply of oxygenated blood via the coronary arteries, which branch off the aorta. Thus, choices (B), (C), and (D) are wrong, since these vessels carry oxygenated blood.

117. C

The three primary germ layers, which arise during the gastrulation stage of embryonic development and from which all organ systems and structures are derived, are endoderm, mesoderm, and ectoderm. Endoderm is the innermost layer of cells from which the following structures arise: the lining of the digestive tract, the lining of the respiratory tract, the liver, the thyroid, the pancreas, and the bladder. Mesoderm is the middle layer of cells from which the following structures arise: skeletal muscle, dermis, bone, blood, the gonads, the kidneys, and the circulatory system. Ectoderm is the outermost layer of cells from which the following structures arise: epidermis (including nails, hair, and the outer layer of skin), the lens of the eye, the pituitary gland, the lining of the mouth and nose, nervous tissue, and the adrenal medulla. Since choice (C) is the only choice not derived from the ectoderm, it is correct.

118. D

In 2-pentene, there is no rotation of substituents attached to the double bond. Therefore, the methyl substituents can be located on the same side of the double bond (*cis*) or on opposite sides (*trans*): The *cis/trans* arrangement of substituents around a double bond is known as geometric isomerism, making **choice (D)** the correct response. *Cis* and *trans* isomers have different physical properties, attributed to a difference in their dipole moments and symmetry. **Choice (A)** is wrong since anomers are cyclic forms of carbohydrates that differ in the configuration about the anomeric carbon (usually carbon 1). Enantiomers are chiral molecules that are non-superimposable mirror images of each other. In addition, they have identical chemical and physical properties (except the ability to rotate plane-polarized light). 2-pentene is achiral, and its isomers have different physical properties, so **choice (B)** is wrong. Conformational isomers arise by the rotation around a single bond, not a double bond. At normal temperatures, these isomers cannot be isolated; therefore, **choice (C)** is also wrong.

Passage IV (Questions 119–123)

119. D

Chlorination of butane results in the formation of 1-chlorobutane and 2-chlorobutane, since butane possesses two types of hydrogen that can be substituted. 1-Chlorobutane is achiral, so Statement III is correct. On the other hand, 2-chlorobutane possesses a chiral carbon, so Statement I is also correct:

$$CH_3CH_2-\overset{\overset{\textstyle H}{|}}{\underset{\underset{\textstyle Cl}{|}}{C}}-CH_3$$

Choice (D) is the only choice that contains both Statements I and III, so it is the correct response.

Statement II is also correct because the reaction occurs through a free radical intermediate; the halogen can add to either side of the molecule, forming a racemic mixture, which has no observed optical rotation.

120. A

The passage tells you that the order of reactivity of the halogens is fluorine, then chlorine, then bromine, then iodine. Bromine produces five times as much tertiary product as primary product, so it seems to be selective about which hydrogen it reacts with. However, with fluorine, equal amounts of product form, so it must be pretty unselective. Therefore, **choice (A)** is correct: Fluorine is the most reactive halogen, but it is the least selective, so there is an inverse relation between reactivity and selectivity.

Choice (B) is wrong. Because fluorine is more reactive than bromine, it will be a better halogenating agent. Choice (C) is also wrong because fluorine is simply more reactive than bromine: It doesn't matter which sort of hydrogen it is substituting. Choice (D) is true in that fluorine forms stronger bonds to primary carbons than bromine, but that doesn't account for the different products that are formed.

121. B

In free radical substitution reactions, only a small amount of initiator is required because a halogen radical is produced in the propagation step, which can drive the reaction without the help of the initiator (resulting in a chain reaction). Therefore, the reaction can be started by light of low intensity to produce a small concentration of halogen radicals. **Choice (B)** is the correct response.

Choice (A) is wrong because these reactions have high activation energies. Choice (C) is wrong because halogen–halogen bonds are quite strong. Finally, **choice (D)** is wrong because alkanes are extremely unreactive molecules.

122. B

A chain termination step is one that ends the reaction chain. The chain in this reaction is kept going by the presence of free radicals: To terminate the chain, the number of radicals must be reduced. This is shown in **choice (B)**, where two radicals combine to form a neutral molecule.

Choice (A) and **choice (D)** are wrong because these are propagation steps; bromine radicals are generated that assist in the reaction, not terminate it. **Choice (C)** is wrong because no radicals are shown here at all. This is actually the overall reaction that occurs between bromine and the alkane.

123. D

The passage states that the most reactive type of hydrogen toward substitution is a tertiary hydrogen. Substitution of the tertiary hydrogen in 2-methylpropane will result in the formation of 2-bromo-2-methylpropane, **choice (D)**.

Choice (B) is wrong because it names the molecule as a butane and the longest carbon chain has three carbons, not four. **Choice (A)** names the molecule as 2-bromomethylpropane. If this were true, propane would have a bromomethyl substituent, not a bromo and a methyl substituent. **Choice (C)** is wrong because it states that the product has a 1-bromo substituent, not a 2-bromo substituent. This product would only be formed if the less reactive primary hydrogen were substituted.

Passage V (Questions 124–129)

124. D

According to the passage, eukaryotic cells contain genes known as proto-oncogenes, which normally code for proteins involved in the regulation of growth. If any of these proto-oncogenes become transformed into an oncogene, then that cell is said to be tumorigenic. A tumorigenic cell is one that gives rise to a tumor, and unlike normal cells, tumor cells don't obey the rules of normal cell growth and, instead, divide indefinitely. Thus, in a tumorigenic cell, you would expect to see an increase in all of the activities and processes associated with cell growth and division, such as mRNA synthesis (transcription) and ribosomal assembly. Likewise, cell division would also increase, since tumor cells replicate at an accelerated rate. Statements I, II, and III are all in correct answer **(D)**.

125. A

A point mutation is the replacement of one nucleotide base pair with another pair of nucleotides in double-stranded DNA. A point mutation is also referred to as a base-pair substitution. Thus, a cellular oncogene activated by point mutation differs from the proto-oncogene from which it was derived by a single base-pair.

126. C

For a proto-oncogene to transform a cell, oncoproteins must be produced from proto-oncogene transcripts. But if complementary nucleic acid sequences are present, the proto-oncogene mRNA will base-pair with the nucleic acids before it can be translated and produce oncoproteins.

According to the passage, cellular proto-oncogenes often become tumorigenic via a point mutation, which leads to the formation of a defective protein, so **choice (A)** is wrong. **Choice (B)** is wrong, since you're told that a mutation that causes a proto-oncogene to produce an excess of its protein product, such as a chromosomal translocation, will convert the proto-oncogene into a tumorigenic oncogene. **Choice (D)** is wrong, since you're told that a mutation that causes the proto-oncogene to undergo gene amplification would also cause an excess of protein product and convert the proto-oncogene into a tumorigenic oncogene.

127. C

A c-onc (proto-oncogene) is a cellular gene found in an organism's own genome. A v-onc is a gene found in the genome of transforming viruses. The v-onc is not normally part of the viral genome; it was incorporated into the viral genome from c-onc genes formerly found in a eukaryotic host cell. If the v-onc gene was captured from a host cell in the form of c-onc RNA, the v-onc gene will have a sequence similar to the sequence of c-onc RNA. The v-onc gene will be similar to the exons the c-onc gene spliced together. So **choice (C)** is the correct answer.

Choice (A) is wrong, since if the v-onc gene contained only c-onc introns, the v-onc gene would code for nonsense. It's the exons that contain the coding sequences. **Choice (B)** is wrong, because although it is true that a v-onc gene has a greater level of expression than its corresponding c-onc gene, expression level is independent of gene sequence. **Choice (D)** is wrong because although the v-onc RNA could be spliced after that had transcribed inside a eukaryotic host cell, that would not explain why the v-onc gene itself had an mRNA sequence resembling that of the c-onc gene.

128. D

The binding of a compound to a growth-factor receptor on the cell surface triggers a series of reactions that activate the protein ras, which in turn triggers another cascade of reactions. The end result is the activation of specific transcription factors and the expression of select genes. This is an example of signal transduction. Likewise, the second messenger system (as utilized by peptide hormones) is put into action by the binding of a molecule to a receptor on the outer surface of the cell membrane. This event triggers a cascade of events in which a signal is transmitted to the interior of the cell. On receipt of a signal from outside the cell, other reaction cascades are initiated inside the cell that result in a specific change in cellular activity. Typically, second messenger systems involve G proteins and cyclic AMP.

Choice (A) is wrong since formation of an antibody-antigen complex occurs within the vessels of the circulatory and lymphatic systems and involves the binding of proteins expressed on the surface of the antigen to the antibody-binding sites of the antibody itself. **Choice (B)** is wrong since the sodium-potassium pump transports sodium and chloride ions across membrane without any signal transduction. **Choice (C)** is wrong because the Krebs cycle, which is a part of cellular respiration, is regulated via a negative feedback mechanism. The synthesis of citrate from oxaloacetate and acetyl-CoA is an important control point in the cycle. ATP inhibits citrate synthase, the enzyme that catalyzes citrate synthesis. As ATP levels increase, citrate synthesis is inhibited.

129. B

A promoter is a region of DNA involved in the binding of RNA polymerase to initiate transcription. The promoter region is located approximately 10–35 base pairs before the first coding base of the gene. The strength of a promoter describes the frequency at which RNA polymerase initiates transcription and appears to be related to the closeness with which its sequences conform to the ideal consensus sequences. So a strong promoter increases the frequency with which RNA polymerase binds to the region and transcribes the gene. Based on this, **choice (B)** is the correct answer.

Choice (A) is wrong since promoters are involved with transcription, not translation. **Choice (C)** and **choice (D)** must be wrong since translocation and mutation typically lead to abnormal gene product, not to an excess of normal gene product.

Passage VI (Questions 130–135)

130. A

An animal's immune system produces antibodies in response to the presence of antigens—substances that are recognized by the animal as being "foreign" or "non-self." Healthy animals do not normally produce antibodies against their own circulating hormones. Since mice and rabbits are not normally exposed to human hormones, injecting them with extract from the human endocrine gland that synthesizes a particular hormone will elicit the production of antibodies specific for that hormone. The antibodies are then isolated from a blood sample for use in an RIA. Thus, **choice (A)** is the correct answer.

Choice (B) is wrong because human endocrine gland cells produce hormones, not antibodies; the B-cells of the immune system produce antibodies. Furthermore, if human endocrine cells could produce antibodies, then they would be able to produce them in vivo.

Choice (C) is wrong because it implies that human hormones will only elicit an immune response in mice and rabbits. Human hormones would do the same in most other mammals, too. Rabbits and mice are commonly used as test animals in laboratories because of certain similarities they share with humans and because they are fast breeders. For your information, exposing chimpanzees to a human hormone extract might not elicit antibody production by the chimp because both species share approximately 96 percent of their DNA.

Choice (D) actually describes the principle behind vaccinations. Vaccination with a weakened or killed form of a pathogen elicits a mild immune response in the organism. This primary exposure to the pathogen results in B-cell proliferation and antibody production. Upon subsequent exposure to the pathogen, the immune response is typically faster and more efficient. However, immunization with a hormone extract will not cause an infection. Viruses and bacteria cause infections.

131. D

ADH, or antidiuretic hormone, is the hormone secreted by the posterior pituitary gland in response to low blood volume or high plasma osmolarity. ADH restores plasma osmolarity or blood volume to normal levels by increasing water reabsorption in the kidneys. Therefore, you would expect the concentration of circulating ADH to be higher in a person suffering from severe blood loss than in a healthy person. Since the RIA for ADH in a healthy person yielded an ADH concentration of 3 pg/mL, then the only possible answer is 5 pg/mL, **choice (D)**, which is the only choice higher in value than the ADH RIA of a healthy person.

132. D

According to the passage, labeled and unlabeled hormones compete for binding sites on the antibody. If there is little unlabeled hormone in the sample, the percentage of antibody-bound radiolabeled hormone will be high; if there is a lot of unlabeled hormone, the percentage of antibody-bound radiolabeled hormone will be low. FSH (follicle-stimulating hormone) stimulates the maturation of an ovarian follicle during a typical menstrual cycle. During pregnancy, however, the menstrual cycle is inhibited because progesterone, which is secreted by the corpus luteum during the first trimester of pregnancy and secreted by the placenta during the remainder of the pregnancy, inhibits FSH secretion. So the concentration of FSH is very low during pregnancy. If an RIA for FSH were done on a woman before pregnancy and again in her 16th week of pregnancy, you would expect the percentage of antibody-bound radiolabeled FSH to be higher during pregnancy since the concentration of FSH in her body will be low. Thus, on Figure 1, the point that corresponds to the before-pregnancy state must the point that corresponds to a higher FSH concentration on the x-axis than the part that corresponds to the pregnancy state. Therefore, **choice (D)** is the correct answer.

Choice (A), choice (B), and choice (C) all show the FSH concentration to be greater during pregnancy than before pregnancy and so are incorrect. Since all of the answer choices except for choice (D) have a higher FSH concentration at the second point, you could have concluded that choices (A), (B), and (C) all imply the same thing and, therefore, must be wrong.

133. B

So long as the antibody binds to the radiolabeled hormone and the unlabeled hormone with equal affinity, then the concept of competition for the binding sites is valid, and so is the RIA. If the antibody preferentially bound the radiolabeled hormone, then the percentage of antibody-bound radiolabeled hormone would always be high, regardless of the concentration of unlabeled hormone in the blood sample being assayed. The standard curve generated from such data would be invalid and, therefore, useless for calculating hormone concentrations. Thus, choice (B) is correct, and choice (A) is wrong.

Choice (C) is wrong because if there were enough antibody in the solution to bind completely all of the radiolabeled hormone and unlabeled hormone, then the two couldn't compete for antibody binding sites. This competition is essential to RIA because the percentage of each of the hormones that binds to the antibody is directly proportional to its concentration in the solution. Choice (D) is wrong because there is no evidence in the passage to support it. Antibodies can only bind to antigens at their antigen-binding sites.

134. B

Insulin is the pancreatic hormone that lowers blood glucose concentration, mainly by stimulating the conversion of glucose into its storage form, glycogen. In response to high blood glucose, the pancreas secretes insulin, and blood glucose concentration decreases. Thus, one hour after an infusion of glucose, you would expect to find a higher concentration of insulin in a blood sample taken from the subject than before the infusion. And in an RIA in which the concentration of unlabeled hormone is expected to be high relative to the concentration of radiolabeled hormone, the percentage of antibody-bound radiolabeled hormone is expected to be low. Thus, if Figure 1 were the standard curve for insulin, the point representing insulin after the glucose infusion must correspond to a higher hormone concentration than the point representing insulin concentration before glucose infusion. Choice (B) is the only pairing of points that show this relationship.

135. C

That the precursor and active forms of a hormone are chemically and structurally similar implies that an antibody developed against either form of the hormone would be capable of binding to both and would do so with equal affinity. The question stem states that the researcher wanted to measure the concentration of the active form of the hormone, since it's the active form that circulates and acts on target cells. However, the researcher used the precursor form to develop the antibodies and generate the standard curve used for the RIA. If the sample to be assayed contained only the active form, the results of the RIA would be valid. However, if the sample of unlabeled hormone to be assayed were somehow contaminated with the unlabeled precursor form, then the antibody would bind to both forms. Now three competitors would be vying for the antigen-binding sites on the antibodies: the radiolabeled precursor form, the unlabeled precursor form, and the unlabeled active form. This means that the percentage of antibody-bound radiolabeled hormone would be atypically low. And since the percentage of antibody-bound radiolabeled hormone is inversely proportional to the concentration of unlabeled hormone in the sample, the calculated concentration of the active hormone would be greater than its actual concentration. Thus, **choice (C)** is correct, and **choice (D)** is wrong.

Choice (A) is wrong for two reasons. First, the standard curve generated using the precursor form of the hormone would be valid, but only for calculating the concentration of either form of the hormone in a sample containing only that form. Second, according to the question, the researcher is looking to measure the concentration of the active form of a particular hormone, not its precursor form. **Choice (B)** is wrong since it proposes that the percentage of antibody-bound radiolabeled hormone would be greater than normal, while in actuality, it would be less than normal.

Discrete Questions

136. A

Osmosis is the tendency of water to flow from regions of lower solute concentration to regions of higher solute concentration. Freshwater fish tend to gain water because of osmosis, and marine fish tend to lose it. If water is flowing into the freshwater fish, then the fish's environment must be hypotonic to its blood; that is, the fresh water has a lower concentration of dissolved solutes than the fish's blood. The marine fish is losing water to its surroundings, which means that its aqueous environment must be hypertonic to its blood. **Choice (A)** is correct. In both cases, the water is flowing from hypotonic regions to hypertonic regions. The term *isotonic* means that there is no difference in osmolarity between two regions; there is no net osmosis between isotonic regions.

137. D

Hemoglobin has four subunits, each with its own heme group, while myoglobin has only one unit and, therefore one heme group. The sigmoid, or S-shape of hemoglobin's O_2-dissociation curve reflects the fact that the saturation of hemoglobin depends not only on the concentration of O_2 in blood but also on the number of subunits that are occupied with O_2 molecules. Cooperative binding means that the binding of the first O_2 molecule to one of hemoglobin's subunits makes it easier for the second O_2 to bind. And the binding of the second makes it easier for the third, and so on. In other words, when the partial pressure of O_2 in the blood is low, it is more difficult for that first O_2 to bind, but because of the cooperativity after the first one binds, it becomes much easier for the other O_2 molecules to bind, causing the curve to rise steeply. Since myoglobin does not have multiple subunits, O_2 cannot bind to it in a cooperative fashion, which is why myoglobin's O_2-dissociation curve is not S-shaped. Its curve reflects the fact that the saturation of myoglobin is directly proportional to the concentration of O_2 in the blood. Thus, **choice (D)** is correct, and **choice (B)** is wrong.

Choice (A) is wrong because *Bohr effect* is the term used to describe hemoglobin's decrease in O_2 affinity at high plasma concentrations of CO_2 and low pH. Choice (C) is wrong because while the difference in the partial pressure of O_2 between muscle tissue and arterial blood is the factor accounting for the diffusion of O_2 into O_2-depleted muscle tissue, it does not account for the difference in the shapes of the two curves.

138. B

All *meta*-directors have a positive charge on the atom directly bonded to the ring or can be polarized to have a partial positive charge there. Most *ortho*- and *para*-directing groups have at least one pair of nonbonding electrons on the atom directly bonded to the ring. Choice (B) is correct because the nitrogen possesses a pair of nonbonding electrons.

The carboxyl group in **choice (A)** will certainly be a *meta* director since the carboxyl carbon is positively polarized. The same thing applies to the ketone group in **choice (C)**: The carbonyl oxygen polarizes the bond so that the carbon has a slight positive charge. Choice (D) is also a *meta* director, since the electron-withdrawing nature of the oxygens ensures that the sulfur atom is positively polarized.

139. A

When an amino acid reaches its isoelectric point, it is in the form of a zwitterion. In this state, the molecule is electrically neutral: The carboxylate group is negatively charged, and the ammonium group is positively charged. As a result, it will not migrate toward either the cathode or the anode when placed in an electric field. Since the amino acid migrates to the anode at pH 8.5, it must have a net negative charge. To attain neutrality and, hence, reach the isoelectric point, the ammonium group has to be protonated, which can be achieved by lowering the pH. Therefore, the isoelectric point must be lower than 8.5, which corresponds to choice (A).

140. C

Both LH and FSH are released by the anterior pituitary under the influence of their respective hypothalamic gonadotropin-releasing factors. However, male and female hormones differ in their pattern of release and physiological function. In males, the release of LH and FSH is relatively constant because they stimulate two continuous processes: testosterone synthesis and spermatogenesis. In females, the release of LH and FSH is strictly cyclic. Prior to ovulation, FSH and LH secretion continuously increase; the increase in FSH stimulates follicle development, and the increase in LH stimulates the development of the corpus luteum following ovulation. The secretion of both hormones drops sharply following ovulation and does not begin to rise again until the onset of the next menstrual cycle. Therefore, the switch from cyclic production of gonadotropin-releasing factors to acyclic production during reproductive development would most certainly affect the release patterns of both of these hormones. Choice (C) is correct.

Passage VII (Questions 141–144)

141. D

In Figure 2, H+ bonds with the oxygen of the carbonyl group. It is then lost in Step 4 to regenerate H_3O^+ and the α-halo ketone. A catalyst is a material that increases the rate of a reaction but remains unchanged itself, so the hydrogen ion fits this definition.

On the other hand, the hydroxide ion is a reactant. In Figure 1, the hydroxide abstracts an α-hydrogen from the ketone in the first step to produce water and the enolate ion. Since the hydroxide anion is used up and not regenerated, it is a reactant and not a catalyst. Therefore, **choice (D)** is the correct response.

142. A

Tautomers are compounds that differ in the arrangement of their atoms but exist in equilibrium with each other. The most common type of tautomerism is that in which molecules differ in the attachment of a hydrogen and the placement of a double bond, namely keto-enol tautomers. In Figure 2, the reactant, acetone, is in its keto form. It becomes protonated by acid to form an intermediate, which then slowly isomerizes to produce the enol form of acetone.

Enantiomers are a subdivision of stereoisomers, so they differ in their spatial arrangement, not their atomic connectivity. The product and reactant in Step 2 do differ in their atomic connectivity, so **choices (C)** and **(D)** are wrong. Geometric isomers are another type of stereoisomer and are defined as compounds that differ in the position of groups around a double bond. The product and reactant do not fit this definition either, so **choice (B)** is wrong.

143. A

Alpha halogenation in basic solution usually doesn't stop at the mono-halogenated product stage because the halogen on the alpha carbon is highly electronegative: It pulls electron density towards it, so the two remaining protons are highly acidic. Since the conditions are basic, these hydrogens can be easily abstracted, and the anion that is formed can attack the positively polarized region of another halogen molecule, resulting in multiple halogenations. Therefore, **choice (A)** is the correct response.

Choice (B) is true in that the base is strong and will abstract protons, but that is not why multiple halogenations occur. **Choice (C)** is incorrect because α-halo ketones are not unstable compounds; they can be isolated quite easily. **Choice (D)** is wrong because abstraction of a proton will result in the formation of a carbanion, not a carbocation, and a halogen would destabilize a carbocation, not stabilize it.

144. C

This question can be interpreted as "What reactants are involved in the rate-limiting step?" Remember that the rate-limiting step is the slow one. Therefore, in Figure 1, the rate depends upon the abstraction of an α-proton from acetone. The two species involved in this reaction are acetone and OH-, Roman numerals I and III, making **choice (C)** correct.

Bromine has nothing to do with the slow step; it is only involved with the fast step, which does not affect the rate. Hence, **choices (B)** and **(D)** are wrong. **Choice (A)** is wrong because the rate of the reaction does not solely depend upon the concentration of acetone.